SHETLAND ISLANDS PILOT

SHETLAND ISLANDS PILOT

Gordon Buchanan

Imray Laurie Norie & Wilson

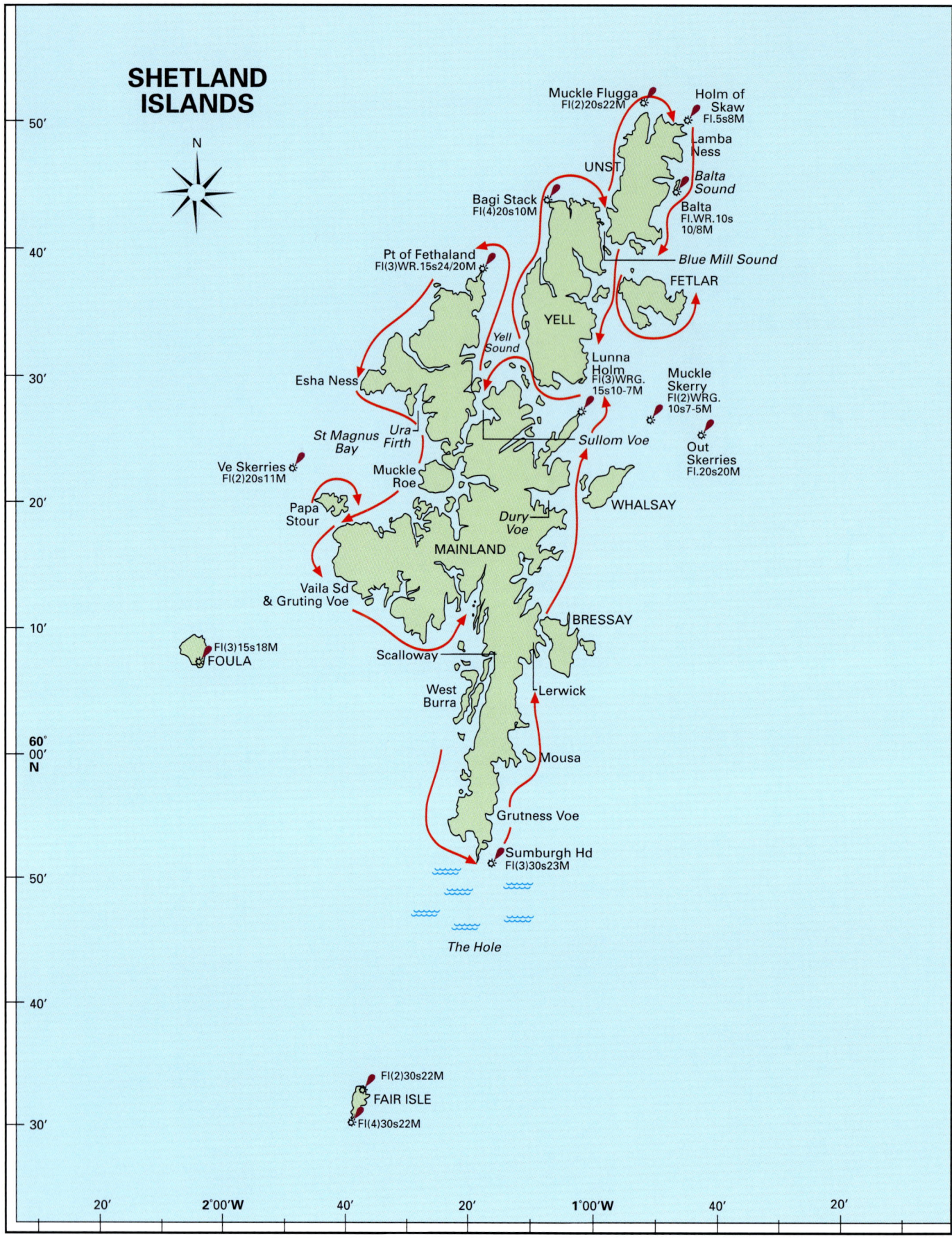

CONTENTS

PREFACE *vii*

INTRODUCTION *1*

FAIR ISLE *9*

MAINLAND, EAST COAST *12*

MAINLAND, WEST COAST *50*

YELL *87*

UNST *97*

FETLAR *104*

OUT SKERRIES *106*

INDEX *108*

Published by
Imray Laurie Norie & Wilson Ltd
Wych House, St Ives
Cambridgeshire PE27 5BT England
☎ +44 (0)1480 462114 *Fax* +44 (0)1480 496109
Email ilnw@imray.com.
www.imray.com
2009

All rights reserved. No part of this publication may be reproduced, transmitted or used in any form by any means – graphic, electronic or mechanical, including photocopying, recording, taping or information storage and retrieval systems or otherwise – without the prior permission of the publishers.

1st edition 2009

© Gordon Garman 2009
Gordon Garman has asserted his rights to be identified as the author of this work in accordance with the Copyright, Designs and Patents Act 1988.
© Photographs Gordon Garman 2009
© Aerial photographs Patrick Roach and
Imray, Laurie, Norie and Wilson Ltd 2007

ISBN 978 085288 977 0

British Library Cataloguing in Publication Data.
A catalogue record for this book is available from the British Library.

Plans
The plans in this guide are not to be used for navigation. They are designed to support the text and should at all times be used with up to date navigational charts.
The plans and tidal information have been reproduced with the permission of the Hydrographic Office of the United Kingdom (Licence No. HO151/951101/01) and the Controller of Her Britannic Majesty's Stationery Office.

Caution
Whilst every care has been taken to ensure accuracy, neither the Publishers nor the Authors will hold themselves responsible for errors, omissions or alterations in this publication. They will at all times be grateful to receive information which tends to the improvement of the work.

Correctional Supplements
This pilot book will be amended at intervals by the issue of correctional supplements which will be published on our website www.imray.com and may be downloaded free of charge. Printed copies are also available on request from the publishers at the above address.

Printed in Singapore by Star Standard Industries Pte

PREFACE

For many years, the waters around the most northerly of the British Isles were only lightly used, and that mainly by fishing vessels who plied the area in search of their catch. Then oil was discovered. The monetary value resulting from finding of one of the world's most sought after commodities meant an influx of new people, new machinery, new vessels and new technology. The Shetland Isles had lost their traditional nature forever, and the transition took some time before the old and new settled into an amicable co-existence.

Despite the dramatic evolution, it was not long before the benefits of a flourishing oil industry were well in evidence. While the fishing industry was showing signs of an early decline, and the knitwear sector, even although world-renowned could not on its own support the community, oil brought a previously unknown prosperity. This meant an immediate demand for better communications such as roads, telephones including mobiles, and for the seaborne aspects, better navigational aids.

This last part has been of direct benefit to those who are prepared to spend the necessary time in reaching these fabulous cruising grounds. The Shetland Islands, all 120 of them, are definitely not all oil terminals and ever bigger tankers. In fact, one could easily spend a month cruising around the island and never see either. What would be seen though is a selection of wildlife in its natural habitat; a selection that includes whales, dolphins, and sea birds of almost every northern species. If that is not enough, the air has a clarity that makes taking each breath a sensuous pleasure.

From a navigators appoint of view, the development of these islands has meant that charts are both comprehensive and regularly updated. All 13 Admiralty charts for the area are now using WGS84 datum so use of GPS is a simple matter with positions being suitable for plotting straight onto the charts. A further benefit of modern Shetland life is that buoyage is now quite comprehensive.

Shetland also boasts its own radio station and although some of the local news may pass over the heads of visitors, the same cannot be said about the regularly updated weather forecasts that include much detail of interest to yachtsmen.

In these directions I have tried to identify some of the many anchorages that are accessible by most cruising yachts of reasonable size. They are not intended to replace Admiralty publications for large commercial vessels, and as a result often show details of small and sometimes shallow but interesting areas. These directions should be used in conjunction with all other available sources of information, in particular, up-to-date charts.

It is always possible that I have missed some hazard, and although the cartography department at Imray Laurie, Norie and Wilson have been superb in spending many hours making sense of my plans, a weather eye on an echo sounder is always prudent.

Acknowledgements

Many people have helped this book to see completion, and in particular I would like to thank John Goode and Willie Wilson for their inspiration. In addition many sailors who are lucky enough to call these waters home, have helped with detail, and in order to avoid the pitfall of omitting any, I thank you all. This guide would not be what it is without you. Finally, many thanks to the Officers and members of Lerwick Boating Club. Their help and hospitality is a superb example to any club throughout the sailing world.

Gordon Buchanan, November 2008

INTRODUCTION

Cruising the Shetland Isles

Well known to ancient Norse mariners, the Shetland Isles offer a fascinating cruising ground for today's less warlike sailors. Although rugged to some the almost treeless landscape offers a multitude of wonderful anchorages. Distances within the Shetland Islands are not great and there are some 120 different islands to explore, but some of the more remote anchorages are shallow enough to be more suited to smaller craft. The wide variety of scenery on offer means that, no matter the size of craft, there will be more than enough of interest to ensure that one visit will certainly not be enough. In addition to the natural attractions, one of the most compelling reasons for making the effort to reach the Northern Isles is the phenomenal welcome that the Islanders reserve for visiting yachts and their crews.

Apart from day sailing boats that are either hauled ashore, or that can return to one of the many marinas each night, any visiting boat must be well equipped. The distances involved in a boat getting to the Shetland Islands on its own bottom tend to ensure that only boats suitable for extended offshore passages are seen cruising here. The weather, even in summer is subject to rapid change, and winds that are predominantly a little stronger than may be more common further South, can also bring fog as well as accompanying larger seas. Tides can also be a dominant factor in forming cruising plans around the Shetland Islands with a number of 'Rosts' that can run at rates of up to eight knots. Wind against tide conditions make for spectacular vistas, but not ones to be experienced at too short a range.

The fact that there are very few trees naturally growing should give some clue to the type of winds that can be encountered during winter gales. Prudent cruising should perhaps be limited to the months from May to September when winds are generally of a more acceptable and predictable nature.

It should be noted that many of the anchorages offer little in the way of facilities, so yachts should be prepared for a degree of self reliance, although most items of a consumable nature for both the boat and its crew are available from the larger towns. A lot of Shetland history is closely related to the sea, so almost anything for a boat or its repair will be available from one of the many boating related businesses, typically along with a friendly Shetland smile. The remoteness of some of the anchorages has been mentioned, and as the sea bed ranges from mud to shingle and sometimes rocks, it is recommended that at least two different patterns of anchors be carried. The commonly used CQR type is quite effective in many places, but can be compromised where there is a thin layer of sand or mud over rock. Whatever type of anchor is used it is worth spending a little more time than usual ensuring that it is well dug in, particularly if leaving the boat unattended.

Due to the wonderful seclusion that many of the Shetland Island areas offer, swinging room is not usually a problem, and although this allows the use of an anchor warp instead of all chain, a good length of chain before the warp should be considered essential due to the sometimes sharp rocks that can be encountered.

Decent size fuel and water tanks are also almost an essential due to the remoteness of some of the best cruising areas. Otherwise regular trips back to the population centres will be required, particularly for fuel if hose delivery is needed.

Charts currently available are all Admiralty issue and although the complete set for the Shetland Islands runs to some 13 sheets, for those carrying a computer, Admiralty Leisure do issue an electronic Plotter version with all the charts included at a much reduced cost.

The main centre in the Shetland Islands is Lerwick, and although some stores are often available in the smaller local shops located around the islands, major storing is best done at either Lerwickon the East coast, or Scalloway on the West coast.

Shetland Islands Tourist Office is located in Market Square, Lerwick, a few steps from the yacht pontoon in Victoria Harbour, and is a superb source of information about almost everything to do, see or that is available throughout the islands. The staff are extremely

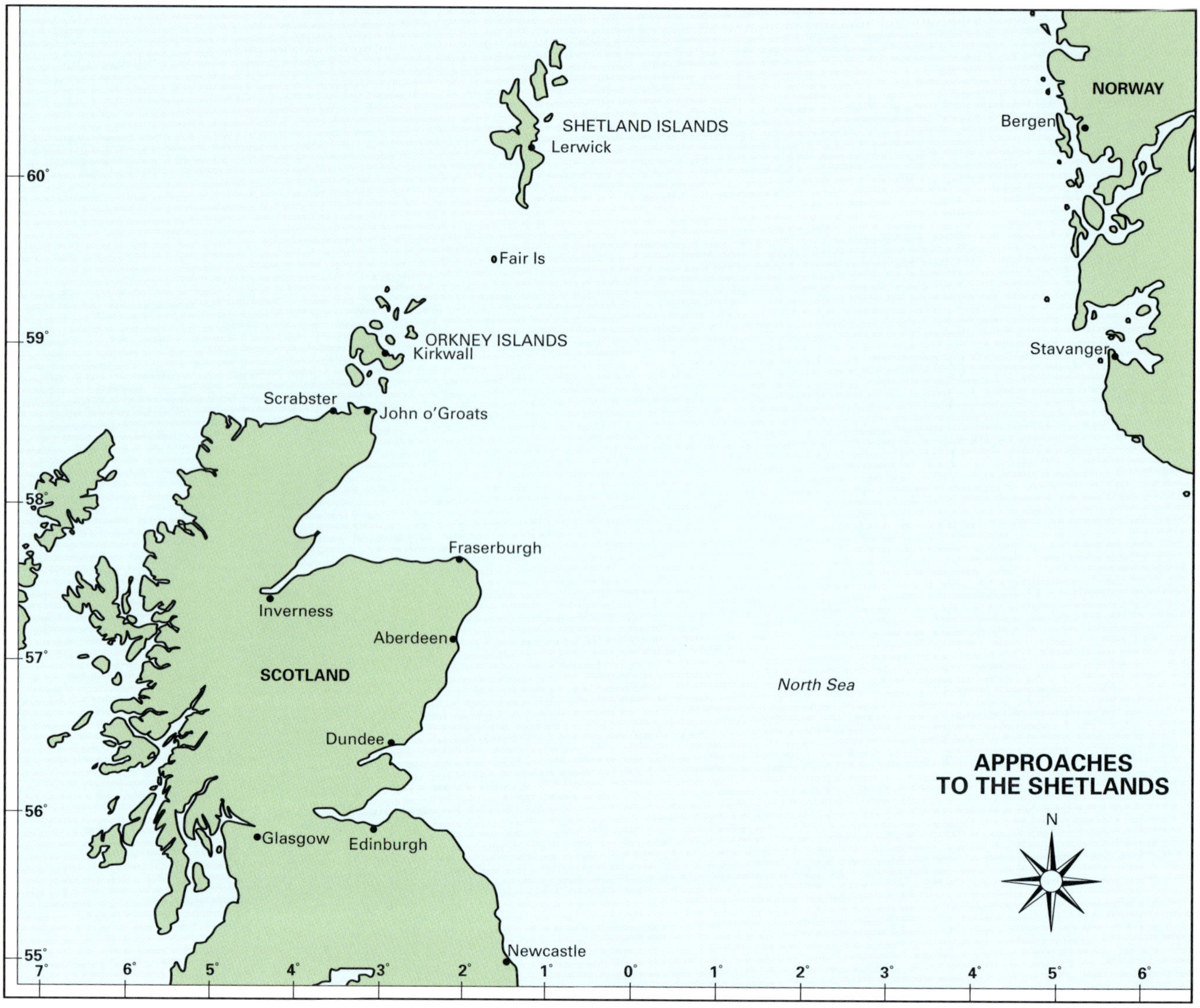
SHETLAND ISLANDS
Lerwick
Fair Is
ORKNEY ISLANDS
Kirkwall
Scrabster
John o'Groats
NORWAY
Bergen
Stavanger
Fraserburgh
Inverness
Aberdeen
SCOTLAND
North Sea
Dundee
Glasgow
Edinburgh
Newcastle
APPROACHES
TO THE SHETLANDS
N
60°
59°
58°
57°
56°
55°
7°
6°
5°
4°
3°
2°
1°
0°
1°
2°
3°
4°
5°
6°

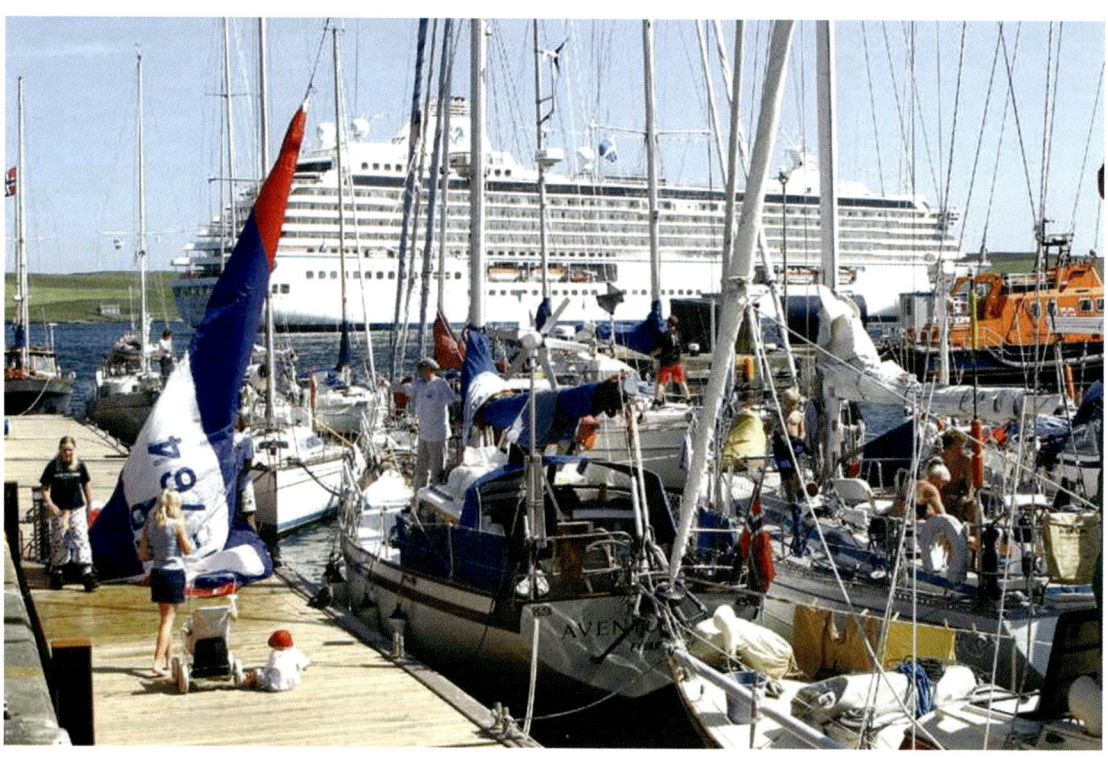

Getting there

The Shetland Isles are centred around the 60th parallel, making them a reasonable distance from the mainland of both UK and Europe. From the UK mainland there are two very useful stopping points; the Orkney Islands and Fair Isle. From Europe distances are not beyond the capabilities of even a small family crew with the distance from Norway being as little as 160 miles.

In order to do justice to a cruise around these wonderful isles, if at all possible, several weeks should be allocated to the venture. Fortunately there are good transport links to and from the Shetland Islands, so crew changes can be accomplished without difficulty. There are air links from Stanstead and Glasgow as well as indirect links from several other UK airports. Ferries, which can also take cars, run daily from Aberdeen to Lerwick.

Sailing from the UK mainland, either the West coast route or Northwards past the East coast are the two options with the former being more exposed to the prevailing Atlantic winds, but with many more stopping points. Many of these are very attractive and most offer shelter from even the worst of Scottish summer weather. One word of warning though, weather in the Shetland Islands is even more extreme than that likely to be experienced on Scotland's West coast, so sailing to these rewarding isles should realistically be restricted to the months of May to September. Notwithstanding these times, good weather can also be experienced from mid May and for the first couple of weeks in September. Temperatures are likely to be a bit lower than further south, but the resulting clarity of the air spectacularly makes up for this. Conversely, summer in the Shetland Isles means that thick mist, or fog for the uninitiated, is likely on average about three days per month.

The West coast route takes one past such beauty spots as Mull, Skye and the Outer Hebrides, with many alternatives on the mainland coast. Oban, Tobermory, Kyle of Lochalsh, and Ullapool provide good centres with almost anything that could be needed by either a weary sailor or his boat. Once past Ullapool on the route north, both Lochinver and Kinlochbervie, being fishing ports, provide last minute stores and refreshments before setting off to round Cape Wrath and setting sail towards the Orkney Islands. The distance to Stromness on the West side of Orkney is about 80 miles and if arriving when the tide is on the ebb, likely to be severely delayed as the flow out of the channel can reach five knots. Better to sail a bit slower and enjoy the sail from the Scottish mainland than to have to wait off the entrance for a couple of hours. The channel is well charted however and for those with a powerful enough engine should pose no real problems, but as with most such channels caution applies when wind is against the tide.

Such is the draw of the Orkney Islands that many boats stay longer than planned, but if the crew can be pulled away, the sail around the Northern Isles of the group and on to Fair Isle is most rewarding with its variety of scenery and wildlife. In these northern waters sightings of minke whales, dolphins, and sea birds galore are likely to make the trip one that sticks in memory for many years. Fair Isle offers a similar draw for its fascinating scenery and even more wildlife. Of the three anchorages on the island, only North Haven is really practical, and as the Observatory is located there, it is almost an essential stopping point. Showers and meals are available at the Observatory, and there is even a small bar where crews from visiting yachts are made most welcome. Many crews are also tempted to join one of the guided wildlife tours that are the raison d'être for the centre's existence. If time is not too pressing these are well worth considering.

The remaining voyage to the Shetland Islands is on a course of almost due North, and if care is taken to keep a few miles to the east of Sumburgh Head, a clear run into Lerwick will avoid The Rost, the stretch of very turbulent water off the southern tip of Mainland Shetland. Most visiting yachts make Lerwick their first stop, so gaining their first experience of Shetland courtesy and hospitality. It is no surprise that many stay much longer than planned. Lerwick itself has much to offer, with attractions ranging from its very friendly sailing club, to a recently opened museum. The sailing club has showers, and laundry facilities that can be accessed 24 hours a day. Get a key for a small refundable deposit from the harbourmaster's office. The tourist office is about 50 metres from the yacht pontoon in Victoria Harbour, and well worth a call, not just for the help on offer regarding the sights around the Shetland Islands, but also for the free use of their internet connections.

An alternative route to the Shetland Islands offers a combination of both east and west coast passages. Heading north past the easier areas of the west coast as far as Fort William then allows a trip through the Caledonian Canal to Inverness. From there a stop at Wick followed by another at Kirkwall provides quite a variety of interests. The trip through the Caledonian Canal is itself a fascinating experience. As all the locks are manned by BWB staff, there is less need for a large and muscular crew than with some canals, and the scenery can only be described as spectacular. It is not the quickest way north, and as the locals say, "It takes two days (for the passage) if you hurry; and two days if you don't." If time allows, a worthwhile variation and this route avoids the sometimes boisterous area around Cape Wrath.

Things to do and see

Such is the diversity of life in our far north islands that there are almost certainly many things of interest to visitors regardless of individual preferences. Wildlife abounds all over the islands, relics from ancient cultures abound, and for those of an energetic nature, there are many areas where walking and trekking offer rewards seldom found elsewhere.

The Shetland Islands are rich in history, and several museums give clues to what life was like in the past. Geographically closer to Scandinavia than to the UK mainland it is not surprising that a substantial part of the local culture is strongly influenced by this connection. However, that is not to say historical interests are the only ones. Shetlanders are very conscious of the benefits of tourism to their economy, and as a result go out of their way to provide a variety of pursuits. For the sailor, even the serious traditionalist, the arrival of some of the long distance races, such as the Round Britain race and the annual Bergen to Shetland race are spectacles not to be missed. This latter race forms part of the Netherlands based 1000 mile race which takes in several Scandinavian countries with Shetland being the only Scottish stop. For those more interested in mechanical means of transport there is a Classic Motor Show at the beginning of June, recently attracting upwards of 180 classic and vintage cars.

Held, unfortunately outwith the sailing season, the highlight of the Shetland year is without doubt, 'Up-Helly-Aa', a festival where the whole community celebrate in their own unique style for a week which culminates on the last Tuesday in January in the ritual burning of a replica Viking Longship. For those who cannot make it to the winter festival there is a fully operational replica Longboat kept afloat off Lerwick Boating Club and it is possible to arrange to sail in her, although whether anyone is likely to be converted from the comforts of a modern yacht to the rigours of a long voyage in such a boat is another matter.

Musical interests are very much to the forefront of Shetland culture with both formal and impromptu music sessions being held all over the islands. One place that is very popular and which offers live music from just about every possible background is The Lounge. Music ranges from pop to folk with just about everything else being performed at some time. The Lounge is situated a few meters up the hill beside the Tourist Office in central Lerwick. Wednesdays and Fridays seem to be the most popular evenings.

If time allows, it is worth hiring a car, as this allows easy and quick access to the three main islands of Mainland, Yell and Unst. The main hire companies are all located on Mainland, but will usually deliver a car to customers almost anywhere within the island group. Local car ferries are both regular, efficient and by UK mainland standards, very cheap. The use of a car certainly expands the horizons without the necessity to walk for many miles between areas of interest.

The lighthouse at Sumburgh Head is well worth a visit, particularly on a clear day. For days when the climate is more in keeping with the latitude, the Shetland Bus Museum at Scalloway is quite fascinating. Having nothing whatsoever to do with motor vehicles, the museum commemorates the brave crews of Norwegian fishing boats who, during the second world war, effectively ran a 'bus' service between the Norwegian coast and Shetland. They carried messages as well as transporting men and women in both directions, some working to gather intelligence, and some

Up Helly-ah
David Spence

Sumburgh Head lighthouse
Roy Longmuir | Dreamstime.com

Unst Boat Haven, Harold's Wick

merely escaping from the enemy in Europe. The fishing boats were either unarmed or at best, very lightly armed, and all sailed right under the noses of the German Navy. Most of the trips were undertaken during the winter months when daylight is limited in these northern waters. As a result storms in the North Sea claimed a number of lives, in addition to those lost due to enemy actions. There is a fascinating book by David Howarth which explains the history of the 'Shetland Bus' and once an appetite for information is whetted at the museum, is a very good read.

The recently opened Shetland Museum in Lerwick is another feature not to be missed, as is the display at the Unst Boat Haven. Other areas that offer a fascinating alternative to formal museum type displays are the prehistoric and Norse settlement at Jarlshof, the Iron Age village at the Old Scatness Broch, and the best preserved Broch anywhere, on the island of Mousa. As there are generally good anchorages on the offlying islands that are close to the various attractions, a visit by boat is a novel way of improving ones knowledge of Shetland history. For those with less interest in ancient lives, the music scene, already mentioned is no less important in the Northern Isles. Each year there is a Folk Festival that attracts some very well known names in addition to some of the highly talented local bands. For those with different tastes there is also a Guitar Festival and Shetland's own Fiddle Frenzy.

Although there are numerous places around these isles that offer decent facilities to visiting yachts, the main centres of Lerwick and Scalloway are definitely better geared to the needs of the serious shopper. Shetland knitwear has long been famous, and with good reason, all over the world. There are several outlets for these rich designs, and some will even make up garments to special order. More generally there are numerous other shops where most items can be obtained, and for the skipper of the boat, an extremely good chandlers, albeit with a slant towards fishing and the commercial sizes of gear. They will, however in typical helpful Shetland fashion, try to obtain almost anything not in stock.

Shetland Museum
Mark Sinclair

INTRODUCTION

helpful and have an almost encyclopaedic knowledge, even about where to get specifically nautical items both of the unusual variety and the more commonly required such as Calor Gas.

For those who cannot take unlimited time from work or other commitments there are both ferry and air services to the Shetland Islands. The ferry leaves from Aberdeen on a daily basis and there are frequent flights from Glasgow, Edinburgh, and Inverness, all of which enable crew changes to be planned well ahead, and there are many hotels and guest houses, should a yacht's arrival be delayed for any reason.

Visited by numerous Scandinavian boats as well as those from UK waters, there are several approaches to the islands. Either from the West coast round Cape Wrath, or from the East coast via the Caledonian canal, or indeed direct from the East coast. Whichever route is taken, a stop at The Orkney islands and Fair Isle allow the voyage to be split into sections that can be covered in day sails.

Cautions for navigators throughout the Shetland Islands include the numerous and often unlit fish farms. Not only do these cause a hazard to navigation, but they must be cleared by some distance when anchoring, unless one wishes to become extremely unpopular, particularly with the owners of the oyster beds. The other side of this rule is that the local seafood is spectacularly good.

Where plans in this book show suggested routes into anchorages that contain fish farms, it is important that such equipment is given a good berth even where the suggested route may appear to suggest otherwise.

Bearings used in the Pilot are all true bearings.

Distances are quoted in nautical miles or cables (¹⁄₁₀ of a nautical mile, or 200 yards.)

Depths are given in metres, and tides are quoted on both a local basis where possible or as a constant on Lerwick.

Pictures are intended to help mariners visualise areas being visited, but should be used in conjunction with the script, plans, and with reference to the relevant chart. Admiralty charts for the Shetland Isles are all WGS84 compliant, so GPS positions can be plotted directly.

Throughout the islands, mobile phone networks seem to provide good communications with few blank areas.

Lastly, it is worth stressing that although some effort is often required to get to these enchanting islands, the energy expended is likely to be repaid many times over. The scenery and wildlife alone make the trip worthwhile, and as for the Shetland people, their attitude to visitors is such that one visit will never be enough.

Viking boat at Lerwick
Tt | Dreamstime

INTRODUCTION

Fact File

Lerwick Port Authority ☎ 01595 692991
VHF Ch 12 (24hour)

Lerwick Boating Club ☎ 01595 692407
(mainly bar hours)

Doctor Lerwick Health Centre, South Road, Lerwick
☎ 01595 693201

Dentist ☎ 01595 695769

Lerwick Coastguard ☎ 01595 692976

Facilities

Fuel and Chandlery
LHD Marine Supplies, Albert Building, Esplanade, Lerwick ☎ 01595 692379.

Charts
LHD Marine Supplies, 1 Alexandra Buildings, Lerwick
☎ 01595 693768.

Gas
Rearo Gas Supplies, Staney Hill, Lerwick
☎ 01595 692807 (Calor Gas only).

Water
Alongside at Victoria Pontoon.

Showers and Laundry
Lerwick Boating Club – keys are available from the Port Authority offices in Albert Building for a small deposit.

Waste disposal
Alongside at Victoria Pontoon.

Slipways
Victoria Harbour and at Gremista Marina.

Bank/ATM
Banks are located in Commercial Street, Lerwick's main street.

Leisure Centre and swimming pool at Clickimin ☎ 01595 741000.

Shetland Islands Tourist Office
Market Square, Lerwick ☎ 01595 693434.

Provisions
Supermarkets: Co-op, Holmsgarth Road, Lerwick, Sommerfield, South Road, Lerwick,

Bonded Stores,
Zetland Bonded Services, 12 Thorfinn Street, Lerwick
☎ 01595 693537 (useful if sailing on to Scandinavia).

Repairs
A. Adamson & Co., 22 Commercial Road, Lerwick
☎ 01595 696656.

Shetland Composites, SBS Base Lerwick
☎ 01595 696426 (grp repairs).

Thule Craft Ltd, Gremista, Lerwick ☎ 01595 692500

Pubs and restaurants
Monty's Bistro, 5 Mounthooly Street, (at side of Tourist Office) Lerwick ☎ 01595 696555.

The Lounge, 4 Mounthooly Street, Lerwick (music & drinks) ☎ 01595 692231.

Grand Hotel, 149 Commercial Street, Lerwick
☎ 01595 692231

Interest

Fort Charlotte is located at the Northern end of Commercial Street and dates back to 1665.

Lodberries Properties built out to sea for the original use of merchants whose goods were shipped directly to and from the buildings using their own jetties.

Shetland Museum and Library has been recently rebuilt at a new site beside Hay's Dock just North of the main shopping street. It includes the fully restored 1825 clock from the original site.

The Knab Located at the South end of the cliff top path from Twageos Point, spectacular views show the old importance of Lerwick as a naval anchorage.

Up-Helly-Aa The traditional world famous Shetland Island festival is held on the last Tuesday of January, so may not be of much interest to visiting yachts, but well worth a visit by other means of transport. An exhibition giving the full flavour of the spectacle is open during the summer months at St. Sunniva Street Galley Shed.

Lerwick

Traditional houses in Lerwick

FAIR ISLE

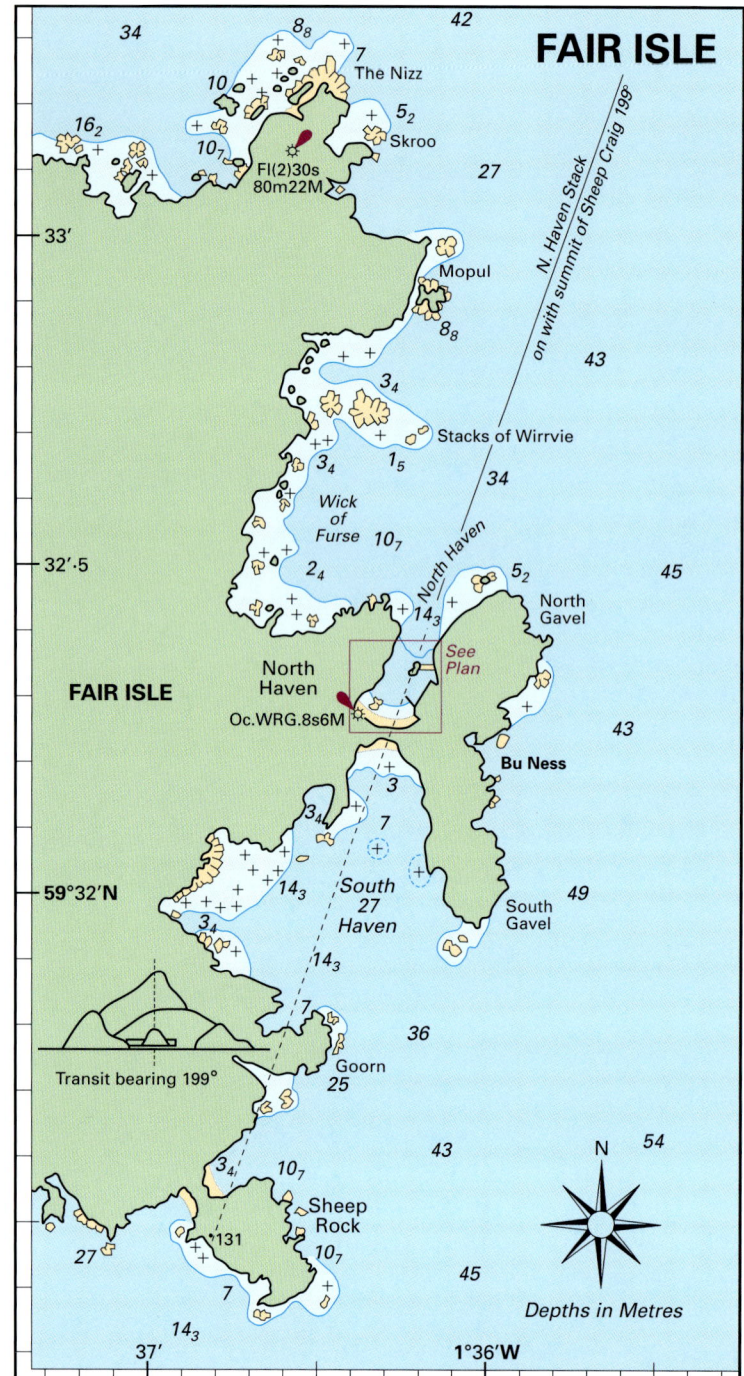

Black lamb enjoying the sun on Fair Isle

Sheep Rock, Fair Isle

FAIR ISLE

South Harbour
⊕ 59°30´·3N 1°39´·0W

South Haven
⊕ 59°31´·8N 1°36´·3W

North Haven
⊕ 59°32´·6N 1°36·1W

CHART
3299

TIDES
-0022 Lerwick

LIGHTS
Skadan Lighthouse Fl(4)30s32m22M 59°30´·829N 001°39´·154W
Skroo Lighthouse Fl(2)30s80m22M 59°33´·120N 001°36´·578W
North Haven Oc.WRG.8s10m6M 59°32´·241N 001°36´·378W

Dangers

If approaching from the South, beware the offlying rocks known as The Keels, and also the tidal race called the Roost of the Keels which extends up to 2½ miles offshore and can cause dangerous overfalls in a wind against tide situation. There is also a tide race at the North of the island, and similar comments apply.

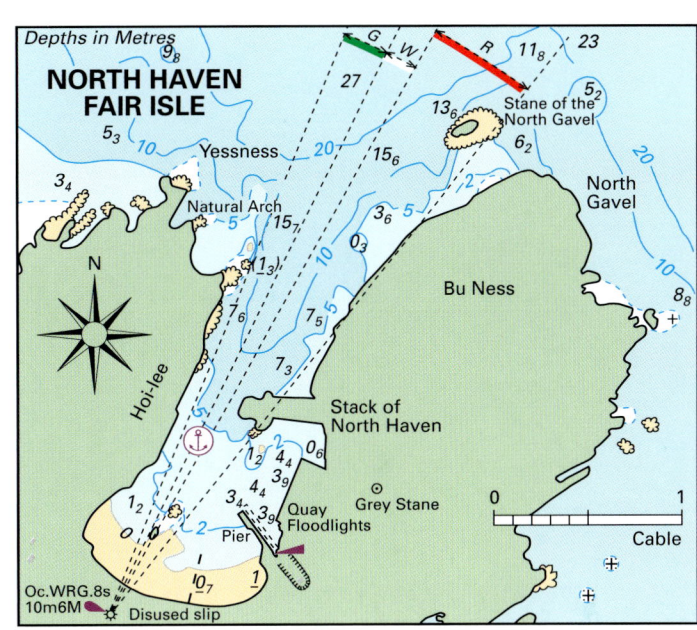

Anchorages

There are three anchorages, but of these only one, North Haven, can be considered of much practical use.

The harbour at North Haven. Fair Isle

FAIR ISLE

North Haven, Fair Isle. The arrow shows the leading light

North Haven

North Haven

A leading light has been erected at the inner end of the bay, but is quite difficult to see, especially if entering on a sunny afternoon when the light will be in your eyes. The light is sectored, but if invisible a line from the top of Sheep Rock over the end of the breakwater leads clear of the few dangers. If entering from the East, leave the rock called The Stane of the North Gavel to port and turn onto a heading of 210°. Once past the end of the breakwater, either tie up alongside, leaving room for the ferry, or anchor off the pier as soundings permit. Bottom is sand over rock.

South Haven

This anchorage lies just South of the narrow causeway that lies at the South end of North Haven, and could provide shelter from seas formed by a strong North East wind. The bottom is rock and holding is either suspect or if the anchor fouls under one of the rocks, likely to be permanent. Entering from the South beware the rocks off the points at both sides of the entrance and also the rock just to the East of the centre of the bay.

South Harbour

The main population centre of the island is located at South Harbour, but the anchorage can only be considered a fair weather stop, and the entrance is littered with rocks, only some of which show above water. Not recommended.

Facilities

The Fair Isle Bird Observatory is located 300m from the pier at North Haven, and offers visiting yachts a warm welcome, with showers, meals and a small bar. It is open from April to September each year. Diesel can be obtained in small quantities by arrangement with the Bird Observatory, and fresh water is available on the pier at North Haven. A small but well stocked shop and Post Office can be reached about 1½ miles to the South. Contact Jimmy Stout ☏ 01595 760222.

Interest

This fascinating island has many high cliffs which is one of the reasons for the existence of the Fair Isle Bird Observatory. Apart from birdlife, many species of whales are regularly sighted from the vantage point of the cliffs, making the island a popular destination for those interested in wildlife. The population of the island is about 70, plus the summer visitors.

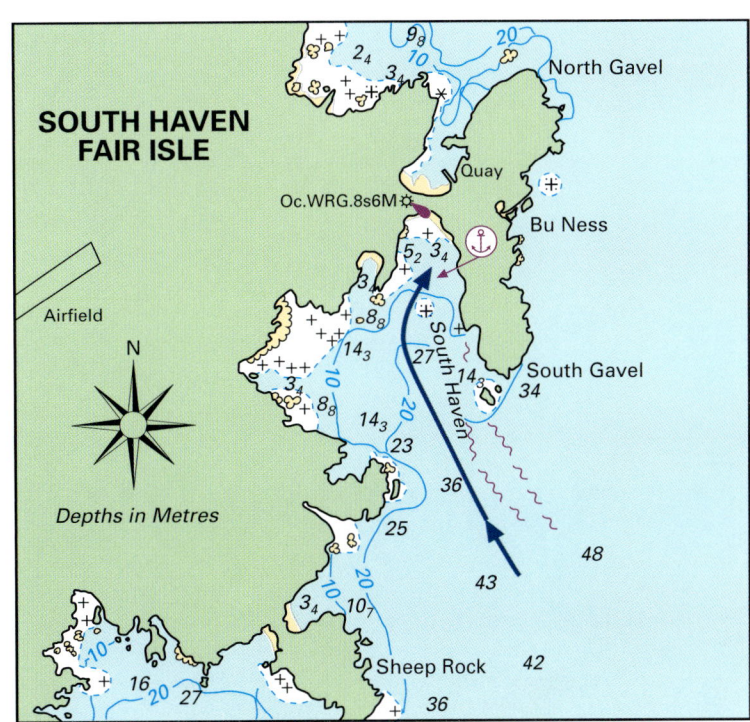

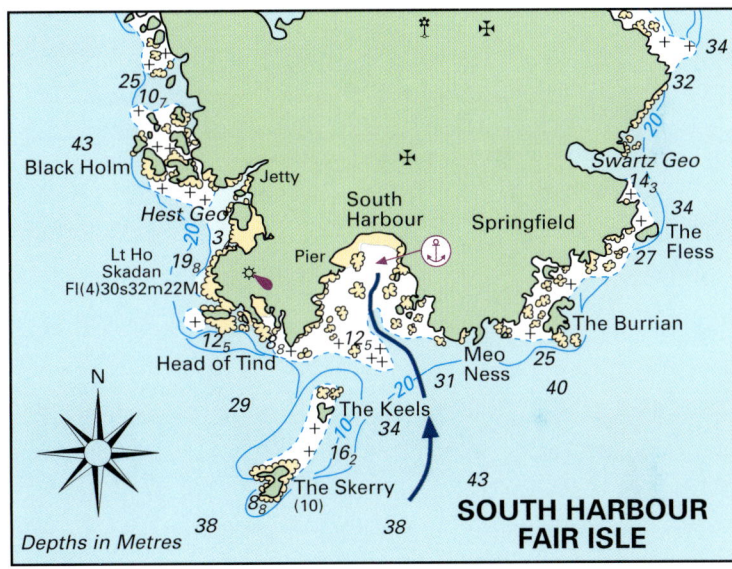

The Keels, rocks off the south end of Fair Isle

MAINLAND SHETLAND EAST COAST

Grutness Voe

⊕ 59°52´·9N 1°15´·7W

CHART
3283

TIDES
+0015 Lerwick

LIGHTS
Sumburgh Head Fl(3)30s91m23M 59°51´·222N 001°16´·515W

Dangers
There are strong tides to the East of Sumburgh Head and in Westerly winds downdrafts can cause unexpected strong gusts for some distance offshore. Proceed at least ½ mile North of Looss Laward before turning into the bay.

Anchorages
The first practical Shetland anchorage when sailing from the South. Grutness Voe must be approached from the North East avoiding the shoals and rocks that extend North of Looss Laward by almost ½ mile. The head of the bay is shallow but the anchorage just North of the jetty in about 4m gives shelter from all but North East winds. Strong South winds create downdrafts due to the height of Sumburgh Head. Unattended yachts should not be left tied to the pier which is reserved for the Fair Isle ferry.

Facilities
Sumburgh airport, water and toilets at pier. Ferry to Fair Isle. Shop, pub and restaurant within walking distance. ☏ 01950 460201. *See also Pool of Virkie.*

Interest
Cliffs at Sumburgh Head with attendant birdlife.

Grutness Voe from the north

Pool of Virkie

⊕ 59°53′·1N 1°17′·5W (Centre of Pool)

CHART
3283

TIDES
+0004 Lerwick

LIGHTS
Entrance 2FG(vert) 59°53′·018N 001°17′·170W

Anchorages
Very sheltered but shallow, and only suitable for small boats or those that can take the ground.

Facilities
Hotel ☏ 01950 460240. Toilets, water and slip at Marina. Contact Brian Halcrow ☏ 01950 477 260.

Interest
Old Scatness and Jarlshof are both interesting archeological sites, one showing how life was lived in this area in the Iron Age. The latter showing that the area was inhabited several thousand years ago. Guides and demonstrations are available during July and August.

Virkie Marina

⊕ 59°53′·1N 1°17′·5W

CHART
3283

TIDES
+0004 Lerwick

LIGHTS
Entrance 2FG(vert) 59°53′·018N 001°17′·170W

Anchorages
A friendly marina and home of the Ness Boating Club, but entrance is narrow and shallow making local advice almost essential. Maximum depth in the marina is 1m and only one visitors berth is available. Check availability before entering by calling Brian Halcrow ☏ 01950 477260.
Ness Boating Club ☏ 01950 460712.

Facilities
See Pool of Virkie - above.

Interest
See Pool of Virkie - above.

Voe Bay

⊕ 59°54′·9N 1°16′·1W

CHART
3283

TIDES
+0004 Lerwick

LIGHTS
None

Dangers
Beware gusts blowing out of the bay in strong west or northwest winds.

Anchorages
If approaching from the South, give Lambogha

Pool of Virkie and Grutness Voe looking south

Head a clear berth of at least one cable and from the above waypoint steer 295° and anchor in 6–7m at least 1½ cables from the head of the bay which shoals. Bottom is rocky so use of a tripping line should be considered.

Facilities
Shops ☏ 01806 588286 at Boddam along the road to the North of the anchorage. Bar and restaurant ☏ 01806 588332.

Leven Wick

⊕ 59°58′·70N 1°14′·80W

CHARTS
3283, 3294

TIDES
+0008 Lerwick

LIGHTS
None

Dangers
There are a number of magnetic anomalies in this area and compasses can be up to 15° in error. Care should be taken if steering a compass course in poor visibility.

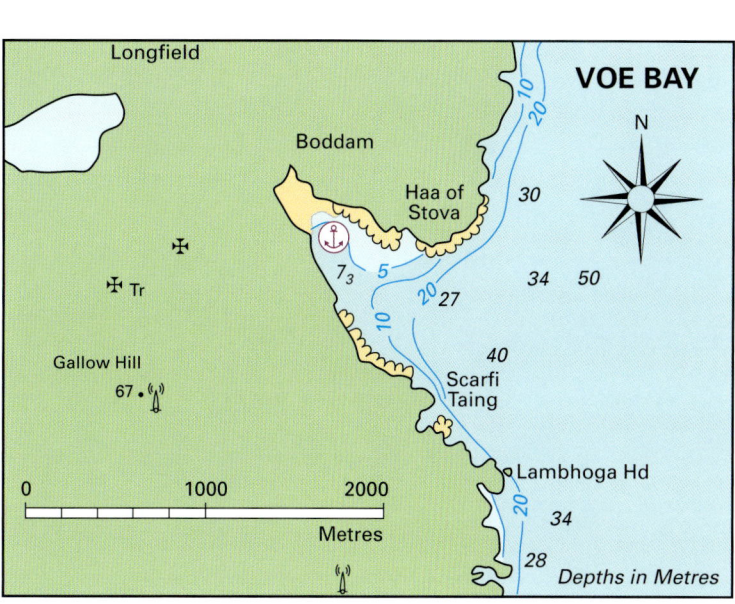

MAINLAND SHETLAND – EAST COAST

Anchorages

Offering some shelter from winds in the South, the shallow area to the North west of Levenwick Ness should be given a berth of at least one cable before turning into the bay. There are two submerged rocks ½ cable off the East shore. Anchor in the centre of the bay in 5m approximately one cable offshore.

Facilities

Shops and hotel at Hos Wick.

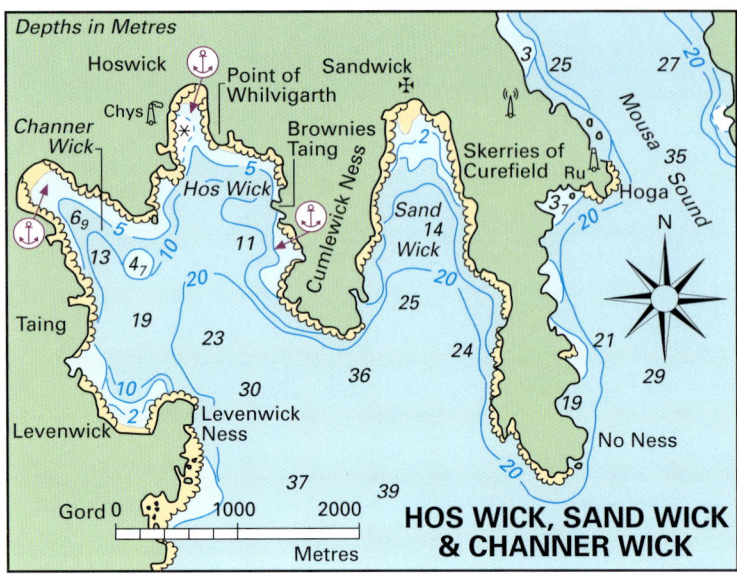

Channer Wick

⊕ 59°58´·70N 1°14´·80W

CHARTS
3283, 3294

TIDES
+0008 Lerwick

LIGHTS
None

Dangers

See above regarding magnetic anomalies. Entrance is clear of dangers beyond one cable of the shore on both sides.

Anchorages

At head of bay in about 5m approximately one cable offshore.

Hos Wick

⊕ 59°58´·6N 1°14´·0W

CHARTS
3283, 3294

TIDES
+0008 Lerwick

LIGHTS
None

Dangers

See above re: magnetic anomalies. Beware rocks which extend ½ cable west of Point of Whilvigarth.

Anchorages

There are two useable anchorages within Hos Wick. The North West corner provides shelter from the North but the head of the bay is shoal. Anchor in the pool one cable North West of Point of Whilvigarth in 5–6m. Bottom sand, but rocks abound if going any further into bay. The second anchorage provides shelter from East winds but can be subject swell. This is South of Brownies Taing in the bay marked Sands of Cumlewick on chart 3294. Anchor in about 6m. Bottom sand.

Facilities

Shops, hotel and pub ☎ 01950 431226 in village.

Hos Wick from the west

Sand Wick Bay

Sand Wick

⊕ 59°58′·6N 1°14′·0W

CHARTS
3283, 3294

TIDES
+0008 Lerwick

LIGHTS
None

Dangers
See above re magnetic anomalies. There are some disused underwater cables in the bay so the use of a tripping line is recommended.

Anchorages
The sides of the bay are clear of dangers ½ cable offshore until Skerries of Curefield 59°59′·397N 001°13′·138W are abeam. Anchorage is possible 1½ cables NW of the Skerries of Curefield on a bearing of 315°. Bottom sand but rocks nearer head of bay.

Mousa Sound

⊕ 59°59′·33N 001°11′·20W

CHART
3283

TIDES
+0008 Lerwick

LIGHTS
Perie Bard Fl.3s20m10M 59°59′·84N 001°09′·51W

Dangers
Passage through the sound is quite straightforward with no hazards beyond two cables of either shore. Tides are surprisingly gentle, with spring tides not causing a flow much over 1·5 knots. Tides generally run approximately NW/SE.

Anchorages
The bay ½ mile North of the Broch (spelt Brough on chart 3283) provides reasonable shelter from Easterly winds, but a tripping line is recommended.

Facilities
There are no facilities on the island other than the ferry from Mainland.

Interest
Perhaps the best preserved Broch (ancient dwelling) in the UK.

MOUSA

⊕ West Ham 59°59′·88N 001°11′·72W
East Ham 60°00′·35N 001°10′·18W

CHART
3283

TIDES
+0010 Lerwick

LIGHTS
Perie Bard Fl.3s20m10M 59°59′·829N 001°09′·490W

Dangers
None in the approaches but there is a drying rock slightly north of half way across the bay just to the west of the jetty.

Anchorages
West Ham To the South of the jetty in 4–5m. Some swell.

East Ham Very temporary anchorage with some shelter from South west winds. Do not go further into the bay than South of the North point.

Facilities
None.

Interest
Ancient broch is a half mile walk South of the anchorage at West Ham. Caves at East Ham.

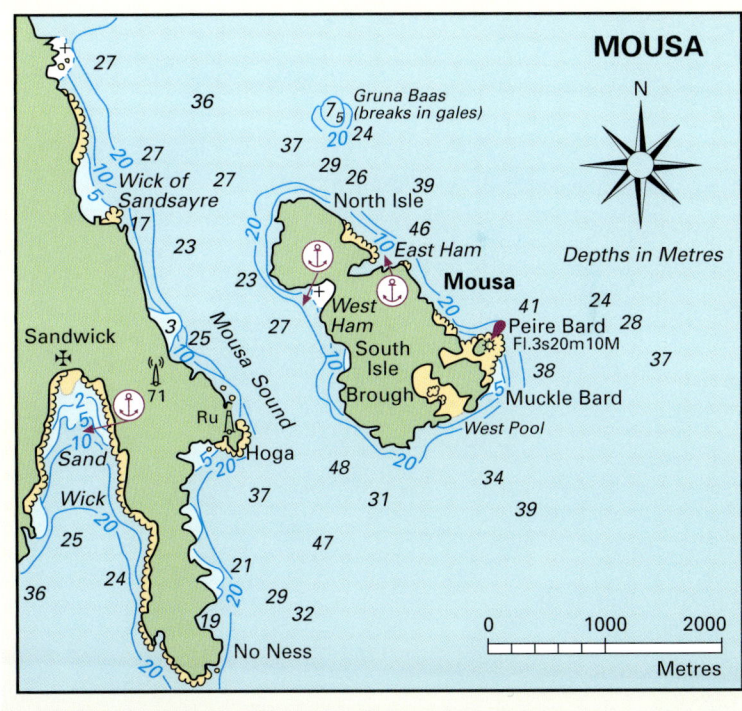

Mousa from the NW

MAINLAND SHETLAND – EAST COAST

Wick of Sandsayre with ferry to Mousa in mid channel

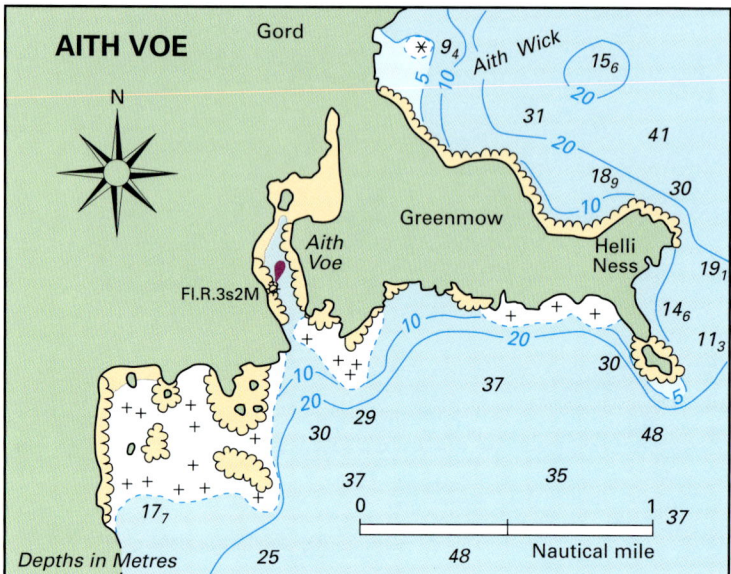

Wick of Sandsayre

⊕ 60°00´·65N 001°12´·70W

CHART
3283

TIDES
+0008 Lerwick

LIGHTS
None

Dangers
Rocks extend just over a cable north from the south point of the bay.

Anchorages
The middle of the bay provides a good anchorage on sand in about 5m.

Facilities
Ferry to Mousa leaves from the small pier in the SW corner of the bay.

Aith Voe

⊕ 60°01´·75N 001°12´·50W

CHART
3283

TIDES
+006 Lerwick

LIGHTS
Aith Voe Fl.R.3s3m2M vis 305°–339° 60°02´·26N 001°12´·90W
Aith Voe Marina Fl.R.5s3m2M 60°02´·41N 001°12´·85W

Dangers
Entrance shoals quickly and East side is littered with rocks.

Aith Voe Marina. The entrance channel is to the left of picture

The harbour area at Aith Voe

Anchorages

Temporary anchorage off the pier and North of Aith Voe light, or follow marked channel to Aith Voe Marina. Entry at night is not recommended as channel markers are unlit. Marina has restricted depths.

Facilities

Slipway, water.

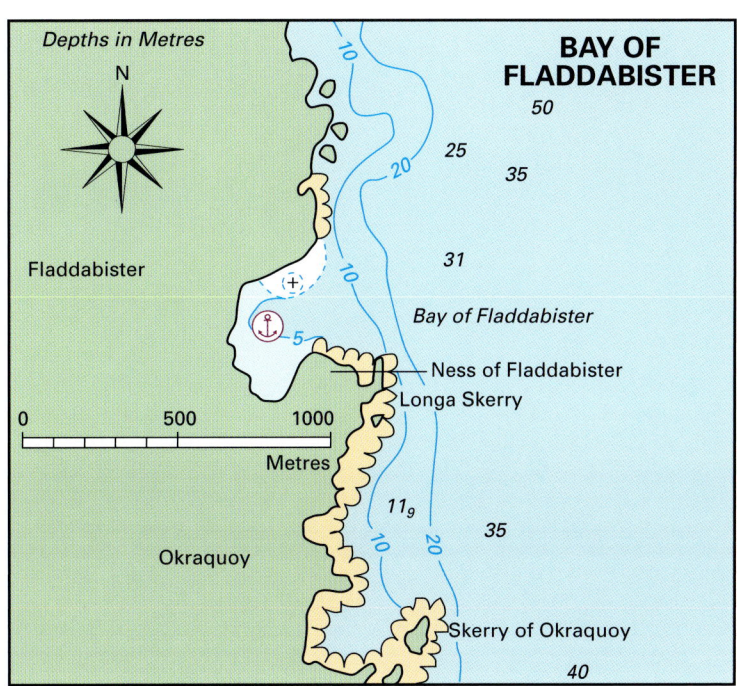

Bay of Fladdabister

Bay of Fladdabister from the NW

⊕ 60°04´·50N 001°12´·00W

CHARTS
3283, 3272

TIDES
+004 Lerwick

LIGHTS
None

Dangers

There is a submerged rock ½ cable off the North shore at the entrance opposite the W point of Ness of Fladdabister.

Anchorages

Temporary anchorage exposed to the East and tripping line recommended as bottom is rocky in places. Anchor in 5–6m.

East Voe of Quarff

⊕ 60°05´·90N 001°12´·80W

CHARTS
3283, 3272

TIDES
+004 Lerwick

LIGHTS
None

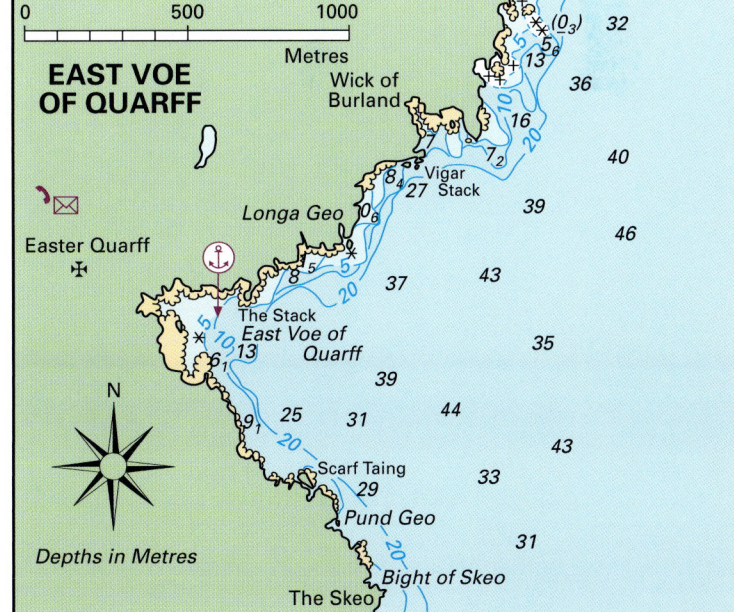

Dangers

A reef extends a cable from the South shore with a sunken rock a further cable off the end of the reef.

Anchorages

Keep to the Northern half of the bay and anchor one cable offshore in 7m.

MAINLAND SHETLAND – EAST COAST

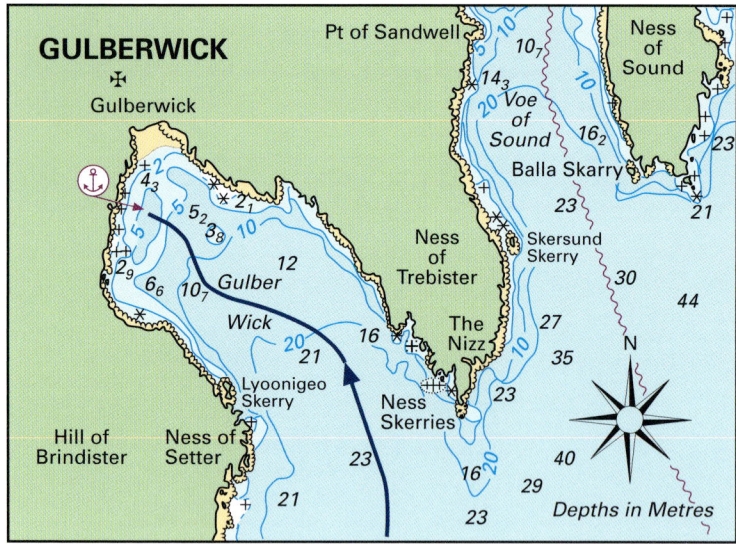

Voe of Sound looking SW

Gulberwick

Gulberwick

See also plan page 19

⊕ 60°06´·85N 001°10´·90W

CHARTS
3283, 3272, 3271 in part

TIDES
+002 Lerwick

LIGHTS
None

Dangers

There are no offlying dangers more than ½ cable offshore. Exposed to winds from the south when a swell makes the anchorage unsuitable.

Anchorages

Anchor a cable from the West shore and clear of the head of the bay which dries. There are several sandy spots in 5m that are easily seen during daylight. Use of these will avoid the many rocky areas, but the sand varies in depth so a tripping line is recommended.

Facilities

At Lerwick, a two mile walk.

Voe of Sound

See plan page 19

⊕ 60°07´·50N 001°09´·75W

CHARTS
3283, 3272, 3271

TIDES
+002 Lerwick

LIGHTS
None

Dangers

A submarine cable runs South from the head of the bay. Beware Skersund Skerry on the west side of the entrance and Balla Skerry on the east side, but otherwise an offing of one cable leads clear of all hazards until abreast Point of Sandwell.

Anchorages

A sandy pool with over 10m of water is positioned one cable to the North East of Point of Sandwell, but due to the presence of underlying rocks a tripping line is recommended.

Facilities

As Lerwick, a 1½ mile walk.

Brei Wick

See plan page 19

⊕ 60°08´·30N 001°08´·70W

CHARTS
3283, 3272, 3271

TIDES
+002 Lerwick

LIGHTS
Cro of Ham on Bressay Fl.3s12m3M 60°08´·26N 001°07´·57W

Dangers

Bressay Sound is ¾ mile wide but beware the rocks one cable off the point at Ness of Sound, thereafter keeping one cable from the shore leads clear of dangers until the reef and submerged rock that runs NE from Skeo Tang. Keep at least two cables to the east.

Anchorages

Anchor in the NE corner in 8m. Rock so tripping line recommended.

Facilities

As Lerwick ½ mile walk, but supermarket ¼ mile.

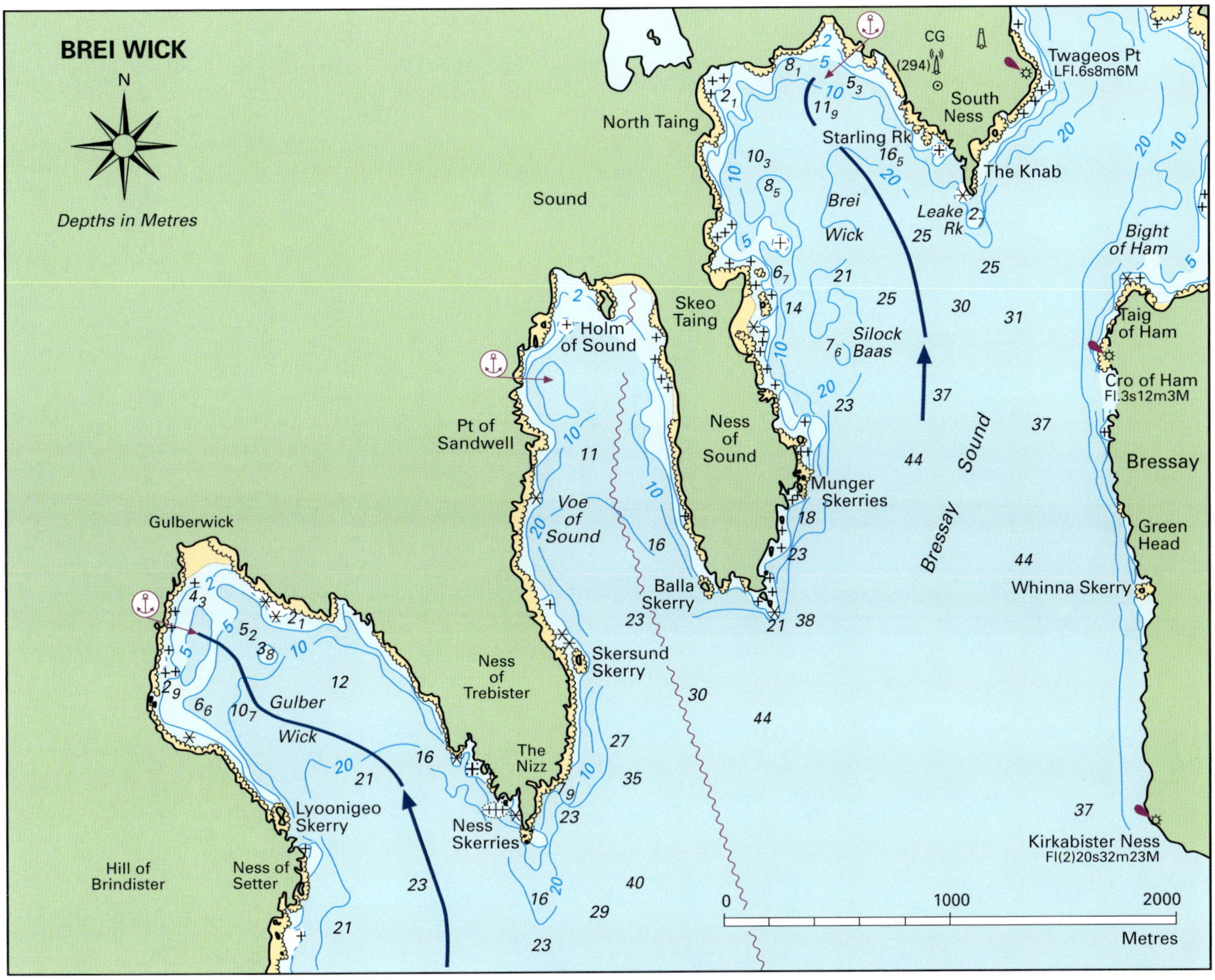

BREI WICK

Brei Wick from the SE
Exposed to the South but a useful anchorage

BRESSAY

⊕ **Bressay Marina** 60°08′·92N 001°07′·18W
⊕ **Aith Voe** 60°11′·24N 001°05′·89W
⊕ **Elvis Voe** 60°11′·07N 001°05′·42W

CHARTS
3272, 3271, 3282, 3283

TIDES
HW Lerwick

LIGHTS
As Lerwick

Dangers
All dangers are quite apparent.

Anchorages
Bressay Marina entrance is shallow but the marina is well sheltered and the visitors berth at the outer end of the pontoon has 2m. See plan page 21.

Aith Voe at the North end of Bressay is almost landlocked and as a result provides good shelter in any wind direction. Keep North of Holm of Beosetter and Holm of Gunnista. Otherwise, keep to mid channel until the Voe opens and anchor as space permits clear of the fish farms in 4–6m. Mainly sand.

Elvis Voe is a useful stop sheltered from East winds. Anchor in 3–4m. Mainly mud.

Bard Head has mooring rings on the west side near to Orkneyman's Cave.

Facilities
Hotel a short distance from the marina. No facilities at the other anchorages. Ferry from Lerwick.

Interest
Gun emplacement on Score Hill. Several ruined churches. Orkneyman's Cave is worth visiting by dinghy, but only in settled weather.

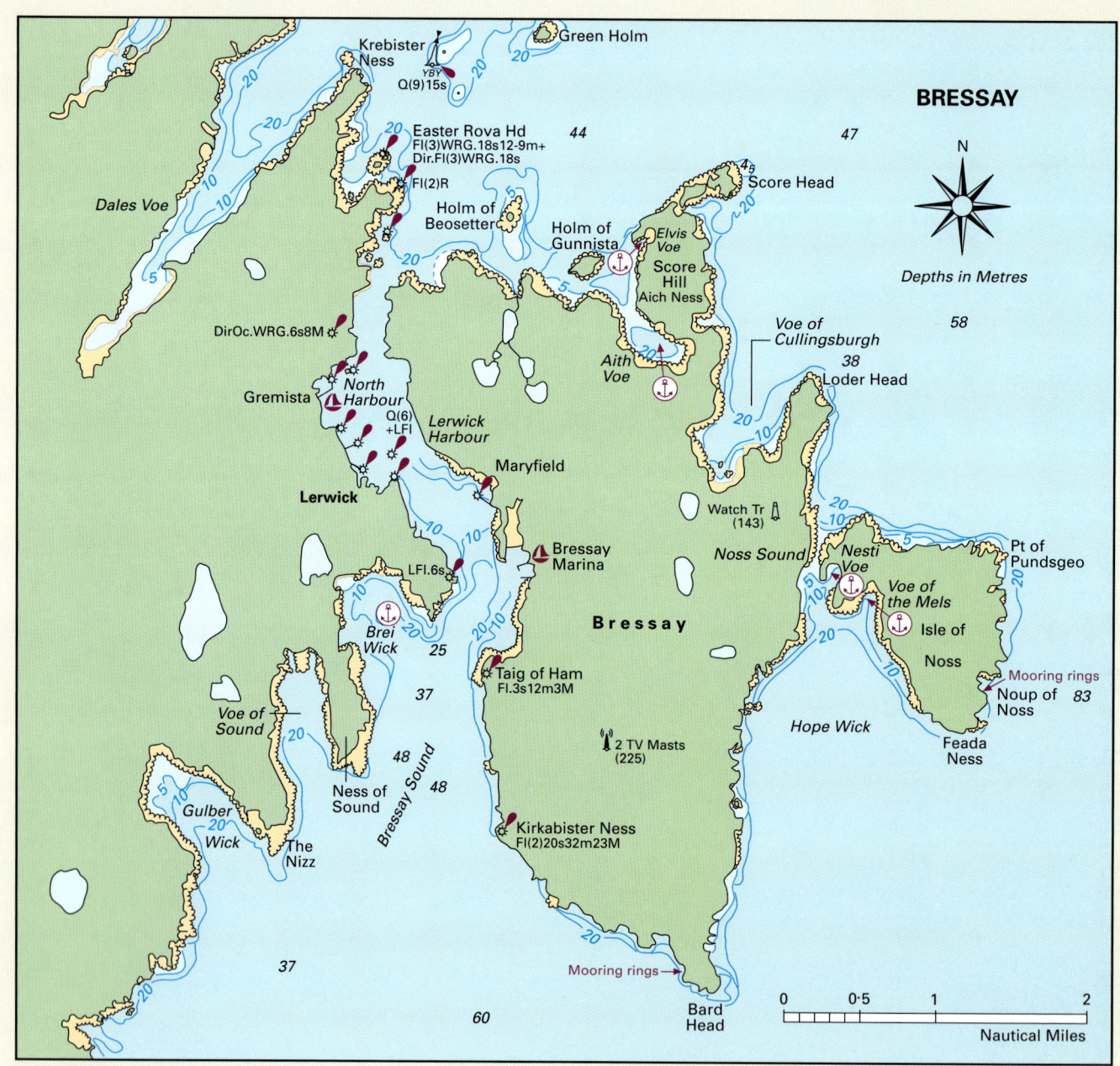

Aith Voe, Bressay offers almost perfect shelter

Bressay from Lerwick

ISLE OF NOSS

See plan page 20
⊕ **Nesti Voe** 60°08´·54N 001°02´·82W
⊕ **Voe of the Mels** 60°08´·53N 001°02´·32W
⊕ **Noup of Noss** 60°08´·23N 001°59´·96W

CHART
3283, 3272

TIDES
HW Lerwick

LIGHTS
None

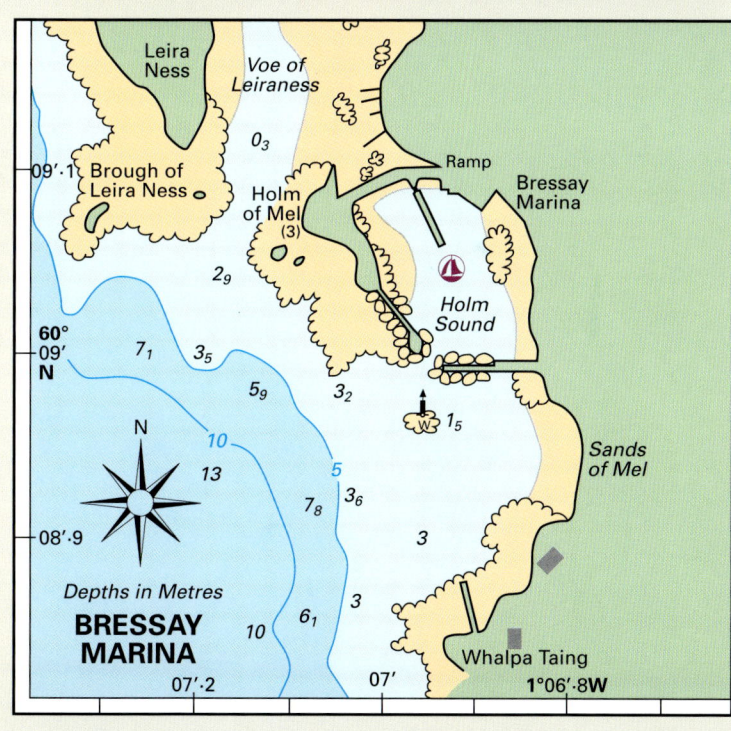

Dangers
The approaches to each anchorage are clear although all three can only be considered temporary stops and a good eye must be kept on the weather. Apart from keeping a reasonable offing at the headlands where tides can run strongly Isle of Noss offers spectacular views of the birdlife which inhabits the island.

Anchorages
Nesti Voe is the small bay to the East of small peninsula that forms part of Noss Sound. There is an underwater rock in the West part of the bay and the inner part dries.

Voe of the Mels is an easier anchorage to enter, the only hazard being a drying rock at the East end of a rocky outcrop which extends almost one cable from the West point. 4–5m.

Noup of Noss is not really an anchorage, there being some rings ashore to which mooring lines can be made fast. These are located under the Noup but the condition of the rings is uncertain. Useful in settled weather when stopping to watch the nesting birds.

Facilities
None.

Interest
Extensive birdlife and Isle of Noss is a nature reserve.

MAINLAND SHETLAND – EAST COAST

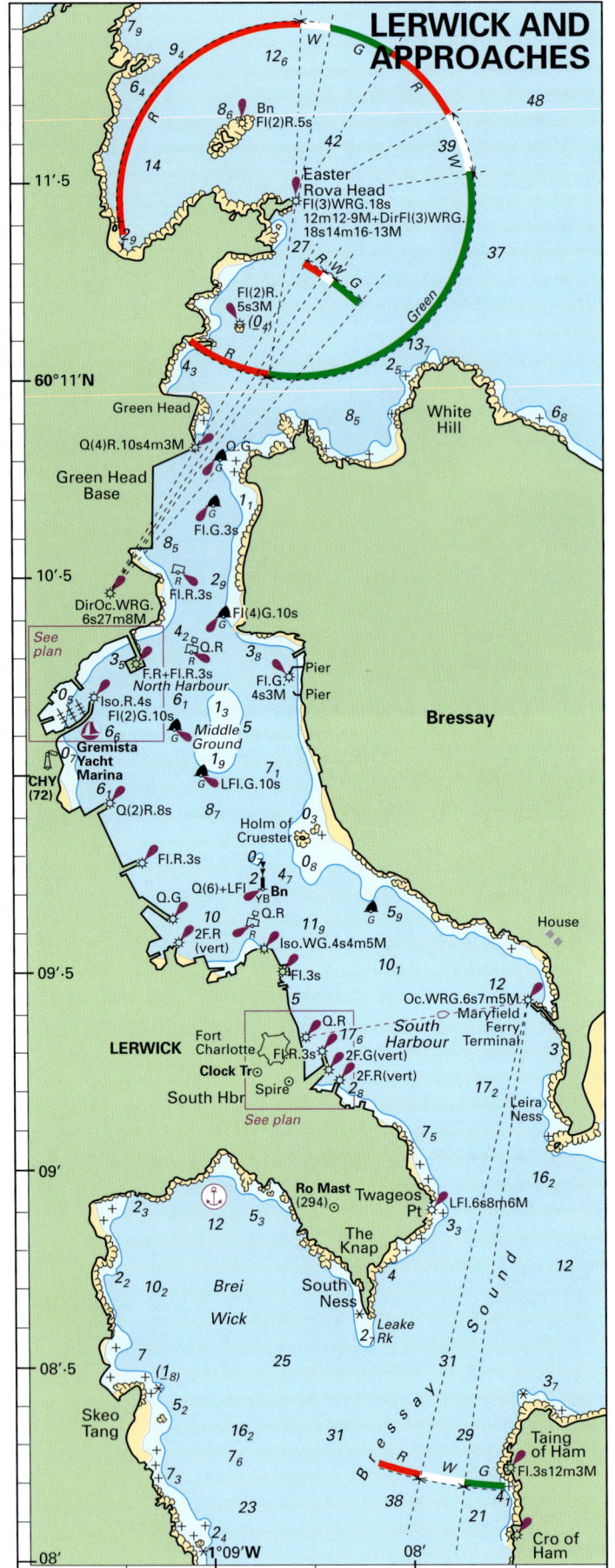

Lerwick

⊕ South entrance 60°08´·55N 001°07´·81W
⊕ North entrance 60°11´·55N 001°07´·96W

CHARTS
3283, 3272, 3271

TIDES
Lerwick, – 001 Dover

LIGHTS
Cro of Ham on Bressay Fl3s12m3M 60°08´·26N 001°07´·57W
Twageos Point Fl6s8m6M 60°08´·91N 001°07´·95W
Maryfield Ferry Terminal Oc.WRG.6s5m5M vis W008° – R013° – G111° – 008° 60°09´·43N 001°07´·45W
Breakwater Head 2F.R(vert)5m4M 60°09´·24N 001°08´·41W
Victoria Pier 2F.G(vert)5m4M 60°09´·26N 001°08´·45W
Albert Dock Fl.R.3s5m 60°09´·30N 001°08´·47W
Spur Jetty Q.R 5m 60°09´·34N 001°08´·55W
North Ness Pier Fl.3s5m 60°09´·57N 001°08´·66W
North Ness Iso.WG4s4m5M, vis shore – W – 158° – G – 216° – W – 301° 60°09´·57N 001°07´·45W
Shearers Quay 2F.R(vert)4m 60°09´·585N 001°09´·129W
Morrison Dock Q.G.4m5M 60°09´·637N 001°09´·229W
Deep water channel Q.R 60°09´·632N 001°08´·831W, Q.G at 60°09´·679N 001°08´·779W
Loofa Baa beacon Q(6)+LFl.15s4m5M 60°09´·72N 001°08´·78W
RoRo pier Fl.R.3s8m2M 60°09´·796N 001°09´·322W
Holmsgarth Jetty Q(2)R.8s6m2M 60°09´·918N 001°09´·549W
Deep water channel LFl.G.10s 60°09´·956N 001°09´·037W, Fl(2)G.10s 60°10´·199N 001°09´·223W
Gremista breakwater Iso.R.4s3m2M 60°10´·199N 001°09´·607W
Gremista Quay F.R & Fl.R.3s(vert)9m2M 60°10´·284N 001°09´·398W
Bay of Heogan pier Fl.G.4s5m3M 60°10´·252N 001°08´·620W
North Entrance Directional light
DirOc.WRG.6s27m8M vis 211°–R–214°–W–216°–G– 221° 60°10´·466N 001°09´·523W
Deep water channel Q.R 60°10´·336N 001°09´·091W, Fl(4)G.10s 60°10´·431N 001°09´·022W, Fl.R.3s 60°10´·524N 001°09´·160W, Fl.G.3s 60°10´·676N 001°09´·052W, Q.G 60°10´·801N 001°08´·989W
North Quay Q(4)R.10s4m3M 60°10´·834N 001°09´·093W
Skibby Baas rock Fl(2)R.5s3M 60°11´·137N 001°08´·830W
Rova Head LH 2Fl(3)WRG.18s14m16/9M White twr vis
090°–R–182°–W–191°–G–213°–R–241°–W–261·5°–G– 009°– R–040° and 176·5°–R–182°–W–191°–G–196·5°
Brethren Rock Q(9)15sYBY 60°12´·350N 001°08´·237W

Note that all above lights are listed in order from south to north.

LERWICK

Dangers

From South give The Knab a clearance of at least one cable to avoid Leake Rock and then keep a cable off but if keeping to the Bressay shore beware the shoal ground around the Brough of Leira Ness (Dr4m). Thereafter the channels are well marked although shore lights at night can cause difficulty in identifying individual lights. Lerwick is a busy commercial port, so a good watch for large vessels, sometimes fast moving, is essential. An additional hazard is that occasional poor visibility can be very localised.

Anchorages

The yacht pontoon is located in Victoria Harbour, the first harbour to Port when arriving from the South, and is in situ from May to September. Additional pontoon berthing is

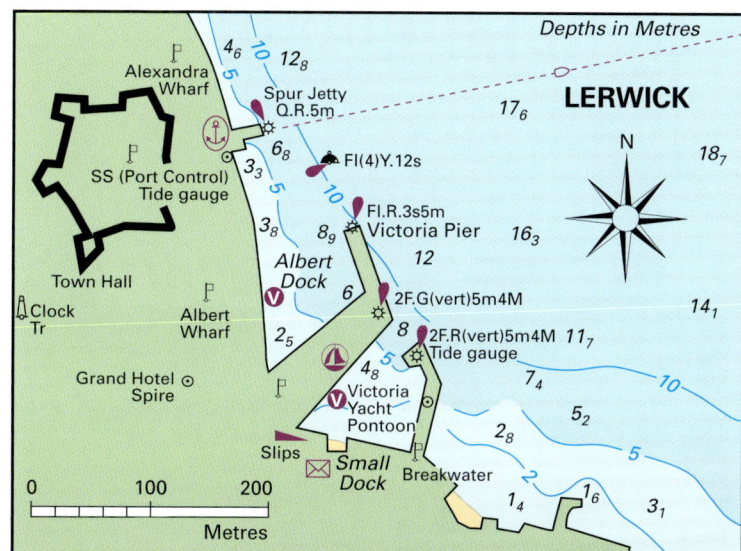

Lerwick from southeast

Knab Head, South Ness with the entrance to Lerwick harbour to the right of the photo

Arrow shows the leading mark for the North entrance to Lerwick

SHETLAND ISLANDS PILOT 23

MAINLAND SHETLAND – EAST COAST

Albert Buildings, Lerwick, home of the Harbourmaster and the local chandler

Commercial Street, Lerwick's main street

Lerwick Boating Club is a few minutes from the town centre

Victoria Harbour pontoon

Lerwick Boating Club is left of centre and Victoria Harbour

available in Albert Dock the next harbour North. This pontoon is sometimes reserved for launches from visiting cruise liners. Before berthing here check with Lerwick Port Authority (VHF Ch12 24hrs).

Facilities

Lerwick is the largest town in the Shetland Islands, and almost any service that a yacht could require is available here. Lerwick Boating Club, whose clubhouse is a short walk south from Victoria Pier, offers visiting sailors a warm welcome. In addition showers and laundry facilities are also available, and for access outwith normal clubhouse opening hours, keys are available from the Port Authority offices in Albert Building for a small deposit. Lerwick Port Authority ☎ 01595 692991, Lerwick Boating Club ☎ 01595 692407.

Entrance to Victoria Harbour with yacht pontoon from the NE

Interest

Be sure to allow more time than originally planned in order to explore the town and its surroundings. The new Shetland Museum is well worth a visit for anybody interested in the sea. Tourist Office in Market Square is very helpful, and provides free internet access. Fort Charlotte commands great views over the harbour area.

Gremista

⊕ 60°10′·18N 001°09′·33W

CHARTS
3283, 3272, 3271

TIDES
As Lerwick

LIGHTS
As Lerwick

Dangers

No offlying dangers, but if using the marina note that the NW isde of the basin is shoal, and an unconfirmed submerged rock has been reported about half distance due north between the second pontoon and the shore.

Anchorages

The only anchorage at Gremista is in the marina, which is owned by a local owners association. Some vacancies can usually be offered to visitors. For availability check at Lerwick Boating Club, or if there is nobody in attendance, Lerwick Port Authority can be helpful.

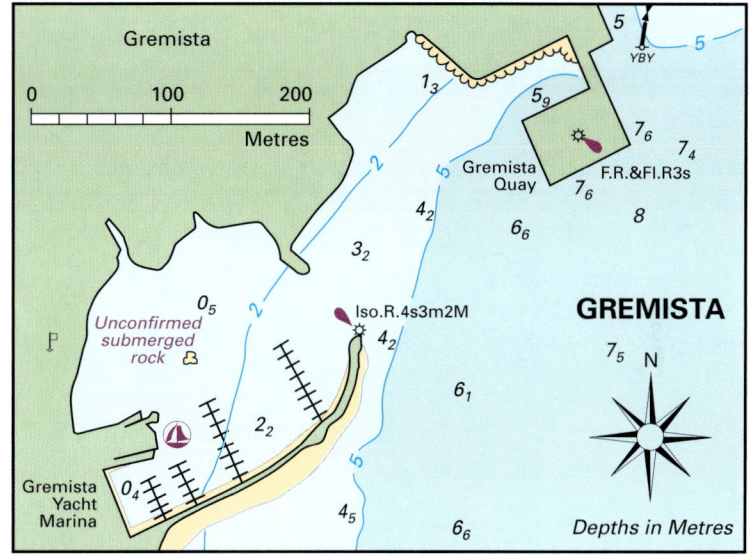

Facilities

Gremista is at the commercial end of Lerwick, and although there are some boat repair facilities close by, and the marina itself has a slipway and crane, the nearest facilities of more common use are in Lerwick. Taxis make the run in a few minutes or a twenty minute walk is enough to reach the Co-op supermarket along the road towards Lerwick.

Interest

Local power station, which overlooks the marina, and uses a substantial proportion of 'recycled' fuel.

Gremista marina is private but a berth can sometimes be found

MAINLAND SHETLAND – EAST COAST

Dales Voe

⊕ 60°12´·49N 001°09´·47W

CHARTS
3271, 3272, 3282

TIDES
-0005 Lerwick

LIGHTS
Brethren Rock Q(9)15sYBY 60°12´·350N 001°08´·237W
The Unicorn VQ(3)5sBYB 60°13´·510N 001°08´·466W
Dales Voe Fl(2)WRG.8s5m W4M, R3M, G3M vis 220°–G–227°–W–233°–R–240° 60°11´·785N 001°11´·218W
Dales Voe Quay 2F.R(vert)9m3M 60°11´·577N 001°10´·606W

Dangers
If approaching from south or east be certain to identify Brethren Rock, and if approaching from north identify The Unicorn, both as light list above. The headlands at Kebister Ness to the south and Fora Ness to the north both require an offing of at least one cable, but if the sectored Dales Voe light can be identified, the white sector leads clear of all dangers until well into the voe.

Anchorages
The best anchorage is SW of Muckle Ayre, but take careful note of soundings in the vicinity of Muckle Ayre. The deep channel (6m) is partially obstructed by a bank extending N and NE from the spit. To enter this anchorage, from a position with Dales Voe light bearing 230° at four cables, steer 230°, noting the fish farm, for 1·35miles.

Facilities
No supplies. Golf course on N side at head of Voe.

Dales Voe anchorage is on the far side of the spit on the left bank

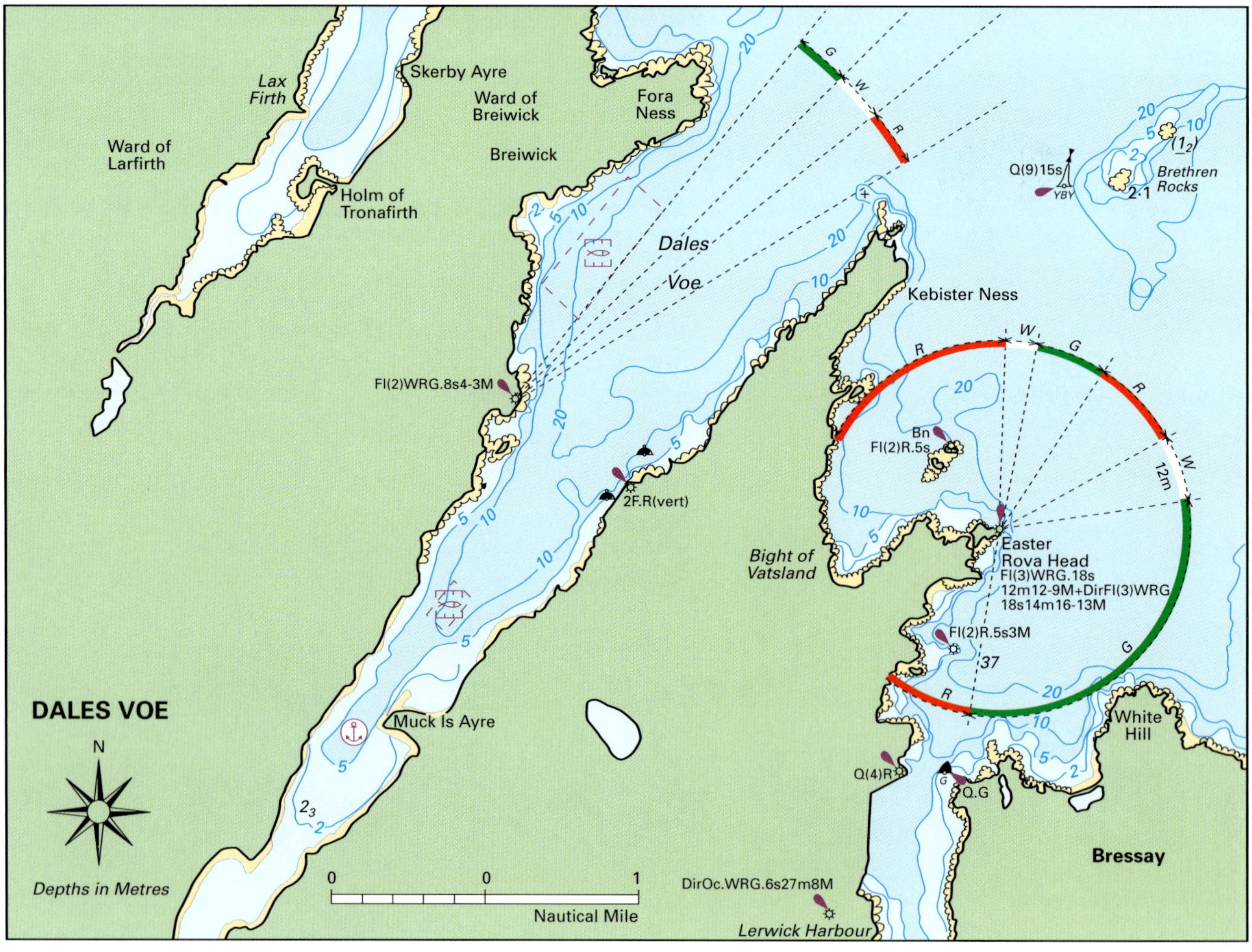

26 SHETLAND ISLANDS PILOT

Foraness Voe

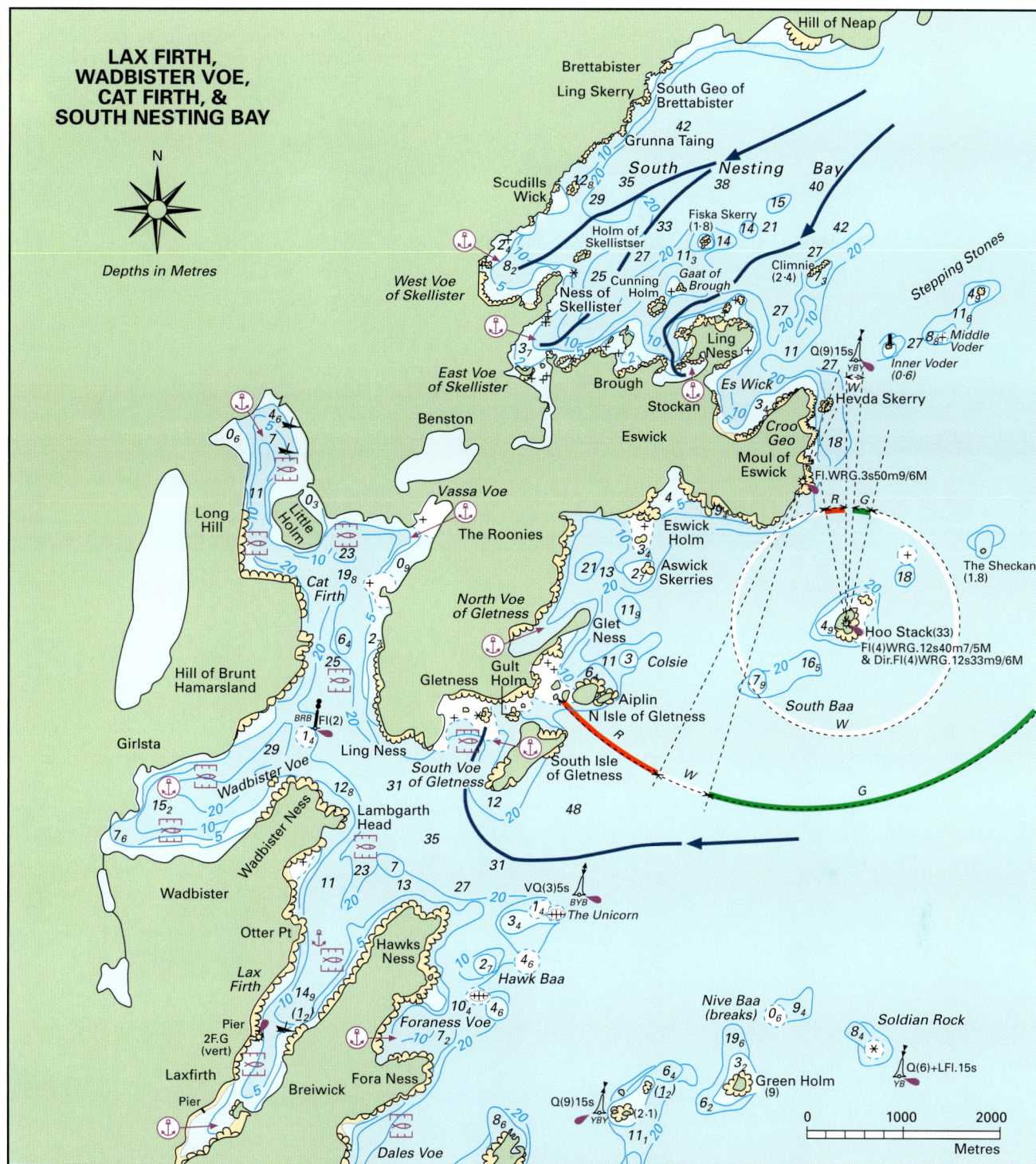

Foraness Voe

⊕ 60°12´·76N 001°09´·27W

CHARTS
3271, 3272, 3282

TIDES
-0005 Lerwick

LIGHTS
As Dales Voe

Dangers
The rocks, shallows and wrecks that lie SW of The Unicorn light require a wide berth, and both headlands are foul, particularly the north headland of Brim Ness. Keep at least one cable off, and ½ cable off the south headland at Fora Ness.

Anchorages
A temporary anchorage, but useful if not wishing to spend the time to reach the head of Dales Voe. From a position due South of The Unicorn light, steer due West for the South headland until two cables off, then turn for the centre of Voe, and once the South shore is visible, anchor as depths permit in the SW corner. Numerous rocks, thus a tripping line is recommended. Exposed to winds from the East. Subject to swell.

Facilities
None.

MAINLAND SHETLAND – EAST COAST

Laxfirth

Laxfirth

See plan page 27

⊕ 60°13´·77N 01°10´·64W

CHARTS
3271, 3272, 3282

TIDES
-0010 Lerwick

LIGHTS
The Unicorn VQ(3)5s BYB 60°13´·510N 001°08´·466W
Laxfirth Pier Head 2F.G(vert)4m2M 60°12´·737N 001°12´·139W

Dangers

From a position at least one cable N of The Unicorn rocks a course of not less than 270° until the Firth is open clears the offlying dangers. Two fish farms obscure the inner Firth and there is a drying wreck and shoal ground on the East shore just N of Laxfirth Pier. Keep to the pier side.

Anchorages

The most sheltered part of Laxfirth is at the head of the Firth opposite the unlit stone pier. Anchor as depths allow in mud.

Wadbister Voe

See plan page 27

⊕ 60°14´·14N 001°10´·82W

CHARTS
3272, 3282

TIDES
-0010 Lerwick

LIGHTS
Hoo Stack Fl(4)WRG.12s40m W7M R5M G5M W pylon vis 169°–R–180°–W–184°–G–193°–W–169°. Same structure Dir Lt 182° Fl(4)WRG.12s33m W9M, R6M, G6M vis 177°–R–180°–W–184°–W–187°, synch with upper light 60°14´·949N 001°05´·362W
The Unicorn VQ(3)5s BYB 60°13´·510N 001°08´·466W
Pillar beacon Fl(2) 60°14´·394N 001°11´·441W

Dangers

Hoo Stack and The Unicorn both deserve a wide berth, and also beware South Baa if sailing from the north. Once inside the entrance to Cat Firth, there is a shoal patch to the South of the Cat Firth beacon. Keep 1½ cables to the south or go north of the beacon. Otherwise sides of Wadbister Voe are clear beyond a cable offshore.

Wadbister Voe is well sheltered

Anchorages

One of many anchorages entered from Cat Firth, Wadbister Voe provides a good anchorage. Unfortunately, chart 3272 does not show the head of the Voe. From the waypoint above, steer 321° for ½ mile until N of the pillar beacon and then turn onto a course of 237° for 1½ miles avoiding the fish farms. Thereafter anchorage may be found at the head of the bay or to the west of the fish farm as depths permit. Tripping line recommended.

Cat Firth

See plan page 27

⊕ 60°14´·05N 001°10´·52W

CHARTS
3272, 3282

TIDES
-0010 Lerwick

LIGHTS
Hoo Stack Fl(4)WRG.12s40m W7M R5M G5M W pylon vis 169°–R–180°–W–184°–G–193°–W–169°. Same structure Dir Lt 182° Fl(4)WRG.12s33m W9M, R6M, G6M vis 177°–R–180°–W–184°–W–187°, synch with upper light 60°14´·949N 001°05´·362W
The Unicorn VQ(3)5s BYB 60°13´·510N 001°08´·466W
Pillar beacon Fl(2) 60°14´·394N 001°11´·441W

Dangers

Entry as above, otherwise fairly straightforward, but note the shoal patch and rock off the spit just over ¾ mile north of the pillar beacon on the east side. This shoal is at the entrance to Vassa Voe *(see next section)*.

Anchorages

From a position abeam the pillar beacon a course of 358° clears any offlying rocks which are all within one cable of the shore. Maintain this course until the channel opens to port, and leaving Little Holm to starboard steer 284° for just under ½ mile. When the channel opens steer 000° towards the head of the Voe and anchor clear of the two wrecks.

Vassa Voe

See plan page 27

⊕ 60°15´·25N 001°11´·03W

CHARTS
3272, 3282

TIDES
-0010 Lerwick

LIGHTS
As above

Dangers

As above until the shoal patch and rock at entrance to Vassa Voe is reached. Several local boats have moorings in the pool to north of the islet, and if room to anchor is available, keep the islet to starboard. A shoal patch and rock are situated off the shore to port almost abeam the north end of the islet so turn towards the centre of the pool and anchor in about 3m.

Anchorages

Very sheltered anchorage with a bottom of mud over rock.

Facilities

New marina is to be built in Vassa Voe. At planning stage in 2007.

South Gletness

See plan page 27

⊕ 60°14´N 001°10´W

CHARTS
3272, 3282

TIDES
-0010 Lerwick

LIGHTS
Hoo Stack Fl(4)WRG.12s40m W7M R5M G5M W pylon vis 169°–R–180°–W–184°–G–193°–W–169°. Same structure Dir lt 182° Fl(4)WRG.12s33m W9M, R6M, G6M vis 177°–R–180°–W–184°–W–187°, synch with upper light 60°14´·949N 001°05´·362W
The Unicorn VQ(3)5s BYB 60°13´·510N 001°08´·466W

Upper Cat Firth with Little Holm in centre of photo

MAINLAND SHETLAND – EAST COAST

Dangers
Apart from the obvious dangers of The Unicorn and Hoo Stack, there is a large fish farm at the entrance to South Gletness. Exposed to the south and north and west parts of the bay are littered with rocks.

Anchorages
Temporary anchorage is available in the East side of the bay west of South Isle of Gletness. From a position half way between the fish farm and South Isle of Gletness identify and then steer for Gult Holm and anchor when North end of Isle of Gletness is abeam. 4–5m over sand.

North Voe of Gletness
See plan page 27

⊕ 60°15´·00N 001° 01´·55W

CHARTS
3272, 3282

TIDES
-0010 Lerwick

LIGHTS
Hoo Stack Fl(4)WRG.12s40m W7M R5M G5M W pylon vis 169°–R–180°–W–184°–G–193°–W–169°. Same structure Dir lt 182° Fl(4)WRG.12s33m W9M, R6M, G6M vis 177°–R–180°–W–184°–W–187°, synch with upper light 60°14´·949N 001°05´·362W

Dangers
If approaching from the NE note The Sneckan which lies just under a mile from Hoo Stack bearing 244°/064° at 60°15´·349N 001°03´·766W, and an unconfirmed rock slightly N of a line between these at 60°15´·328N 001°04´·639W.

Anchorages
This very pleasant anchorage, sheltered from all but N and E is entered between Glet Ness and Aswick Skerries. Be certain to identify Glet Ness and do not mistake North Isle of Gletness for the entrance, after which keep a cable off the point and then proceed mid channel to the head of the bay and anchor in 4m on sand.

South Nesting Bay
See plan page 27

⊕ 60°17´·40N 001°04´·90W

There are three useable anchorages in this bay, all but the last are completely exposed to the N and E although the scenery makes a visit worthwhile. From the N, South Nesting Bay is approached with Hill of Neap and its off lying Hog Island and Stany Hog to starboard. If approaching from S or E, more care is required to avoid the various rocks that lie approximately in a line from Out Skerries to Moul of Eswick.

CHARTS
3284, 3282

TIDES
-0014 Lerwick

LIGHTS
Hoo Stack Fl(4)WRG.12s40m W7M R5M G5M W pylon vis 169°–R–180°–W–184°–G–193°–W–169°. Same structure Dir Lt 182° Fl(4)WRG.12s33m W9M, R6M, G6M vis 177°–R–180°–W–184°–W–187°, synch with upper light 60°14´·949N 001°05´·362W
Moul of Eswick Fl.WRG.3s50mW9M R6M G6M; W twr vis 028°–R–200°–W–207°–G018°–W–028° 60°15´·731N 001°05´·884W
Inner Voder Fl(2)6s7m5M, Racon(M) 10–8M 60°16´·447N 001°04´·912W

Dangers
From the N keep a cable offshore when rounding Stany Hog until the above waypoint is reached. From S keep Hoo Stack bearing 182° until Inner Voder is abeam to starboard then turn on to a course of 303° heading for Fiska Skerry (dr 1·8m distance 1M). Beware the drying rock, Climnie to the NE and the off lying rocks 1½ cable N of Ling Ness.

West Voe of Skellister
See plan page 27

Leave Fiska Skerry one cable to port and then steer for Holm of Skellister. Leave to port if heading for West Voe of Skellister and anchor in middle of bay in 7m. Tripping line recommended.

Gletness looking southeast

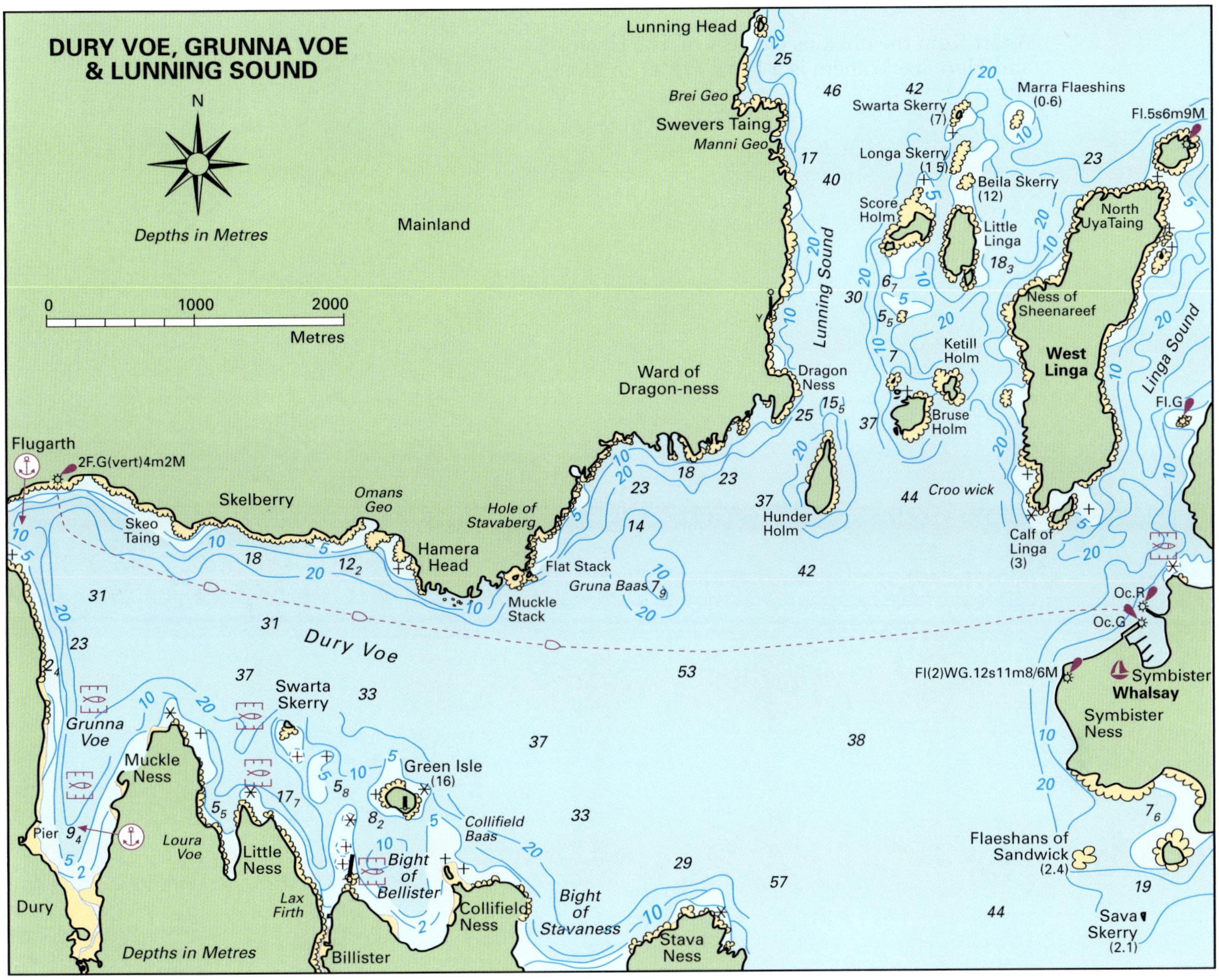

DURY VOE

East Voe of Skellister

See plan page 27

As above but leave Holm of Skellister to starboard and anchor in 5m but beware the rocks that extend ½ cable from both N and S shores. Tripping line recommended.

Dock of Lingness

See plan page 27

Probably the best anchorage in South Nesting Bay but depths are less than 2m. Leaving Fiska Skerry, Gaat of Brough and Cunning Holm to starboard, and from a position due S of Cunning Holm steer 159° to enter the bay. Leave the small islet in the entrance to port and anchor as depths permit. The local landowner is reputed to have had trouble with crews from visiting yachts disturbing livestock and is not enthusiastic about visitors.

Dury Voe

⊕ 60°20´·20N 001°05´·26W

CHARTS
3284, 3282

TIDES
-0014 Lerwick

LIGHTS
Flugarth Ferry Terminal 2F.G(vert)4m2M 60°21´·104N 001°10´·258W

Dangers

Few hazards that are not obvious if course is set to keep at least a cable N of Green Isle and Swarta Skerry. If proceeding to Grunna Voe, keep at least a cable off the point at Muckle Ness in order to avoid an off lying rock.

Left
Dock of Lingness, a lovely anchorage on the southeast side of South Nesting Bay

Right
Dury Voe Ferry Terminal for Whalsay

MAINLAND SHETLAND – EAST COAST

Anchorages

Dury Voe is the home to one of the connecting terminals for the Whalsay ferry, but otherwise does not provide much in the way of shelter except in winds from the W. There is a temporary anchorage just to the W of the ferry pier at Flugarth in 5–6m.

Facilities

Ferry to Whalsay. Shops at Laxo, a ½ mile walk.

Grunna Voe

See plan page 31

⊕ 60°20´·48N 001°09´·80W

CHARTS
3284, 3282

TIDES
-0014 Lerwick

LIGHTS
Flugarth Ferry Terminal 2F.G(vert)4m2M 60°21´·104N 001°10´·258W

Dangers

An isolated rock off Muckle Ness is easily avoided by keeping a cable off, and if the same clearance is maintained off either shore, the only hazards are the fish farms.

Anchorages

Sheltered anchorage at the head of the Voe just N of the small stone pier in 7–8m.

Lunning Sound looking N

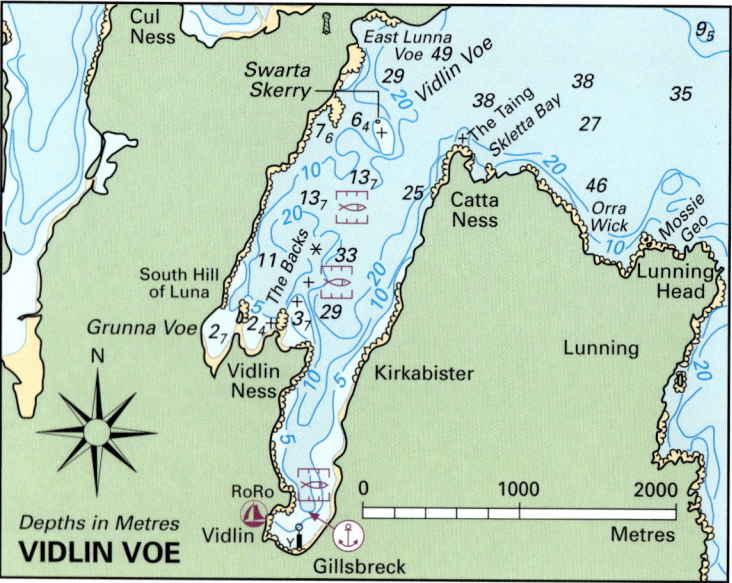

Lunning Sound

See plan page 31

⊕ 60°20´·80N 001°04´·80W

CHARTS
3284, 3282

TIDES
-0017 Lerwick

LIGHTS
None

Dangers

The above waypoint assumes passage is to be made after exiting Dury Voe, and by keeping to the W of Hunder Holm. The shores beyond ½ cable are clear but the tides can reach up to five knots and strong eddies can be experienced particularly on the east side of the channel. Passage should be timed to coincide with slack water.

Interest

Fascinating rock formations on the cliffs from Hamera Head to Dragon Ness.

Vidlin Voe

⊕ 60°24´N 001°06´W

CHARTS
3284, 3282

TIDES
-0020 Lerwick

LIGHTS
None

Dangers

An off lying rock is situated N of Catta Ness. Keep at least a cable off shore. Swarta Skerry, a dangerous rock lies almost mid channel once the Voe is open. Keep one cable off the East side to avoid this and two shallow patches ¼ and ½ mile NE of Vidlin respectively. There are several fish farms in the Voe.

Anchorages

Marina at head of Voe which has a minimum depth of 1·75m. If this is too shallow anchor off the marina in 3–4m, clear of the ferry terminal. Contact Johnny Johnson ☏ 01806 577326 for queries about the marina.

Facilities

Toilets, water, waste disposal, shop ☏ 01806 577285 and post office.

Vidlin Voe

WERST LUNNA VOE

Vidlin Marina

Hamna Voe (Boatsroom Voe)

See plan page 35

⊕ 60°26´·12N 001°06´·16W

CHARTS
3284, 3282

TIDES
-0025 Lerwick

LIGHTS
Lunna Holm Fl(3)WRG.15s19m W10M, R7M ,G7M W twr shore–R–090°–W–094°–G–209°–W–275°–R–shore 60°27´·342N 001°02´·521W

Dangers
If rounding Lunna Ness and Lunna Holm note the offlying dangers of Swarta Skerry and Longa Skerry to the East of Lunna Holm. After rounding Lunna Holm, aim for a point 1½ cables off Point of Feorwick, and then head for the point at Ness of Setter until the Voe is open and the point of the spit on the east side of the Voe is bearing 187°. This course avoids the shallows at Stoura Baa and the obstruction NE of the Ness of Setter. There are rocks extending 1¼ cables NNW of the spit and the west shore is shallow opposite these rocks.

Anchorages
Once past the above obstructions head for the West arm of the bay and anchor in 7–8m. Very sheltered and good holding.

Facilities
Marina is in course of planning (2007). Contact Terry Scott ☎ 01595 859444.

Hamna Voe looking north

West Lunna Voe

See plan page 35

⊕ 60°24´·55N 001°08´·62W

CHARTS
3284, 3282

TIDES
-0025 Lerwick

LIGHTS
None

Dangers
Apart from fish farming activity the passage between Wether Holm and Ness of Setter is clear, and from the above waypoint a course of 133° leads to the anchorage in the East side of the bay. The bay to the West side of the middle spit is either shoal or occupied by fish farming

Lunna Voe, the fishing boat leaving the Voe shows the correct leading line

SHETLAND ISLANDS PILOT 33

MAINLAND SHETLAND – EAST COAST

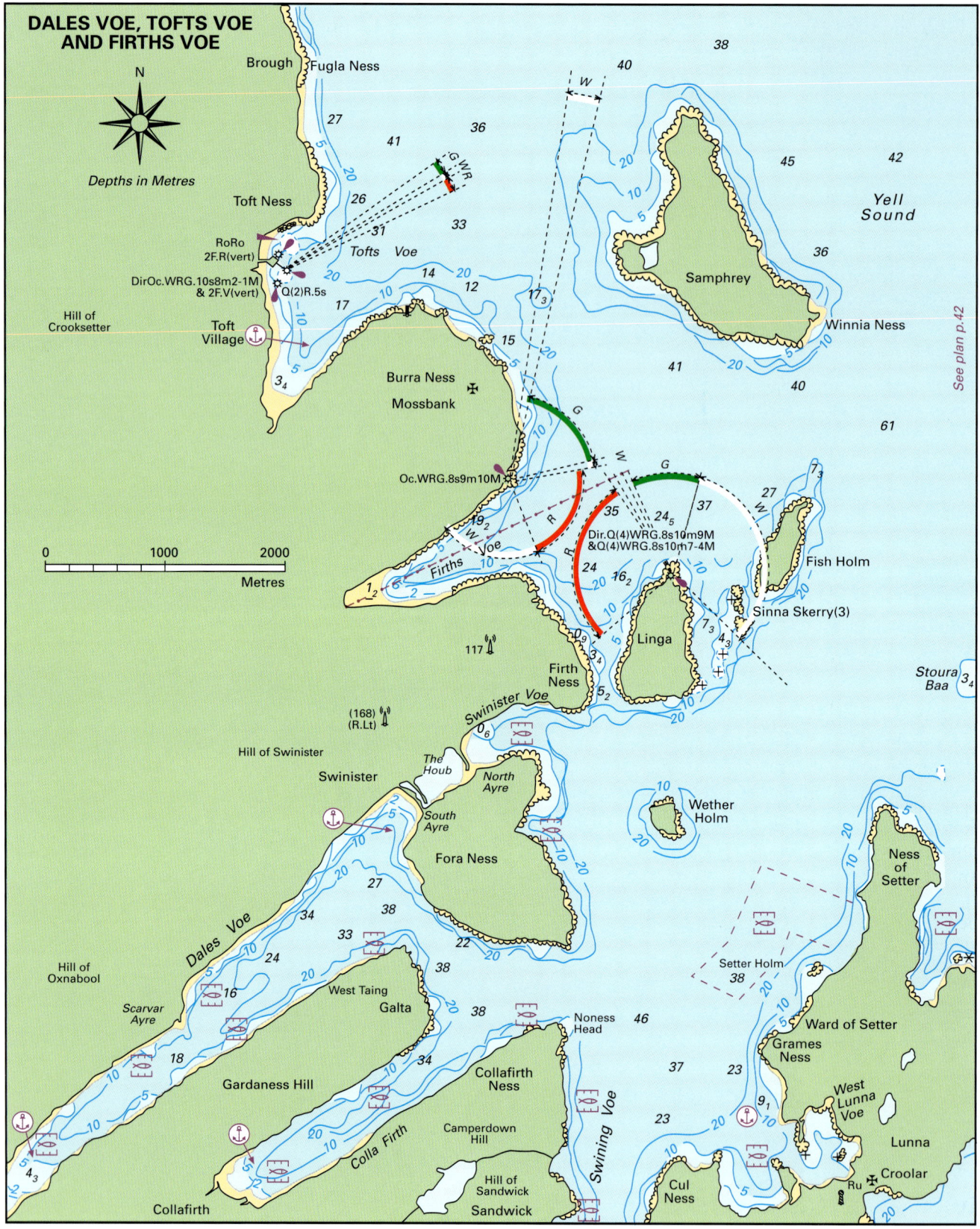

34 SHETLAND ISLANDS PILOT

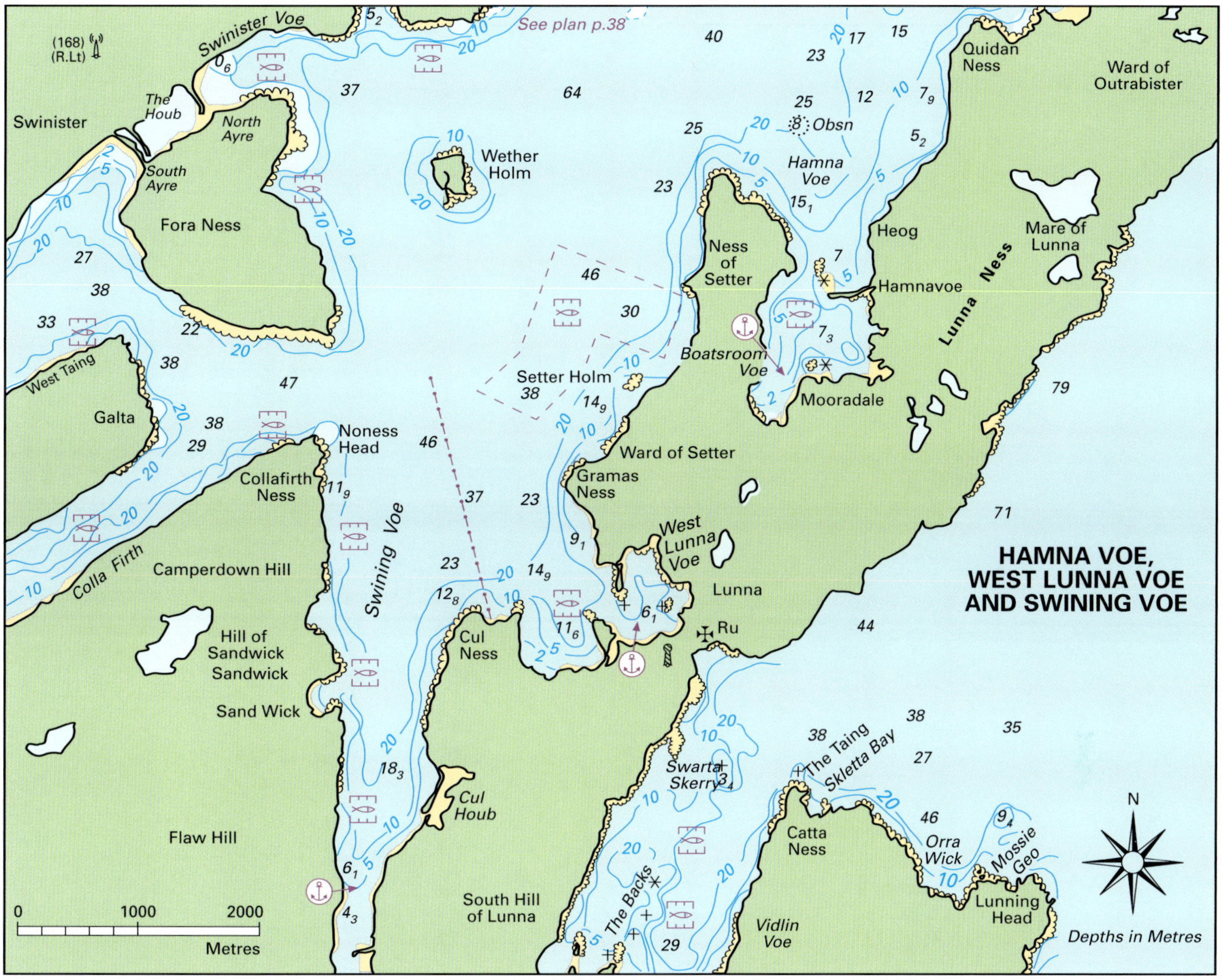

SWINING VOE

equipment. Keep clear of the rocks ½ cable S of Skeo Ness and the rock due W ½ cable N of the opposite point.

Anchorages
The pier on the SE side of the bay is used by local fishing boats but is too shallow for yachts. Anchor in 6–8m W of the pier. The accompanying photograph shows the rock to the N of the pier.

Facilities
None.

Interest
Extensively used during the Second World War as a base for the 'Shetland Bus', the fishing boat operations between Norway and UK.

Dangers
Apart from fish farming activity the Voe is clear provided course is set ½ cable offshore until depths fall below 10m. The head of the Voe is shoal for three cables. Subject to squalls with strong winds from S or W.

Anchorages
As depth permits towards the head of the Voe.

Facilities
None.

Swining Voe

⊕ 60°24´·50N 001°09´·50W

CHARTS
3284, 3282

TIDES
-0025 Lerwick

LIGHTS
None

Swinning Voe

WHALSAY

Whalsay

WHALSAY

See plan page 37

⊕ **Symbister** 60°20´·74N 001°01´·95W
⊕ **North Voe** 60°20´·92N 001°01´·70W

CHARTS
3284, 3282

TIDES
-0030 Lerwick

LIGHTS
Symbister Ness Fl(2)WG.12s11m W8M, G6M, W twr vis: shore–W–203°–G–shore
60°20´·428N 001°02´·283W
Symbister Bay N Breakwater Hd Oc.G.7s3m3M
60°20´·629N 001°01´·716W
East Breakwater Hd Oc.R.7s3m3M
60°20´·667N 001°01´·659W
South Breakwater Hd Q.G.4m2M
60°20´·575N 001°01´·629W. PHM Fl.R.5s
60°20´·537N 001°01´·575W
Marina N pontoon 2F.G(vert)
60°20´·503N 001°01´·592W
Marina W pontoon 2F.R(vert)
60°20´·501N 001°01´·701W
Skate of Marrister Fl.G.6s4m4M
60°21´·346N 001°01´·382W
Suther Ness Fl.WRG.3s10m W10M, R8M, G7M; vis: shore–W–038°–R–173°–W–206°–G–shore
60°22´·114N 001°00´·186W
Wether Holm Fl.5s6m9M; W clad metal framework twr 60°22´·339N 001°01´·328W

Dangers
The entrance to Symbister harbour is quite straight forward but note the channel markers and the shoal ground to the east side. The area south of the north marina pontoon is also shoal. Deep draft yachts should arrange a berth on the north side if at all possible. There is a dangerous rock ½ cable north of Salt Ness point at the entrance to North Voe and the bottom is reported to be foul with old moorings.

Anchorages
Symbister marina provides good shelter and easy access to the local town and pier. North Voe is less disturbed by the slight noise from the frequent ferry services and provides a reasonable anchorage in 3–5m.

Note the fish farm and shoal patches shown on Plan A in chart 3284.

Facilities
Leisure Centre and all other facilities. Whalsay Boating and Sports Club ☎ 01806 566681.

Interest
Britain's most northerly 18 hole golf course is on Whalsay. Museum.

Lunning Sound

See plan page 31

⊕ **North entrance** 60°22´·79N 001°03´·81W
⊕ **South entrance** 60°20´·96N 001°03´·65W

CHARTS
3284, 3282

LIGHTS
Symbister Ness Fl(2)WG.12s11m W8M, G6M, W twr vis: shore–W–203°–G–shore 60°20´·428N 001°02´·283W
Suther Ness Fl.WRG.3s10m W10M, R8M, G7M; vis: shore–W–038°–R–173°–W–206°–G–shore 60°22´·114N 001°00´·186W
Wether Holm Fl.5s6m9M; W clad metal framework twr 60°22´·339N 001°01´·328W

Dangers
The islets between Mainland and West Linga create a confused tidal flow through the sound, and flow at spring tides can reach six knots. There are several eddies on the side of the islets, and the stream southbound tends to set through between Hunde Hom and mainland and towards the islets at the north end.

Looking SE past Symbister Ness to Flaeshans of Sandwick

Lunning Sound from the south

WHALSAY

Passage notes

The Sound presents no real difficulties if spring tides are avoided and a course is set 1½ cables from the Mainland side. The tide runs north from +0220 Lerwick and the south-going stream commences -0430 Lerwick.

Linga Sound

⊕ **North entrance** 60°22'·83N 000°59'·95W
⊕ **South entrance** 60°20'·71N 001°02'·44W

CHARTS
3284, 3282

LIGHTS
Symbister Ness Fl(2)WG.12s11m W8M, G6M, W twr vis: shore–W–203°–G–shore 60°20'·428N 001°02'·283W **Symbister Bay N Breakwater Hd** Oc.G.7s3m3M 60°20'·629N 001°01'·716W
East Breakwater Hd Oc.R.7s3m3M 60°20'·667N 001°01'·659W
Skate of Marrister Fl.G.6s4m4M 60°21'·346N 001°01'·382W
Suther Ness Fl.WRG.3s10m W10M, R8M, G7M; vis: shore–W–038°–R–173°–W–206°–G–shore 60°22'·114N 001°00'·186W
Wether Holm Fl.5s6m9M; W clad metal framework twr 60°22'·339N 001°01'·328W

Dangers

The tides run very strongly, reaching six knots at springs, hence the danger of being pushed off course must be countered. Fortunately, the area is well charted. Tides as Lunning Sound above.

Passage notes

From north, the southeast corner of West Linga bearing 212° leads clear of both Baa of Wether Holm, ½ mile NE of Wether Holm, and the dangerous rocks ¼ mile N of Kirk Ness. Keep at least 1½ cables off West Linga in order to avoid The Flaeshans, a rocky area off the east side. The Skate of Marrister beacon must be cleared to the west by at least a cable. When opposite Bight of Cudda a course with the Symbister East Breakwater head bearing more than 180° leads clear. Keep towards the Whalsay side until south of Calf of Linga in order to avoid the rocks lying up to a cable of the Calf. Seas break at Symbister Ness and all around Flaeshans of Sandwick and Sava Skerry, an offing of 1½ cables at Symbister Ness and a course of not less than 180° leads clear.

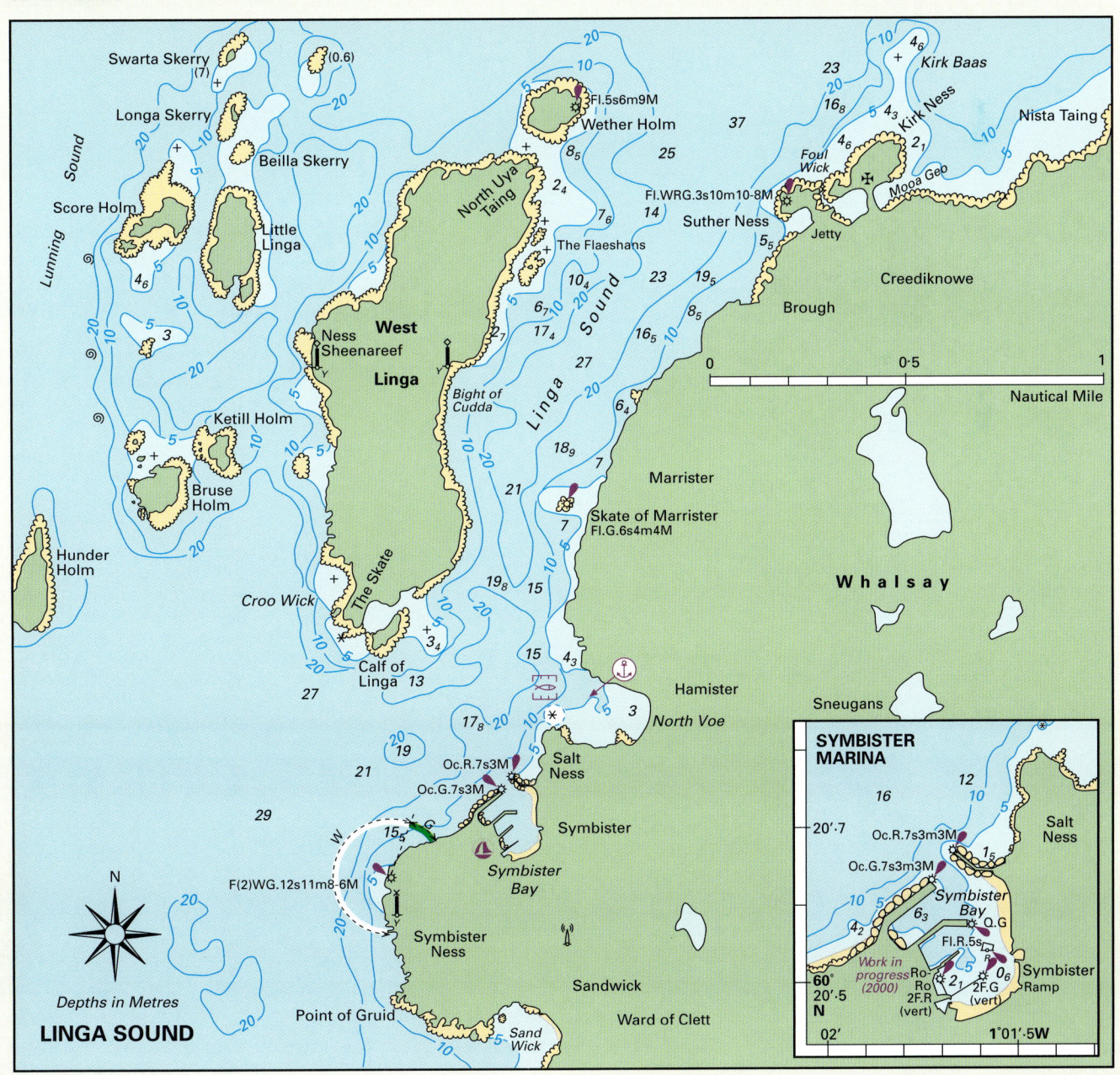

SHETLAND ISLANDS PILOT 37

MAINLAND SHETLAND – EAST COAST

Colla Firth from the south, the harbour is just out of the photo on the left

Colla Firth

See plan page 34

⊕ 60°25´·02N 001°09´·88W

CHARTS
3284, 3282

TIDES
-0025 Lerwick

LIGHTS
None

Dangers

The only hazards are within ¾ cable of the shore until the head of the Voe when there is a shoal patch that extends over a cable from the SW corner. Fish farms may be encountered. Exposed to Easterly winds.

Anchorages

At the head of the Voe in 8m on sand.

Dales Voe

See plan page 34

⊕ 60°25´·05N 001°10´·86W

CHARTS
3284, 3282

TIDES
-0025 Lerwick

LIGHTS
None

Dangers

Beware the shoals that extend up to ½ cable off West Taing at the entrance and Scarvar Ayre on the N side half way to the head of the Voe.

Anchorages

There are two anchorages, the first is at the N end W of the West point of Fora Ness on mud in 10m. The second is at the head of the Voe, again on mud, in 5m. Well sheltered but subject to squalls.

Entrance to Dales Voe looking E

38 SHETLAND ISLANDS PILOT

Firths Voe

See plan page 34

⊕ 60°27´·09N 001°10´·11W

CHARTS
3284, 3292, 3298, 3282

TIDES
-0025 Lerwick

LIGHTS
Lunna Holm Fl(3)WRG.15s19m W10M, R7M, G7M W twr shore–R–090°–W–094°–G–209°–W–275°–R–shore 60°27´·342N 001°02´·521W
Linga Is. Dir Lt 150°Q(4)WRG.8s10m W9M, R9M, G9M vis 145°–R–148°–W–152°–G–155°.
Q(4)WRG.8s10m W7M, R4M, G4M, same structure vis, 052°–R–146°, 154°–G–196°–W–312° synch. 60°26´·794N 001°09´·114W
Firths Voe N shore Oc.WRG.8s9m W15M, R10M, G10M, W twr vis, 189°–W–194°–G–257°–W–261°–R–339°–W–066°.

Dangers

There are no geographical dangers but a main oil pipe from the Brent Oilfield comes ashore in the Firth.

Anchorages

Due to the oil line above, anchoring is not recommended.

Tofts Voe

See plan page 34

⊕ 60°28´·27N 001°11´·15W

CHARTS
3298, 3282

TIDES
-0105 Lerwick

LIGHTS
Tofts Pier Dir Lt 241° (24H) DirOc.WRG.10s8m W16M, R10M, G10M, vis 236°–G–240°–W–242°–R–246°. By day W2M, R1M, G1M 60°27´·958N 001°12´·326W.
There are two other lights used by the ferry for manoeuvring purposes. These are 2F.R(vert), and Q(2)R.5s N and S of the pier respectively.

Dangers

When passing between Burra Ness and Samphrey Island a clearance of 1½ cables leads clear of offlying hazards, but note the currents which can reach speeds of over six knots and can result in very turbulent waters.

Anchorages

The ferry terminal makes this a rather disturbed anchorage although more peace can be obtained in the SW corner in 7–8m on sand.

Facilities

Ferry to Whalsay, limited shops and café.

Toft pier looking towards Yell

Yell Sound

⊕ North entrance 60°39′·65N 001°13′·90W
South entrance 60°28′·09N 001°01′·30W

CHARTS
3282, 3298

TIDES
The flood, South-going, stream starts at -0520 Lerwick.
The ebb, North-going, stream starts at +0110 Lerwick.

LIGHTS
From north entrance southwards:
Bagi Stack Fl(4)20s45m10M 60°43′·530N 001°07′·530W
Gruney Is Fl.WR.5s53m W8M, R6M; W twr, vis 064°–R–180°–W–012°. Racon(T)14M 60°39′·147N 001°18′·168W
Point of Fethaland Fl(3)WR.15s65m W24M, R20M vis 080°–R–103°–W–160°–206°–W–340° 60°38′·045N 001°18′·691W
Muckle Holm Fl(4)10s32m10M 60°34′·822N 001°15′·993W
Little Holm Iso.4s12m6M 60°33′·407N 001°15′·845W
Outer Skerry Fl.6s12m8M 60°33′·031N 001°18′·298W
Ness of Quey Firth, Stream Taing Oc.WRG.6s22m W21M, R8M, G8M, W twr vis: shore (through S & W) –W–290°–G–327°–W–334°–W–shore 60°31′·427N 001°19′·571W
Ness of Sound Fl(3)WRG.12s18m W9M, R6M, G6M; vis shore –G–345°–W–350°–R–160°–W–165°–G–shore 60°31′·337N 001°11′·272W
Brother Isle, North Head Dir. Lt 329°. Fl(4)WRG.8s16m W10M, R7M, G,7M, vis 323·5°–G–328°–W–330°–R–333·5° 60°30′·940N 001°14′·096W
Lamba, South Head Fl.WRG.3s30m W8M, R5M, G5M; W twr vis shore–G–288°–W–293°–R–327°–W–044°–R–140°–shore. Dir Lt 290·5° Fl.WRG.3s24m W10M, R7M, G7M, vis 285·5°–G–285·5°–G–288°–W–293°–W–295·5° 60°30′·721N 001°17′·825W
Tinga Skerry Q(2)G.10s9m5M 60°30′·484N 001°14′·849W
Little Roe Fl(3)WR.10s16m5/4M 60°29′·989N 001°16′·453W
Mio Ness Q(2)WR.10s12m W7M, R4M, W twr vis 282°–W–238°–R–282° 60°29′·660N 001°13′·669W
Gluss Isle Ldg Lts 194·7° (H24) Front 60°29′·771N 001°19′·427W F 39m19M on Gy twr H24. Rear 0·75M from front F 69m19M on Gy twr H24 at 60°29′·039N 001°19′·814W both lts 9M by day
Skaw Taing Ldg Lts 150·5° Front Fl(2)WRG.5s21m W8M, R5M, G5M; Or and W structure vis 049°–W–078°–G–147°–W–154°–R–169°–W–288° 60°29′·096N 001°16′·846W. Rear 195m from front Fl(2)5s35m8M vis W145°–156° 60°29′·002N 001°16′·737W
Ulsta Ferry Term, Bkwtr Head Oc.RG.4s7m R5M, G5M; vis shore–G–354°; 044°–R–shore. Same structure; Oc.WRG.4s5m W8M, R5M, G5M; vis: shore–G–008°–W–036°–R–shore 60°29′·736N 001°09′·471W
Bay of Ulsta Fl(2)G.4s 60°29′·523N 001°09′·424W
Tofts Pier Dir Lt 241° (24H) Dir. Oc.WRG.10s8m W16M, R10M, G10M, vis 236°–G–240°–W–242°–R–246°. By day W2M, R1M, G1M 60°27′·958N 001°12′·326W
There are two other lights used by the ferry for manoeuvring purposes. These are 2F.R(vert), and Q(2)R.5s N and S of the pier respectively.

Firths Voe, N shore Oc.WRG.8s9m W15M, R10M, G10M, W twr vis, 189°–W–194°–G–257°–W–261°–R–339°–W–066° 60°27′·205N 001°10′·618W
Linga Is. Dir Lt 150°Q(4)WRG.8s10m W9M, R9M, G9M vis 145°–R–148°–W–152°–G–155°. Q(4)WRG.8s10m W7M, R4M, G4M, same structure vis, 052°–R–146°, 154°–G–196°–W–312° synch. 60°26′·794N 001°09′·114W
The Rumble Fl.10s8m4M 60°28′·165N 001°07′·265W
Lunna Holm Fl(3)WRG.15s19m W10M, R7M ,G7M W twr shore–R–090°–W–094°–G–209°–W–275°–R–shore 60°27′·342N 001°02′·521W

Dangers

Apart from the strength of some of the currents, there are numerous rocks and islands within Yell Sound. In addition the whole area comes under the jurisdiction of Sullom Voe Port Operations due to the very large amount of oil related shipping. Sullom Voe Harbour Radio (VHF Ch 14) willingly give details of shipping movements and it is recommended that yachts transiting the Sound contact them for advice. From the north, Yell Sound is almost 3½ miles wide and if course in mid channel is maintained, there are no significant dangers for the first three miles. Muckle Holm, lying mid-channel can be left on either hand, but beware the shoal area to the south of the island. A further mile south lies Little Holm, which is best passed to the west, and this almost dictates that Muckle Holm is also left to port when going south. To the east and south of Little Holm there are four shoal areas that create overfalls, and are best avoided. These are Beaufort Bank, South Ladie Bank to the east, and The Fiord and Linna Baa to the south. The latter two are both shallow enough to be a serious hazard to shipping. Tides, which generally run at less than two knots in the outer part of the Sound, begin to reach speeds of over two knots, and more in the vicinity of these banks. Flow is generally in line with the shores.

South of The Fiord and Linna Baa there are three channels which can be used to reach the east side of Yell, or for passage to the south and Lerwick. These are the channel between Lamba and Tinga Skerry, the only one not subject to severe overfalls. Next to the east is the passage between Tinga Skerry and Brother Isle. This is subject to severe turbulence, particularly in wind against tide situations. The Eastmost channel is between Brother Isle and Yell, and between Uynarey and Yell. Some of the effects of the overfalls at the north end of Brother Isle can be avoided by keeping nearer to the Yell shore, particularly when west of Ness of Sound. Tides here run at up to seven knots. Be sure to keep at least four cables North of Brother Isle in order to avoid the rocks around Stoura Baa.

If using either of the passages West of Brother Isle, be sure to keep at least three cables off Mio Ness, and note that there is an onshore set of the current, particularly south of Tinga Skerry. The shoal area, Sligga Skerry, to the northwest of Bigga should be carefully noted, otherwise apart from the flow reaching six knots towards the south end of the channel between Bigga and the Mainland shore, a course in mid channel leads clear of dangers. Similar comments apply to the channel east of Bigga although currents are very slightly less. There are areas of turbulence to both west and east of the south end of Bigga.

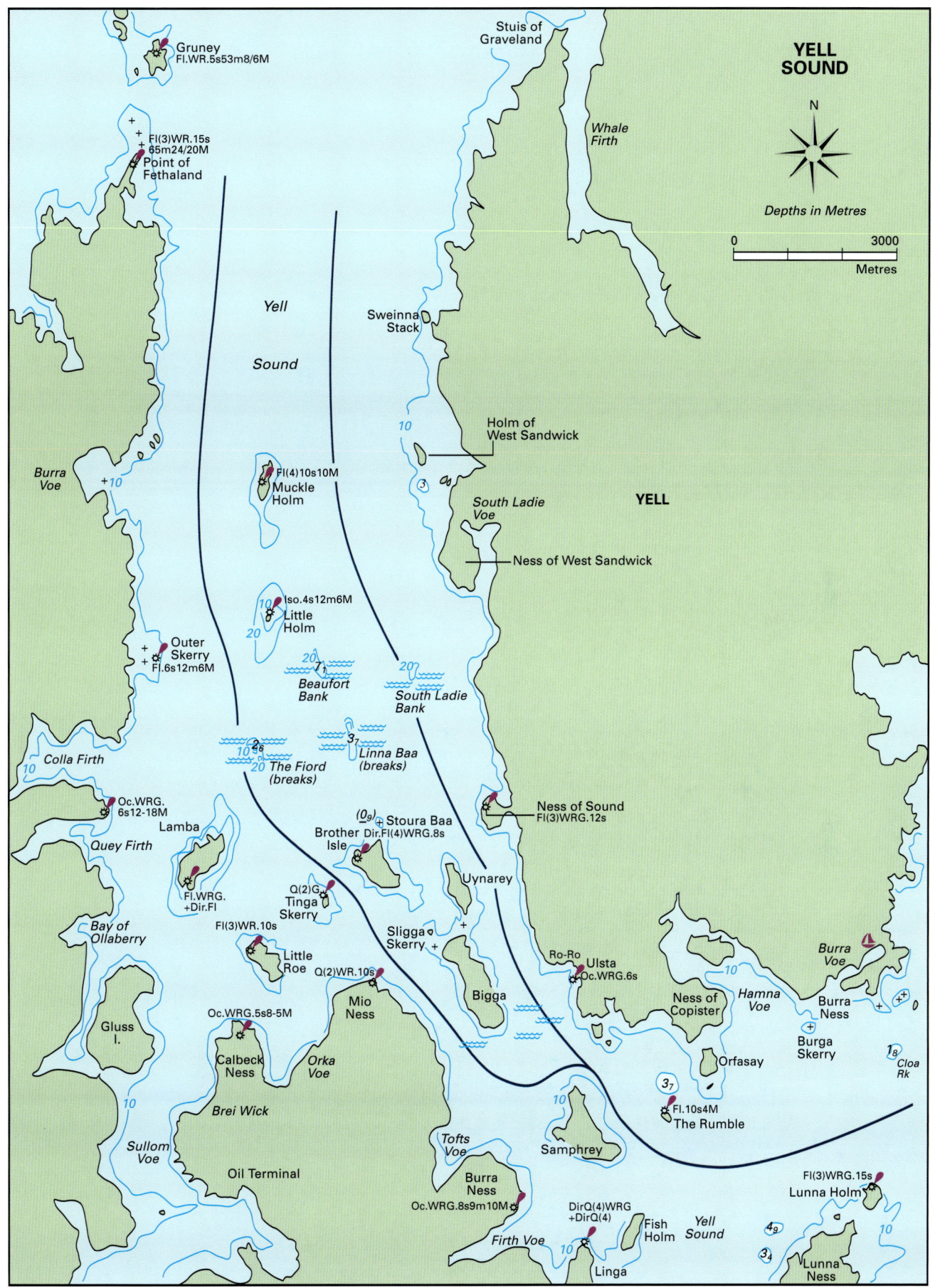

MAINLAND SHETLAND – EAST COAST

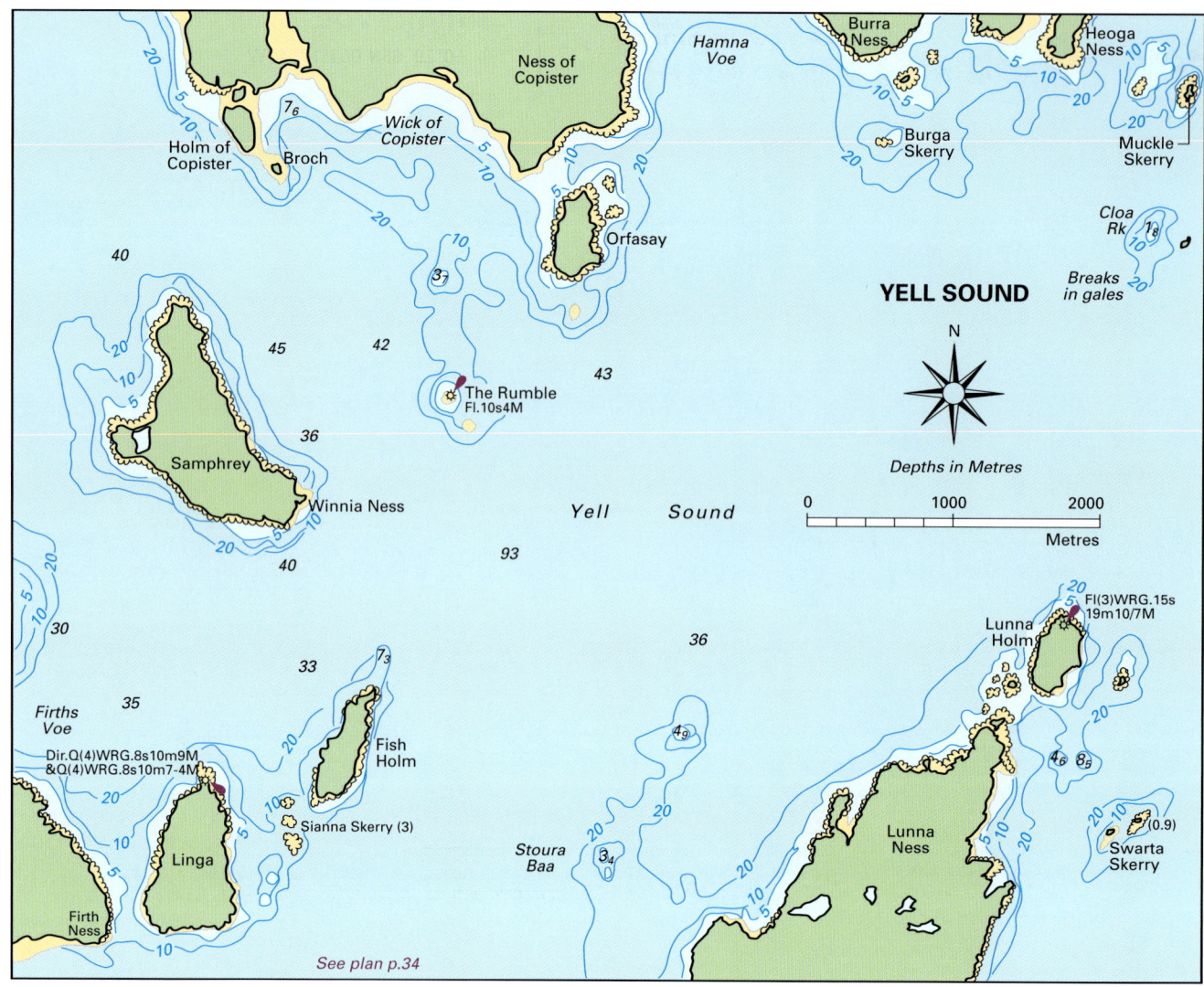

The main, and preferred channel is south of Samphrey, and although the tidal flow reaches at least six knots between Samphrey and the Mainland, a course eastwards from the south of the island leads clear of the dangerous shoal marked at the channel's southern end by The Rumble.

Note that there is a drying rock just over one cable southeast of the light on The Rumble. If using the channel between Samphrey and Yell make absolutely certain that the current does not set one inshore of The Rumble, and note that there are eddies and counter currents to the South of Holm of Copister.

The East entrance to Yell Sound is clear if course is set well South of Cloa Rock, ¾ mile south of Muckle Skerry of Neapaback. Burga Skerry, three cables South of Burra Ness should also be given a good offing.

Orka Voe

⊕ 60°29′·76N 001°15′·06W

CHARTS
3297, 3298, 3282

TIDES
-0028 Lerwick

LIGHTS
Mio Ness Q(2)WR.10s12m W7M, R4M, W twr vis 282°–W–238°–R–282° 60°29′·660N 001°13′·669W

Dangers
Overfalls extend at least ¼M off Mio Ness, and gas pipelines come ashore in the Voe.

Anchorages
The head of the Voe has been partially filled in, and the rest is deep and restricted by the gas pipelines. Anchoring not recommended.

Facilities
None.

Sullom Voe

⊕ 60°29´·66N 001°17´·47W

CHARTS
3281, 3282, 3297

TIDES
−0135 Lerwick

LIGHTS
Primary lights:
Lamba, South Head Fl.WRG.3s30m W8M, R5M, G5M; W twr vis
shore–G–288°–W–293°–R–327°–W–044°–R–140°–shore. Dir Lt 290·5° Fl.WRG.3s24m W10M, R7M, G7M, vis
285·5°–G–285·5°–G–288°–W–293°–W–295·5°
60°30´·721N 001°17´·825W
Little Roe Fl(3)WR.10s16m W5M, R4M, W structure, Or band vis 036°–R–095·5°–W–036° 60°29´·992N 001°16´·452W
Skaw Taing Ldg Lts 150·5° Front Fl(2)WRG.5s21m W8M, R5M, G5M; Or and W structure vis
049°–W–078°–G–147°–W–154°–R–169°–W–288°
60°29´·096N 001°16´·846W. Rear 195m from front Fl(2)5s35m8M vis W145°–156° 60°29´·002N 001°16´·737W
Gluss Isle Ldg Lts 194·7° (H24) Front 60°29´·771N 001°19´·427W F 39m19M on Gy twr H24. Rear 0·75M from front F 69m19M on Gy twr H24 60°29´·039N 001°19´·814W both Lts 9M by day.
Ness of Bardister Oc.WRG.8s20m W9M, R6M, G6M Or and W structure vis
180·5°–W–240°–R–310·5°–W–314·5°–G–030·5°
60°28´·187N 001°19´·623W

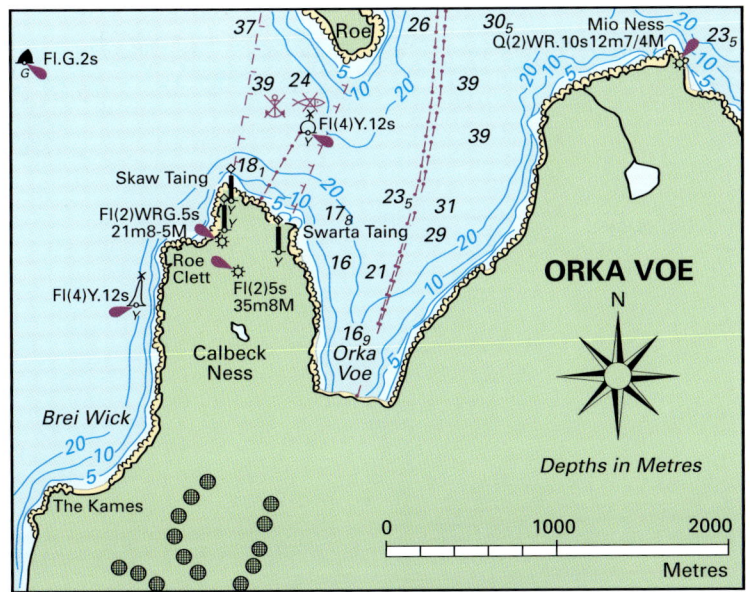

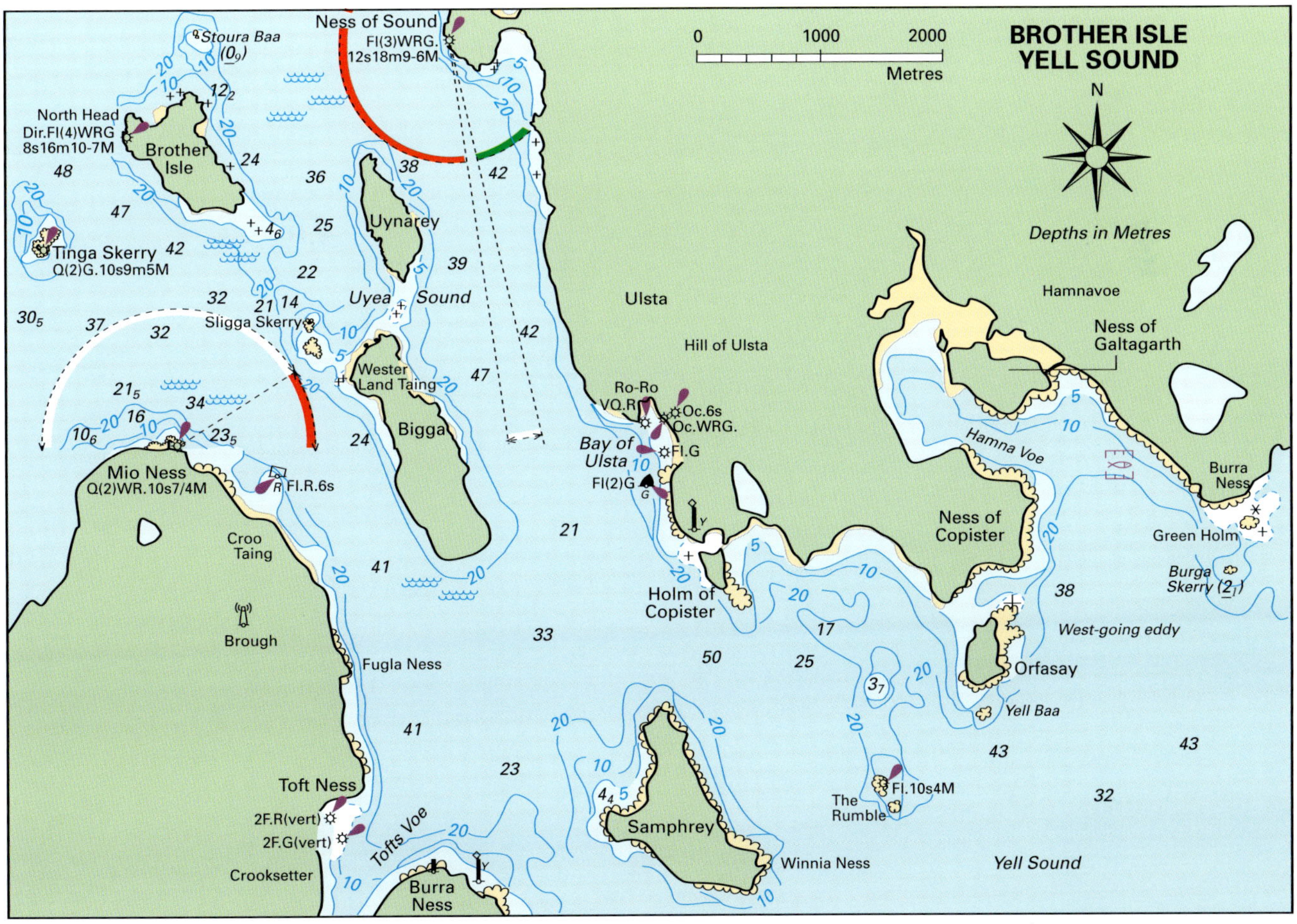

SHETLAND ISLANDS PILOT 43

Fugla Ness Lts in line 212·3° Common front Iso.4s27m14M 60°27'·449N 001°19'·552W synch. with rear Lts. Rear Iso.4s45m14M 60°27'·248N 001°19'·726W. Rear Iso.4s45m14M 60°27'·266N 001°19'·789W
Ungam VQ(2)5s2m2M 60°27'·232N 001°18'·609W
Sella Ness Dir Lt 133·5° Oc.WRG.10s19m W16M, R3M, G3M, vis 123·5°–g–130·5°–Al WG (white phase inc with brg) –132·5°–W–134·5°–Al WR (R phase inc with brg) –136·5°–R–143·5°, H24. By day Oc.WRG.10s19m W2M, R1M, G1m as above all 60°26'·758N 001°16'·655W
Sella Ness Point Q.G.14m6M 60°26'·877N 001°16'·639W
Channel lights:
No 5 buoy Fl.G.2s 60°29'·672N 001°18'·177W
Boom mark Fl(4)Y.12s 60°28'·897N 001°17'·436W
No 4 buoy Fl(3)G.10s 60°28'·767N 001°18'·590W
Boom mark Fl(4)Y.12s 60°28'·128N 001°18'·731W
No 3 buoy Fl(4)R.10s 60°28'·232N 001°18'·402W
NW Jetty light 2F.R(vert)7m3M 60°27'·888N 001°18'·437W
No 2 buoy Fl(2)G.5s 60°27'·613N 001°18'·862W
No 1 buoy Fl.G.2s 60°27'·275N 001°18'·167W
SE Jetty light F.R(vert)7m3M 60°27'·306N 001°17'·145W
Boom mark Fl.Y.2s 60°27'·045N 001°17'·287W
Tug Jetty, Garths Voe 2F.G(vert)8m3M 60°26'·812N 001°16'·298W
Boom mark, Voe of Scatsta Fl(4)Y.12s 60°26'·597N 001°16'·950W
PHM Fl(2)R.10s 60°26'·834N 001°17'·898W
Boom mark Fl(4)Y.12s 60°27'·030N 001°18'·947W
Boom mark Fl(4)Y.12s 60°26'·395N 001°19'·464W
Boom mark Fl(4)Y.12s 60°26'·844N 001°20'·317W
Boom mark Fl(4)Y.12s 60°24'·562N 001°20'·787W

Once past the oil terminal, Sullom Voe is a most attractive cruising area

Dangers

The oil terminal makes this part of the Shetland Islands by far the busiest with a huge number of shipping movements, some of which are severely restricted in their ability to manoeuvre. Vessel movements within the west channel of Yell Sound and particularly within Sullom Voe **must be reported** to Harbour Control on VHF Ch 14. Commercial traffic has priority making it imperative to keep to the western edges of any channels. Tides are generally slight and by keeping a couple of cables from the shores, particularly the west side, most dangers can be avoided. There is a channel inside Ungam which avoids the busy area in the main channel. This passage is best accomplished by keeping to a course between No. 2 buoy and the Boom Mark to the S of Ungam. If proceeding to the head of Sullom Voe, note the spit extending 1½ cables from the west side at the south end of The Narrows. The Boom Marks identify booms that can be positioned without notice in the event of any oil spill hazard. Chart 3297 shows various 'No Anchoring' areas.

Anchorages

There are several anchorages within Sullom Voe. Although the area around the oil terminal is not attractive to yachtsmen, there are some very appealing spots that seem a world away from the frantic activity in the commercial area. From the N entrance the anchorages are:

Yarfils Wick, Gluss Isle and Dale Voe are all usable as temporary anchorages and are easily entered using Chart 3298, but are all exposed to wash from passing commercial vessels.

Garths Voe is not recommended due to the volume of shipping activity. This is the main tug dock for Sullom Voe oil terminal.

MAINLAND SHETLAND – EAST COAST

Delting Boating Club slipway and the new Brae marina

Voe of Scatsta is very shallow and although generally clear of commercial activity, the airport runway is only a few metres away. There is a Boom Mark buoy in the centre of the bay, and although not used very often, there may be little warning of it being activated.

Houb of Lunnister is the first anchorage on the West shore, North of The Narrows but is exposed to the East. Entry is easy and anchorage is on sand and weed towards the North of the bay in 3–4m.

Bight of Haggrister is immediately to starboard after passing The Narrows, but beware of The Spit which can be avoided by keeping 1½ cables off. The best area is in the NW corner in 6–7m. Bottom is mainly small stones but a tripping line is recommended.

Voxter Voe on the East side is mainly shallow but provides more shelter from East winds although strong gusts can blow down the valley behind the Voe.

Note that the Voe dries for a significant distance from both the head and South shore. Anchor in 5–6m on sand. Some weed.

Ell Wick is an attractive and apart from the nearby road, peaceful anchorage at the head of Sullom Voe. Anchor in 6–7m. Bottom is mainly gravel, but a tripping line is recommended. The nearby road leads to Brae, a pleasant walk of about ¾ mile. The unnamed inlet to the NW of Ell Wick is another very attractive anchorage but note the dangers. These are a sunken rock off the East shore and a drying rock at the entrance to the bay just off the North shore. Keep at least 70m off the East shore to avoid the sunken rock and anchor towards the N shore in 7–8m. Bottom rock so tripping line is recommended.

Facilities

Brae is within walking distance and provides most services, including pubs, restaurants, hotels, shops and Delting Boating Club *(See Brae page 57).*

Gluss Voe

See plan page 45

⊕ 60°30´·08N 001°19´·50W

CHARTS
3298, 3297, 3281

TIDES
-0130 Lerwick

LIGHTS
Gluss Isle Ldg Lts 194·7° (H24) Front 60°29´·771N 001°19´·427W F 39m19M on Gy twr H24. Rear 0·75M from front F 69m19M on Gy twr H24 60°29´·039N 001°19´·814W both Lts 9M by day.
Lamba, South Head Fl.WRG.3s30m W8M, R5M, G5M; W twr vis shore–G–288°–W–293°–R–327°–W–044°–R–140°–shore. Dir Lt 290·5° Fl.WRG.3s24m W10M, R7M, G7M, vis 285·5°–G–285·5°–G–288°–W–293°–W–295·5° 60°30´·721N 001°17´·825W

Dangers

The Voe is long with steep sides but few dangers provided course is set ½ a cable offshore. From the waypoint above a course of 202° for 1¼ miles leads to the pool at the head of the Voe. Well-sheltered and clear of the tide in Yell Sound.

Anchorages

Good anchorage at the head of the Voe, but note that the West side of the pool dries. Anchor in 5–6m on a bottom of mud and sand.

Bay of Ollaberry

See plan page 45

⊕ 60°30´·19N 001°19´·50W

CHARTS
3298, 3297, 3281

TIDES
-0130 Lerwick

LIGHTS
Gluss Isle Ldg Lts 194·7° (H24) Front 60°29´·771N 001°19´·427W F 39m19M on Gy twr H24. Rear 0·75M from front F 69m19M on Gy twr H24 60°29´·039N 001°19´·814W both Lts 9M by day.
Lamba, South Head Fl.WRG.3s30m W8M, R5M, G5M; W twr vis shore–G–288°–W–293°–R–327°–W–044°–R–140°–shore. Dir Lt 290·5° Fl.WRG.3s24m W10M, R7M, G7M, vis 285·5°–G–285·5°–G–288°–W–293°–W–295·5° 60°30´·721N 001°17´·825W

Bay of Ollaberry

COLLA FIRTH

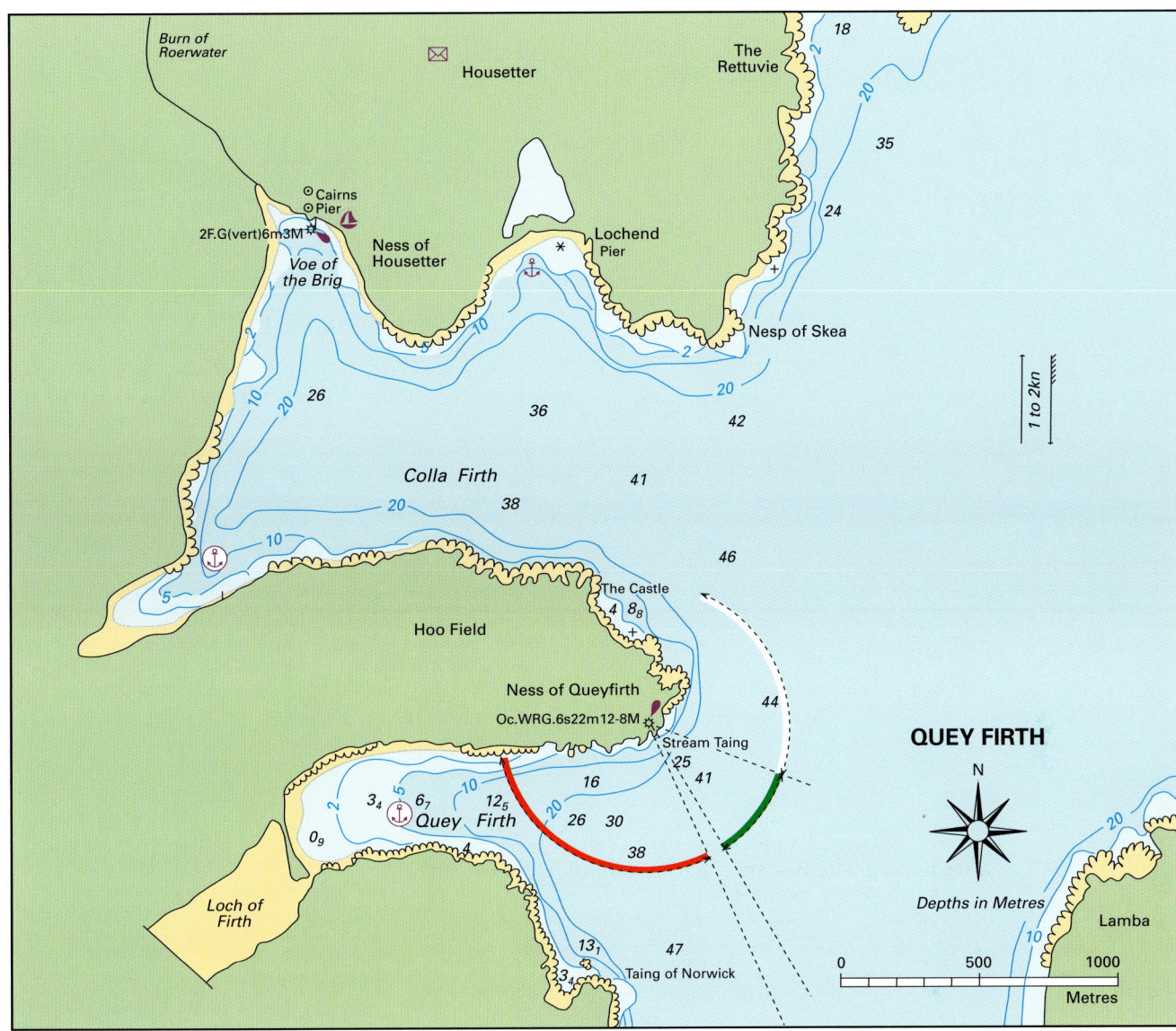

Dangers
Keep ½ cable off both Otter Head on the north side of the bay and East Ness on the south side. Also note that the Bay shoals up to ½ cable in the SW corner, otherwise entry is straight forward. Exposed to east winds.

Anchorages
Good anchorage if time does not permit a visit to Gluss Voe. Anchor in middle of bay South of small pier in 5m.

Facilities
Shop at Ollaberry.

Quey Firth
⊕ 60°31´·19N 001°19´·55W

CHARTS
3298, 3281

TIDES
-0136 Lerwick

LIGHTS
Stream Taing Oc.WRG.6s22m W21M, R8M, G8M, W twr vis: shore (through S & W)
–W–290°–G–327°–W–334°–W–shore 60°31´·427N 001°19´·571W

Dangers
Shores are clean ½ cable off, but head of bay shoals for fully ¼ mile.

Anchorages
Reasonable holding on sand in middle of bay, but Colla Firth may be preferred as an overnight anchorage.

Colla Firth
⊕ 60°31´·90N 001°19´·06W

CHARTS
3298, 3282

TIDES
-0136 Lerwick

LIGHTS
Stream Taing Oc.WRG.6s22m W21M,R8M, G8M, W twr vis: shore (through S & W)
–W–290°–G–327°–W–334°–W–shore 60°31´·427N 001°19´·571W

Dangers
Colla Firth is clear of dangers if course is set at least a cable from the shores. Exposed to the east.

SHETLAND ISLANDS PILOT 47

MAINLAND SHETLAND – EAST COAST

Colla Firth from the south

Colla Firth harbour and marina

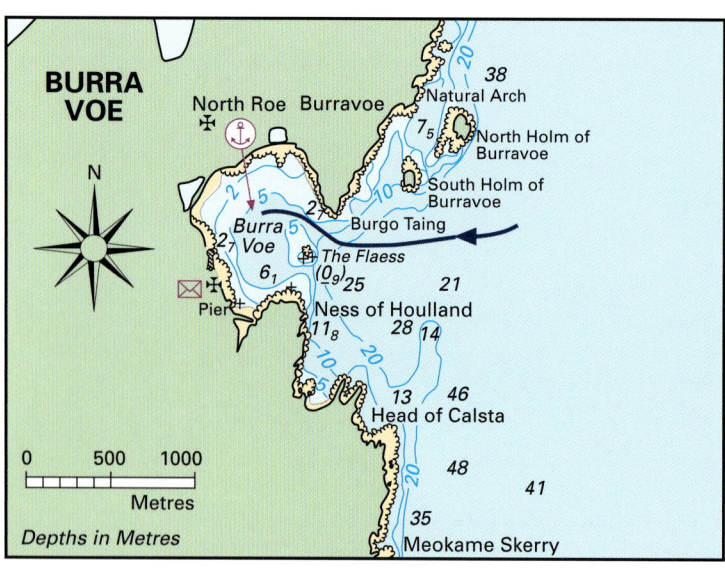

Anchorages

There are two bays on the North shore, the Easterly one is both shallow, and the bottom is rocky making anchoring problematic. A tripping line is recommended. The West bay, marked on chart 3298 as Voe of the Brig, is home to Colla Firth pier and a small marina. The pier provides a good degree of shelter to the marina although some swell can reach the marina in strong Easterly winds. The outside of the pier is used by large vessels and the inside of the pier is used by fishing boats, but yachts can tie alongside if too big for the marina berths. The marina has a depth of 2m.

The bay at the South West corner of Colla Firth provides anchorage in 4–5m and is clear of the commercial activity associated with the main pier mentioned above.

Note that the head of the bay shoals for fully some 1½ cables. Subject to some swell in Easterly winds.

Facilities

At Brae or Ollaberry.

Burra Voe

⊕ 60°34′·80N 001°18′·61W

CHARTS
3298, 3282, 3281

TIDES
-0136 Lerwick

LIGHTS
Muckle Holm Fl(4)10s32m10M 60°34′·822N 001°15′·993W

Dangers

Rocks known as The Flaess obstruct the middle of the entrance to Burra Voe and there is a rocky outcrop off the point on the north side of the entrance and a shoal patch off the south point which has a dangerous rock at its north end. In

Burra Voe is shallow towards the head of the bay

Yell Sound the two Holms, North Holm of Burravoe and South Holm of Burravoe should be given a berth of at least ½ a cable. Do not attempt to pass inshore of these.

Anchorages

The best anchorage is on the North side of the Voe, and is reached by passing North of The Flaess which extend further than is apparent from chart 3298. Keep no more than ⅓ South of Burgo Taing and anchor on a line keeping the South end of Muckle Holm in line with Burgo Taing in about 4–5m. Bottom is mainly stone and shingle. A tripping line is recommended.

Facilities

Shops and post office. Shops at North Roe, ½ mile.

Point of Fethaland

⊕ 60°38´·73N 001°18´·36W (Middle of channel)

CHARTS
  3298, 3282, 3281

TIDES
  -0140 Lerwick

LIGHTS
Gruney Is. Fl.WR.5s53m W8M, R6M; W twr, vis 064°–R–180°–W–012°. Racon(T)14M 60°39´·147N 001°18´·168W
Point of Fethaland Fl(3)WR.15s65m W24M, R20M vis 080°–R–103°–W–160°–206°–W–340° 60°38´·045N 001°18´·691W

Dangers

If rounding from Yell Sound to the west coast of Mainland Shetland, the inner passage between Point of Fethaland and Gruney Is. keeps clear of the very turbulent waters to the north of Grunay Is. and Gaut Skerries. Care is needed as tides still run strongly and constant watch must be taken to ensure that the chosen course is maintained. Beware the drying rocks of both Inner and Outer Booth. The following directions lead clear.

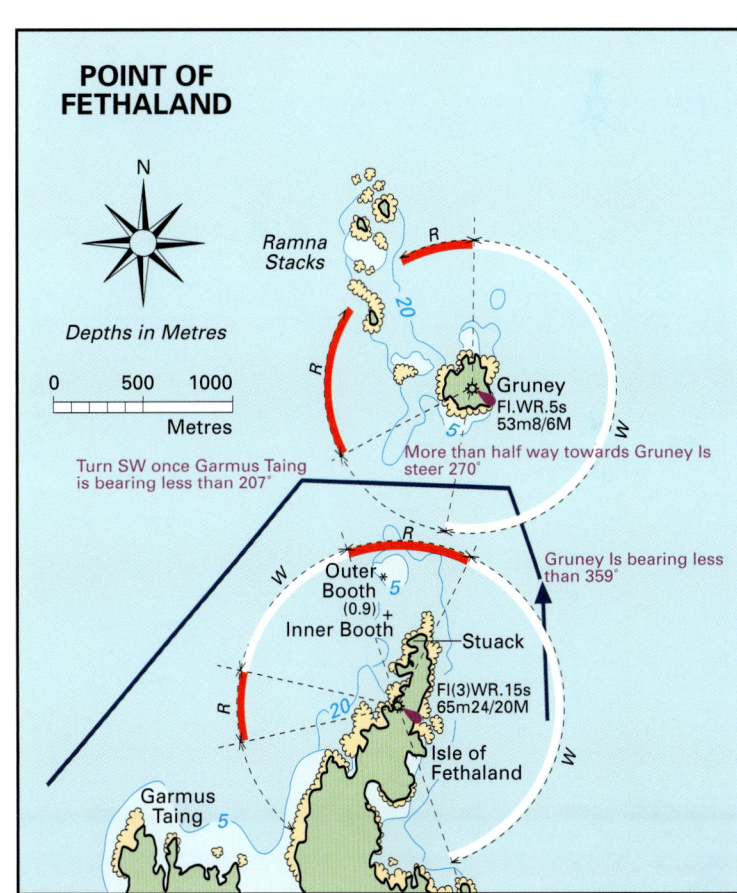

Passage

From the Eastside of Mainland to West stay at least two cables offshore and keep Gruney Is. bearing less than 359° until at least half way Northwards between Stuack off the Point of Fethaland and Gruney Is. Then turn West until Garmus Taing is bearing less than 207° before turning SW onto a course to clear Garmus Taing and Birdik Is.

MAINLAND SHELTAND WEST COAST

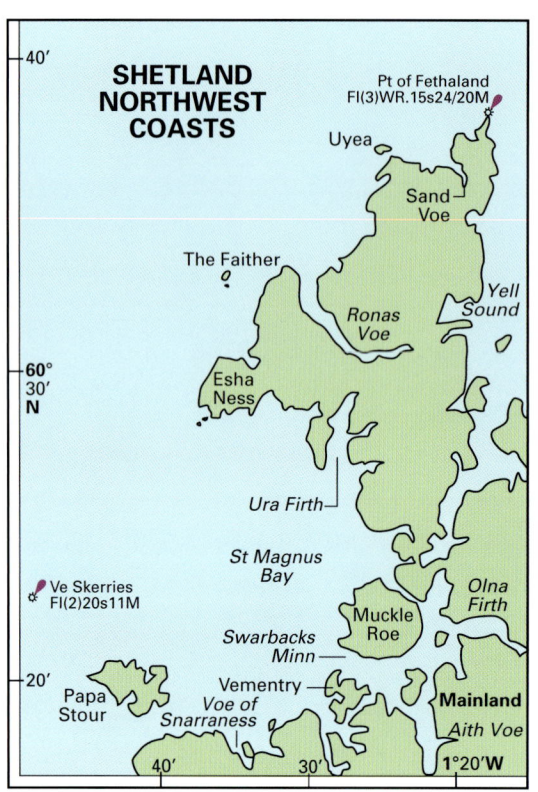

Sand Voe

⊕ 60°36´·85N 001°21´·47W

CHARTS
3298, 3281

TIDES
-0159 Lerwick

LIGHTS
Gruney Is. Fl.WR.5s53m W8M, R6M; W twr, vis 064°–R–180°–W–012°. Racon(T)14M 60°39´·147N 001°18´·168W
Point of Fethaland Fl(3)WR.15s65m W24M, R20M vis 080°–R–103°–W–160°–206°–W–340° 60°38´·045N 001°18´·691W

Dangers

If approaching from the west do not pass inshore of Uyae Baas and note the extensive shoal bewteen Uyae Is. and the entrance to Sand Voe.

Note also the isolated rock ½ cable off the point that lies ¼ mile west of the entrance.

Anchorages

The entrance is between high cliffs on both sides and is only two cables wide, the best anchorage being on the west side in about 5m. Beyond the narrows there is an extensive sheltered area but with depths of only 1–2m.

Ronas Voe

See plan page 51

⊕ 60°33´·70N 001°30´·26W

CHARTS
3295, 3281

TIDES
-0205 Lerwick

LIGHTS
None

Dangers

The spectacular scenery of Ronas Voe also gives reason for the difficulties that can be encountered. The channel between the hills generates ferocious squalls, and these can be strong enough to cause anchoring problems. Shoal patches extend from the west shore (see

Sand Voe ofers very good shelter

50 SHETLAND ISLANDS PILOT

RONAS VOE

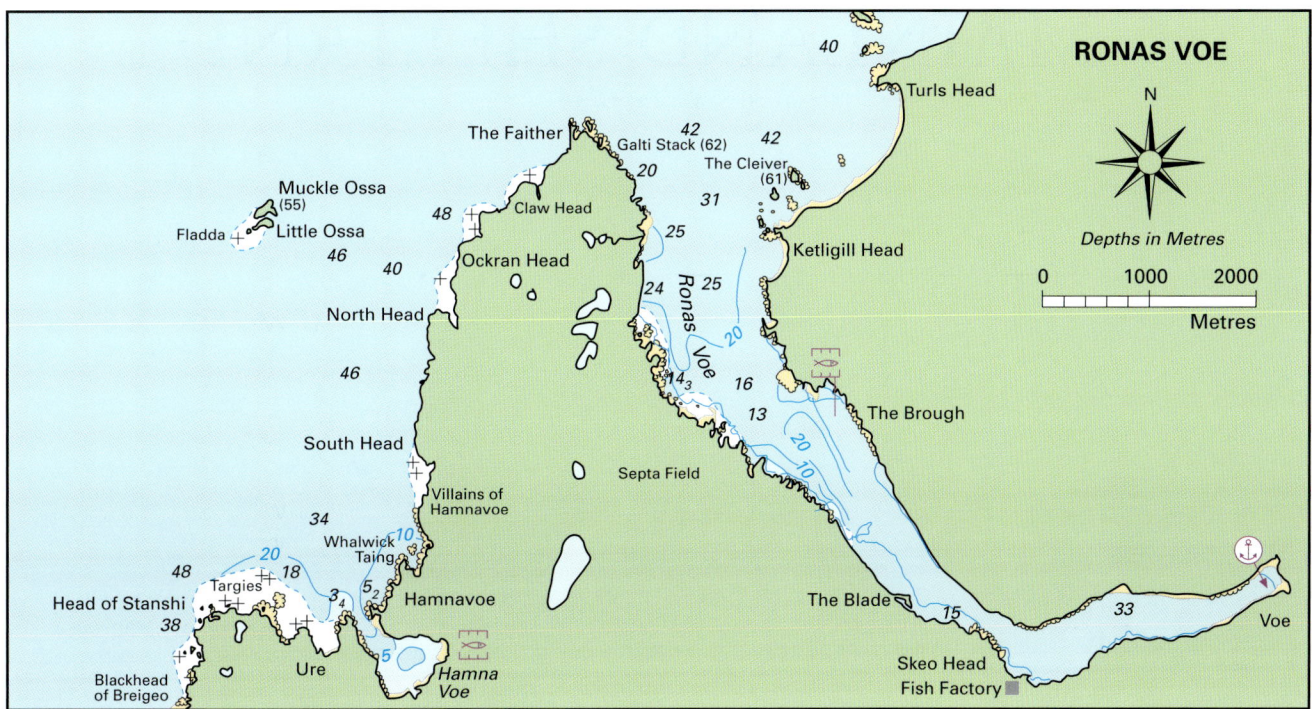

Orr Wick at the head of Ronas Voe

chart 3295) almost from the entrance to the Narrows with a shoal that extends 1½ cables offshore and begins ½ mile to seaward of The Blade only ending at The Narrows. Keep to the north side of the Voe. Several fish farms.

Anchorages

The head of the Voe provides a pleasant and peaceful anchorage in settled conditions, but beware the variable gusts that affect the Voe even this far from the open sea. Anchor in 5–6m on mud. The Fish Factory at Skeo Head has a pier, and although the staff offer kindness typical of Shetland, this is maintained as a commercial facility.

Facilities

At Ollaberry, 2½ miles from head of Voe.

Interest

Ronas Hill is the highest hill in the Shetland Isles reaching 459m. For the energetic, views from the top are spectacular.

South Head

The view to South Head from seaward is spectacular but be sure to keep an absolute minimum of ¼ mile offshore. The cliffs behind South Head are named The Villains of Hamnavoe, not without reason.

Ronas Voe can be subject to severe squalls

South Head

SHETLAND ISLANDS PILOT 51

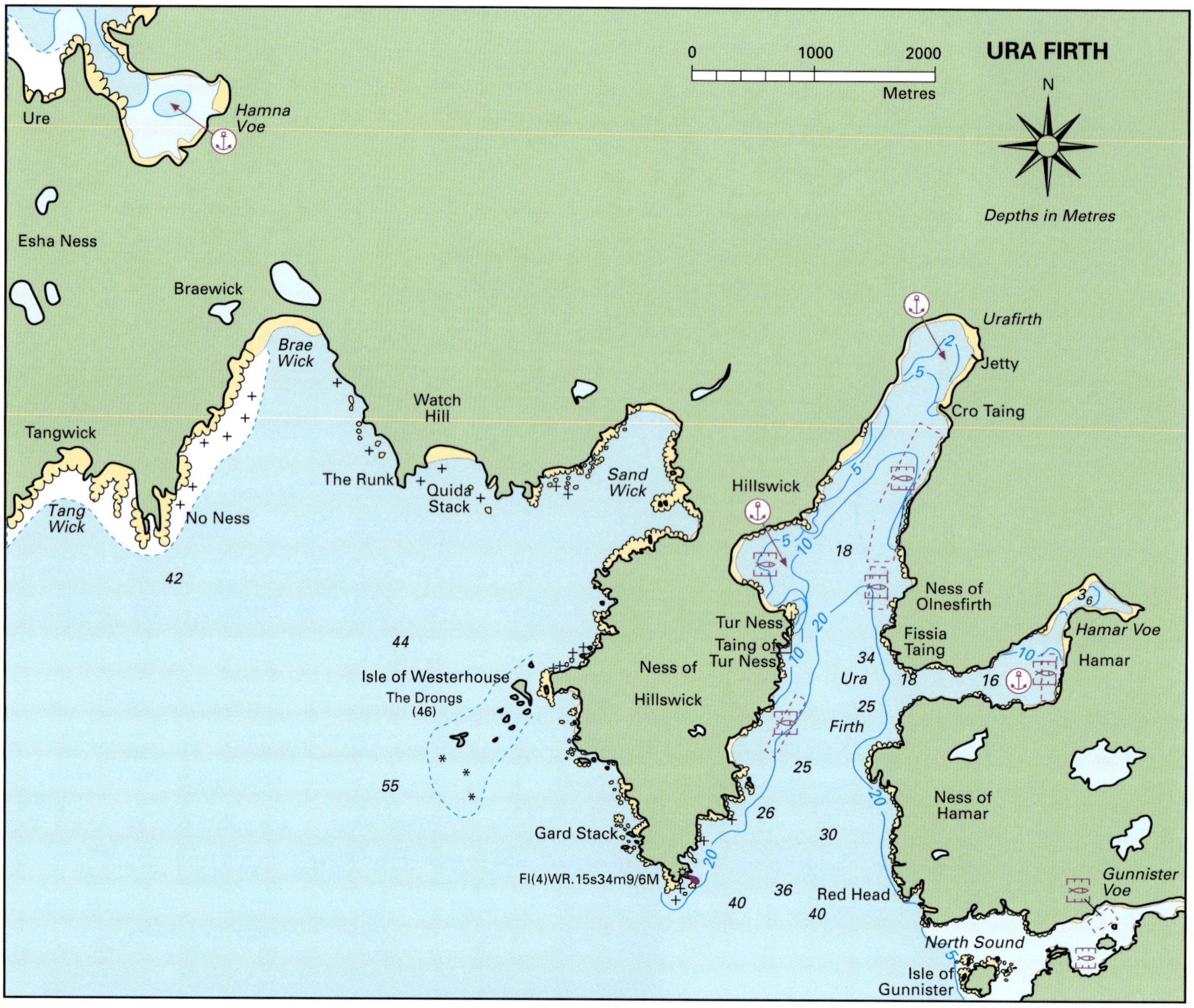

MAINLAND SHETLAND – WEST COAST

Hamna Voe

Hamna Voe

See plan page 51

⊕ 60°30′·23N 001°34′·96W

CHART
3281

TIDES
-0200 Lerwick

LIGHTS
None

Dangers

A narrow entrance with rocks on both sides requires care. Identify the house on the shore in the SW corner and a leading line of 151° leads clear of the rocks. Local knowledge is recommended for first time visitors.

Anchorages

As depths permit clear of fish farming equipment.

Brae Wick

⊕ 60°28′·68N 001°33′·18W

CHART
3281

TIDES
-0205 Lerwick

LIGHTS
Esha Ness Fl.12s61m25M 60°29′·334N 001°37′·663W

Dangers

If approaching from the north keep a good offing from Head of Stanshi to Skerry of Ehsaness and particularly note the onshore tidal set between The Bruddans where rocks extend fully two cables offshore, and Skerry of Eshaness. Once east of Skerry of Eshaness note the rock ½ cable S of Dore Holm.

Anchorages

Brae Wick can only be considered a temporary anchorage, and many rocks, some uncharted, extend for some distance off each shore. Not recommended.

Sand Wick with the Drongs in the distance

Sand Wick

⊕ 60°28′·31N 001°31′·32W

CHART
3281

TIDES
-0210 Lerwick

LIGHTS
Esha Ness Fl.12s61m25M 60°29′·334N 001°37′·663W

Dangers
Similar comments apply to those about Brae Wick above, plus the prevailing winds blow straight into the bay. Some slight incursion into the bay can give spectacular views of The Drongs, the fearsome looking 'teeth' off Houlma Sound.

Anchorages
Not recommended.

Ura Firth

See plan page 52

⊕ 60°26′·90N 001°28′·88W

CHARTS
3281, 3295

TIDES
-0220 Lerwick

LIGHTS
Ness of Hillswick Fl(4)WR.15s34m W9M, R6M vis: 217°–W–093°–R–114° 60°27′·201N 001°29′·791W

Dangers
The entrance to Ura Firth is quite straight forward provided care is taken to avoid the rock lying 1½ cables south of Ness of Hillswick light on bearing of 175/355°. Otherwise a course keeping a cable off each shore leads clear of dangers. If approaching from the west in rough weather note the area SW of the above light where heavy seas break.

Anchorages
There are three recognised anchorages, all of which can be reached in almost any weather. There are numerous fish farms, some unlit.

Ura Firth

The anchorage at Urafirth, at the head of the Firth is partially sheltered by Cro Taing, but some swell reaches the upper part of the Firth in SW winds. Avoid the shoal area off Cro Taing and anchor as depths permit in about 3m towards the head of the Firth.
Note the drying area on the E shore.

Hillswick

See plan page 52

⊕ 60°28′·44N 001°28′·66W

CHARTS
3281, 3295

TIDES
-0220 Lerwick

LIGHTS
Ness of Hillswick Fl(4)WR.15s34m W9M, R6M vis: 217°–W–093°–R–114° 60°27′·201N 001°29′·791W

Dangers
Entry to the bay is easy provided the shoal ground at Taing of Turness is avoided. Keep at least 1½ cables off the point before turning into the anchorage.

Anchorages
On the West shore, Hillswick is the only one with any facilities, but also has the poorest holding on sand over rock, making a tripping line a strong recommendation. Anchor in 5–6m.

Facilities
Hotel ☏ 01806 503372, shops, water, fuel.

MAINLAND SHETLAND – WEST COAST

Hamar Voe

See plan page 52

⊕ 60°27′·93N 001°28′·11W

CHARTS
3281, 3295

TIDES
-0220 Lerwick

LIGHTS
Ness of Hillswick Fl(4)WR.15s34m W9M, R6M vis: 217°–W–093°–R–114° 60°27′·201N 001°29′·791W

Dangers
The only hazards to be encountered are shoal and outlying rocks off the headlands to the south of the entrance to Hamar Voe and these are easily avoided by keeping ½ cable offshore.

Anchorages
The outer part of the Voe offers secure anchorage in deep (15m) water clear of the fish farm. The inner part is very sheltered and reached by keeping to the centre of the channel, and then turning to starboard when the bay opens. Anchor in about 3m.

Gunnister Voe

See plan page 52

CHARTS
3295, 3281

Dangers
There are two entrances, the north of Isle of Gunnister being marked dangerous on chart 3295, partly due to the overfalls that occur and to the various unmarked rocks. The south channel is used by local small boats in connection with the fish farms located behind Holm of Gunnister.

Anchorages
It may be possible to find anchorage at the head of the Voe clear of the fish farms, if pilotage can be provided by a local boat.

Hamar Voe

Gunnister Voe

Mangaster Voe

See plan page 52

⊕ 60°24′·02N 001°26′·25W

CHART
3281

TIDES
-0220 Lerwick

LIGHTS
None

Dangers
Egilsay Is and Black Skerry lie in the entrance. The channel N of Egilsay Is. is not used, there being many rocks and breaking water. The south entrance is narrow due to a fish farm in the entrance and dangerous rocks SW and SE of Black Skerry. Keep ½ cable off the mainland side. Many fish farms.

Anchorages
At the head of the Voe clear of the fish farms. Well sheltered.

Roe Sound

See plan page 55

⊕ 60°24′·02N 001°26′·25W

CHART
3281

TIDES
-0220 Lerwick

LIGHTS
None

Egilsay Island at the entrance to Mangaster Voe

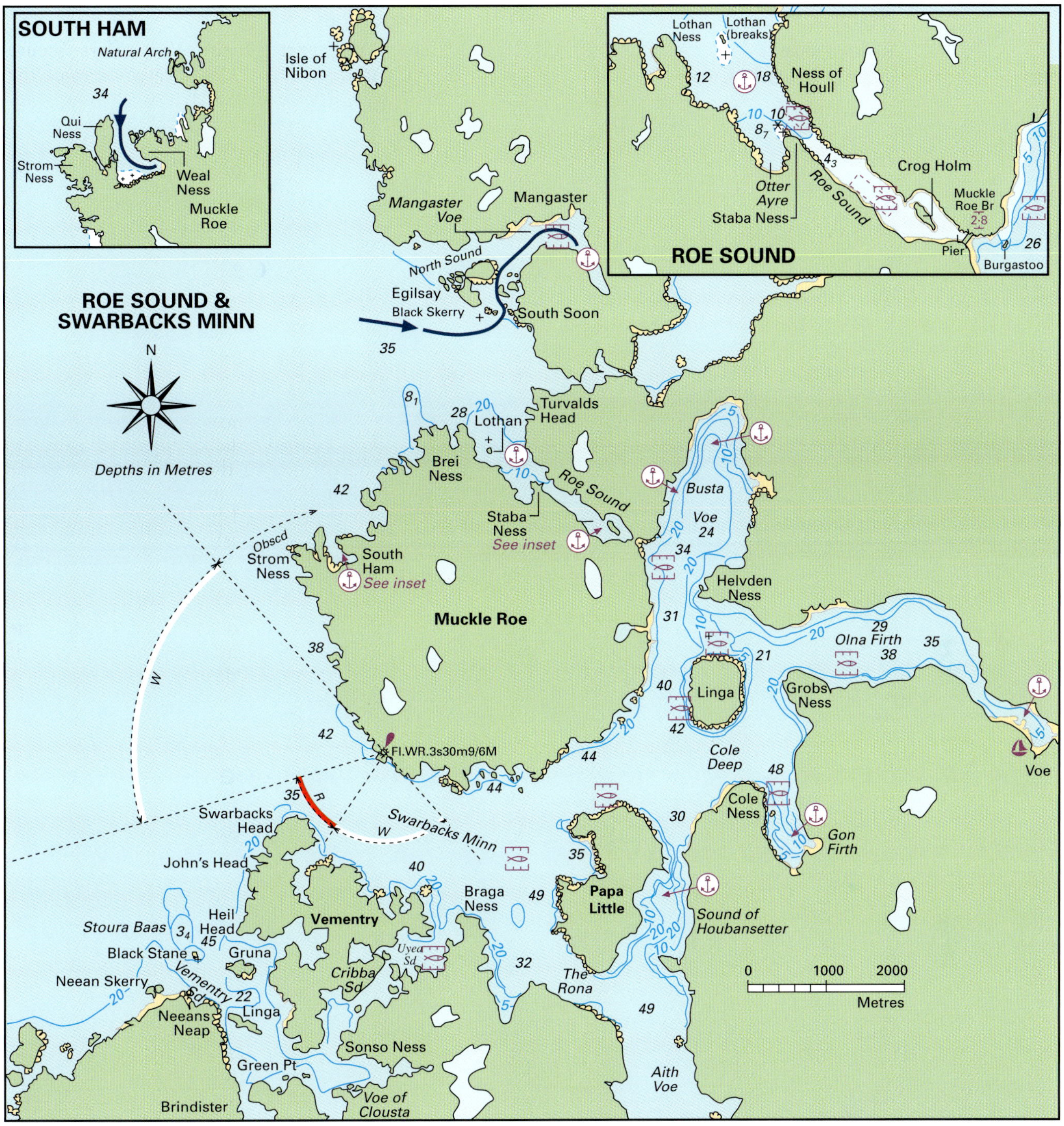

ROE SOUND

Dangers
Entered between Turvalds head and Brei Ness, both of which should be given a berth of at least 1½ cables in order to avoid offlying rocks. Almost in the centre of the entrance lies The Lothan, a shoal patch with breaking water extending ½ mile SE and marked at its outer end by a drying rock. This can be passed on either side but the N shore is cleaner. A spit extends fully 1½ cables NW of the point at Staba Ness. Keep to the centre of the channel between Staba Ness and the N shore.

Anchorages
Although some swell can reach the anchorage just W of Crog Holm, it is normally quite sheltered. There is a small marina on the NE side of Crog Holm, reached by the passage to the E of Crog Holm.

Facilities
Busta House Hotel 1½ miles from marina.

Roe Sound looking northwest

MAINLAND SHETLAND – WEST COAST

South Ham

See plan page 55

⊕ 60°23'·73N 001°27'·88W

CHARTS
3295, 3281

TIDES
-0220 Lerwick

LIGHTS
None

Dangers
The entrance is less than a cable wide, and the Ham is exposed to the west. The south shore is rocky and shoals. A lunch stop only. Mainly shallow.

Anchorages
Anchor in the SE corner as depths permit.

Facilities
None.

Interest
Interesting cliff formations.

Swarbacks Minn

⊕ 60°21'·14N 001°29'·14W

CHARTS
3295, 3281

TIDES
-0220 Lerwick

LIGHTS
Muckle Roe Fl.WR.3s30mW9M, R6M; vis: 314°–W–041°–R–075°–W–137° 60°20'·970N 001°27'·061W

Dangers
A fabulous cruising area giving a flavour of the all that is good in Shetland waters. Entered between Murbie Stacks to the N and Swarbacks Head on the S side, off which lies Swarbacks Skerry, the passage is clear if the shores are cleared by a cable. Incoming tide can reach three knots. If heading for Uyea Sound note the drying rocks ½ cable off the east side of Holms of Uyea Sound. There is a

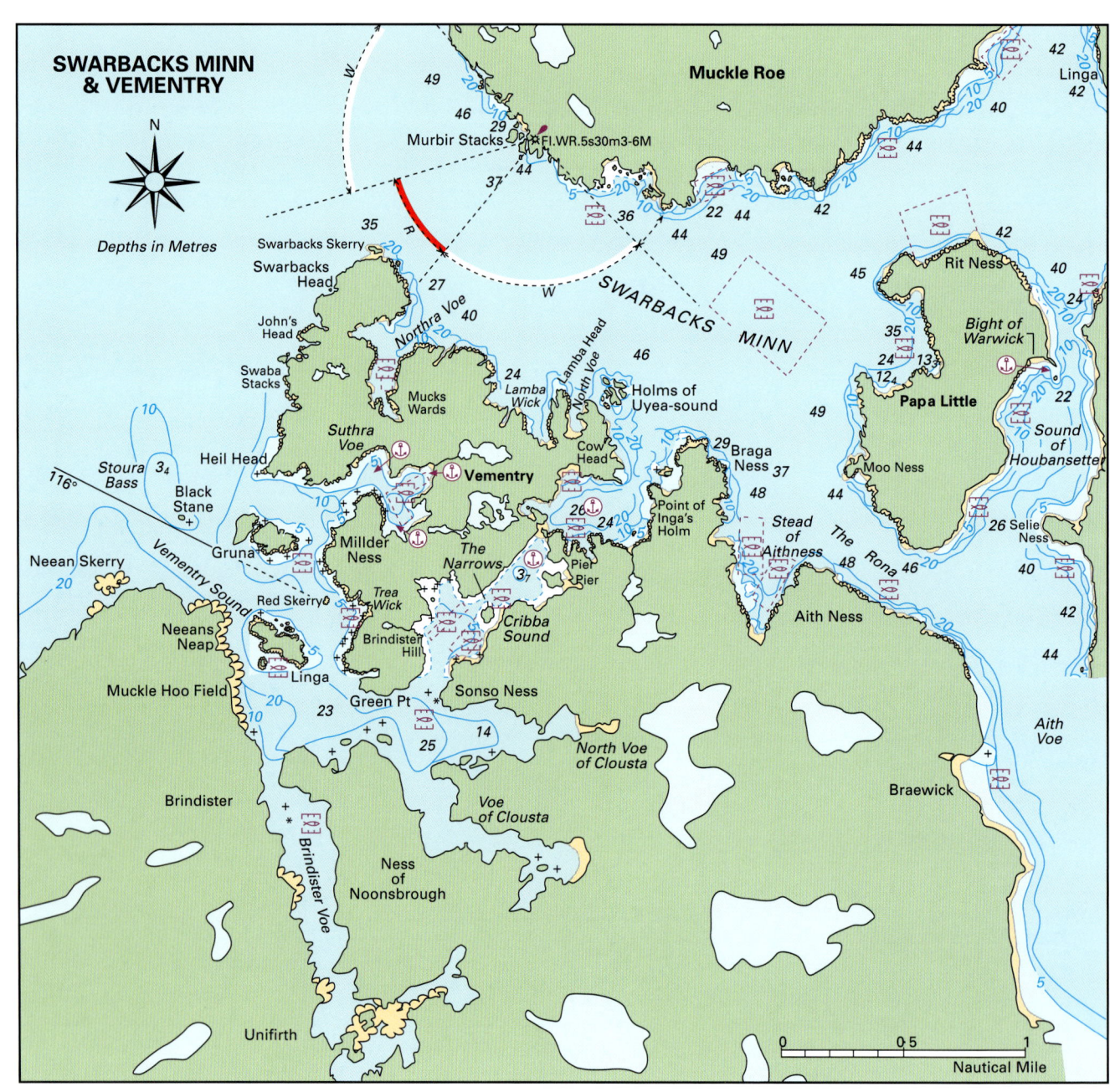

shoal area with a dangerous rock, Groin Baa, two cables N of Linga over which seas break. Otherwise an offing of a cable leads clear to the different Voes and Firths. The clear waters of Swarbacks Minn have encouraged considerable fish farming activity; some are unlit.

Busta Voe

See plan page 55

⊕ 60°22′·04N 001°22′·26W

CHARTS
3295, 3281

TIDES
-0220 Lerwick

LIGHTS
None

Dangers

Keep a cable off the point at Hevden Ness and note the dangerous rock which lies one cable N of the headland. Burgastoo is a rock drying 8m S of the point on the west side just N of Muckle Roe Bridge. Apart from the Houb of Burravoe, which dries, there are no real dangers if a reasonable distance is kept from the shores.

Anchorages

Off the hotel at Busta clear of the moorings in 4–6m. There is a small harbour just below the hotel but this is only suitable for small craft, although convenient if visiting the hotel.

Brae is also used as an anchorage off the sailing club in 5–7m, but due to swell when wind is in the South, this has mainly been superseded by the new marina located on the W side a cable S of the club.

Facilities

Busta House Hotel ☎ 01806 522506. All facilities are available at Brae.

Olna Firth

See plan page 55

⊕ 60°21′·73N 001°20′·61W

CHARTS
3295, 3281

TIDES
-0220 Lerwick

LIGHTS
Voe Pier 2F.G(vert) 60°21′·072N 001°15′·987W

Above
Busta Pier and bay

Below
The small marina at Muckle Roe. The island, Crog Holm, in the centre of photo

MAINLAND SHETLAND – WEST COAST

Marina and harbour, Voe, Olna Firth

Dangers
The entrance is clear if approaching from the south between Linga and Grobbs Ness apart from a fish farm off the mainland side. From the north of Linga beware Groin Baa, a dangerous rock which lies slightly south of mid channel. The deep water approach a cable off Linga, avoiding the fish farm is the preferred course. There is a drying rock a cable off the south shore about a mile from Grobbs Ness, but otherwise the Firth is clear of dangers.

Anchorages
There is a small marina at Voe at the head of the Firth, with nearly 4m. The area East of the marina is shoal, otherwise anchor as depths permit clear of the fish farms. Bottom mud.

Facilities
Most facilities available at Voe including pub and restaurant ☏ 01806 588332.

Gon Firth
See plan page 55

⊕ 60°20´·85N 001°20´·69W

CHARTS
3295, 3281

TIDES
-0220 Lerwick

LIGHTS
None

Dangers
No real hazards although the west and south shores shoal for up to a cable offshore.

Anchorages
In the South East corner clear of the fish farms in about 4–6m. Bottom mud.

Facilities
None.

Sound of Houbansetter
See plan page 56

⊕ 60°20´·58N 001°22´·32W (North entrance)

CHARTS
3295, 3281

TIDES
-0220 Lerwick

LIGHTS
None

Dangers
The usable part of the north channel is less than one cable wide, but a course maintaining the west point of Sellie Ness on a bearing of 188° leads clear.

Note that the spit at the East extremity of Papa Little dries for almost a cable to the south.

Anchorages
The best anchorage is at the North end of Bight of Warwick in 5–6m. Sheltered from North winds. Entry from the South via The Rona is clear of dangers apart from the drying rock ½ cable off Sellie Ness.

Facilities
None.

AITH VOE

Papa Little
See plan page 56

⊕ 60°19´·76N 001°22´·48W

CHART
3295

TIDES
-0220 Lerwick

LIGHTS
None

Dangers
The anchorage is reached from the Sound of Houbansetter. If approaching from the north, clear the spit on the Papa Little shore by at least a cable, and approaching from the south also clear Selie Ness on the Mainland shore by at least a cable in order to avoid the offlying rock.

Anchorages
Anchor in Bight of Warwick clear of the fish farm. Particularly in North winds, the preferred anchorage is to the North of the bay behind the spit in 5m. Good holding and sheltered.

Facilities
None.

Aith Voe
See plan page 59

⊕ 60°19´·03N 001°22´·78W

CHARTS
3295, 3281

TIDES
-0220 Lerwick

LIGHTS
Aith Breakwater Q.G.5m3M 60°17´·210N 001°22´·419W

Dangers
If entering from The Rona, note the rocks that extend almost ½ cable off Keen Point. There are few dangers in the Voe, the only one of note is the rocky outcrop on the east side ¼ M from the entrance to Aith Voe. Otherwise keep ½ cable offshore.

Anchorages
Off Breiwick House An occasional anchorage in 3–4m. Beware the rock which lies just off the North end of the bay.

East Burrafirth on the East side 1M North of Aith. It is possible to anchor in behind the fish

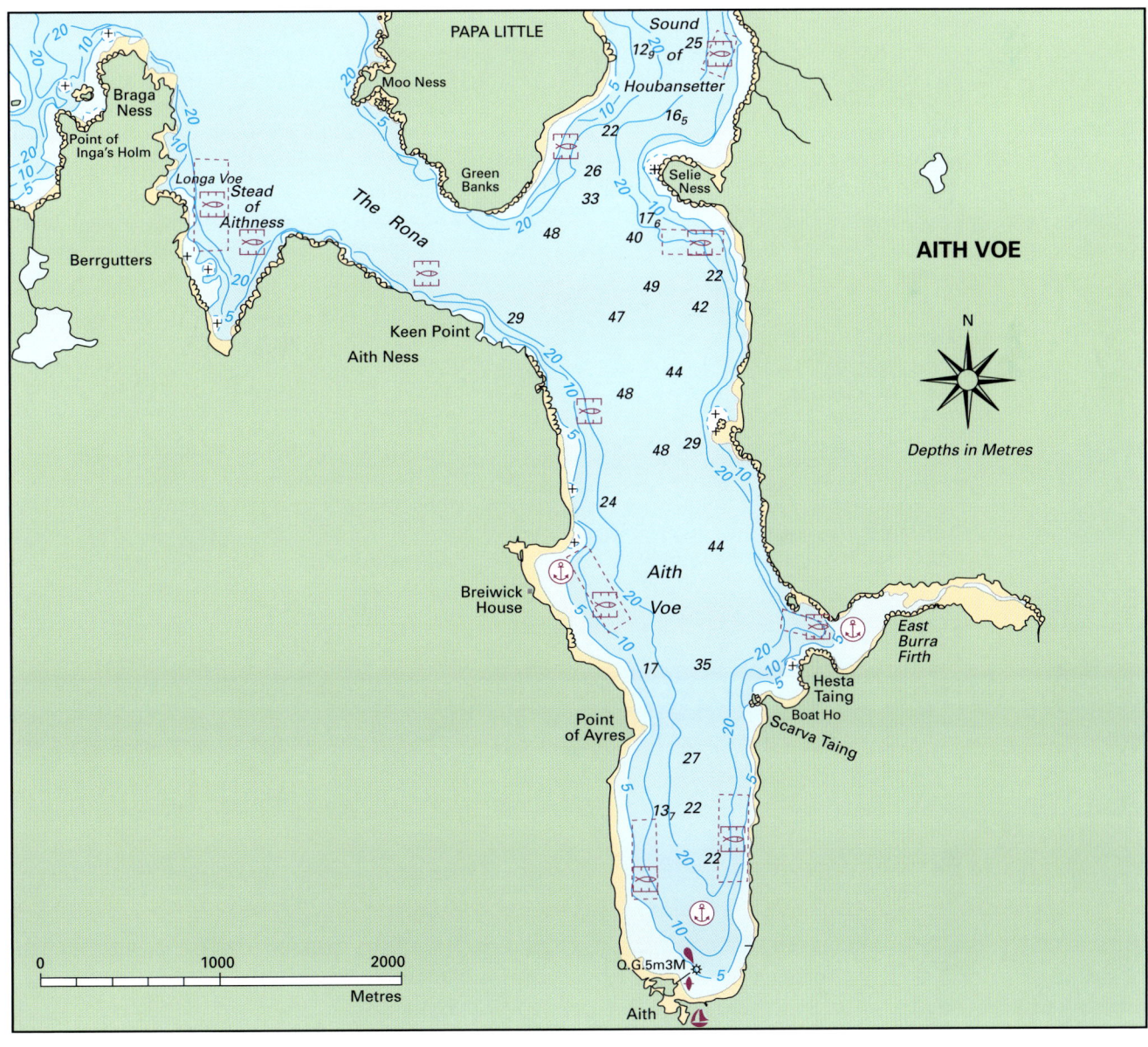

Aith at the head of Aith Voe. The marina can just be seen to the left of picture

farm located at the mouth of the Firth in 4–5m. The Fiurth dries for some considerable distance and if leaving to head for Aith note the drying rock which lies to the West of Hesta Taing.

Aith now has a small marina although depths within are quite restricted (1·2m at low water). There is a visitors berth on the inside of Aith pier more suitable for larger boats. Do not obstruct the Lifeboat berth at the outer end of the pier.

Facilities

All facilities including a leisure centre and swimming pool.

Uyea Sound

⊕ 60°19'·90N 001°25'·90W

CHARTS
3295, 3281

TIDES
-0220 Lerwick

LIGHTS
None

Dangers

A little extra care is required than for most of the anchorages in Swarbacks Minn, but if care is taken to avoid the rocks off The Holms of Uyea Sound and the east shore is given a berth of ¾ cable, passage into the pool is quite straight forward. Pay particular note of the dangerous rocks 0·6 cable off the point at Braga Ness, and at a similar distance off the Point of Ingas Holm. At the south end of the pool there is a shallow (1m) channel with strong tides which leads to Cribba Sound.

Anchorages

The bay on the North side provides good shelter clear of the fish farm.

Facilities

None.

Vementry

See also plan page 55

⊕ 60°20'·00N 001°29'·83W (for Suthra Voe)
⊕ 60°19'·62N 001°31'·26W (for Cribba Sound, Voes of Clousta and Brindister Voe).

CHARTS
3295, 3281

TIDES
-0213 Lerwick

LIGHTS
None

Dangers *See plan page 55*

Entry to the west side of Vementry requires careful navigation due to the many rocks and shoals. If heading for Suthra Voe, beware the shallow area, Stoura Baas, that extends ½M NNW from Black Stane, and over which seas break in even moderately fresh winds.

Note the rock off Heill Head.

If heading south of Gruna for the other Voes, care must be taken to avoid the numerous rocks off Neean Skerry to the south and Black Stane to the north. A course with Red Skerry bearing 116° leads clear. If visibility does not allow positive identification of Red Skerry, Gruna just open of Black Stane and a course ½ cable off leads towards Red Skerry. From Red Skerry note that the passage between Linga and Vementry is shoal for fully one cable from the Linga side and rocks lie off the Vementry side for nearly ½ cable. This leaves a navigable channel only ½ cable wide. If proceeding to Cribba Sound note that the passage between Green Point on Vementry and Green Holm off Ness of Noonsbrough is no more than ½ cable wide being bounded on both sides with rocky reefs which extend nearly 1½ cables from each shore, creating a dog leg approach. Also note rocks off Sonso Ness.

Anchorages

Suthra Voe provides good shelter but is much used by fish farms. The entrance is narrow and there are rocks on each side. Steer for mid channel and keeping at least ½ cable offshore then head for any of the three bays. Anchor as depth permits.

Cribba Sound also provides good shelter, the favoured anchorage is at the NE end but keep to mid channel when transiting the narrows in Cribba Sound.

Facilities

None.

Interest

First World War gun emplacement at Swarbacks Head.

Voes of Clousta (N & S)

⊕ 60°19′·62N 001°31′·26W (for Cribba Sound, Voes of Clousta and Brindister Voe).

CHART
3281

TIDES
-0213 Lerwick

LIGHTS
None

Dangers
The only chart covering this area gives very little detail so caution is advised if approaching either of these Voes. See above for directions on passing between Green Holm, off Ness of Noonsbrough and Green Point on Vementry.

Anchorages
The North Voe of Clousta is the easier entrance but like the South Voe, an interesting place to visit. A cautious approach with a good eye on the echo sounder can be rewarding in good visibility. Many fish farms.

Facilities
None.

Brindister Voe

⊕ 60°19′·62N 001°31′·26W (for Cribba Sound, Voes of Clousta and Brindister Voe).

CHART
3281

TIDES
-0213 Lerwick

LIGHTS
None

Dangers
The easiest approach to Brindister Voe is by leaving Linga to Port but see above for directions as far as Neeans Neap. The passage between Linga and mainland is clear of dangers beyond ½ cable offshore, but note the rocky outcrop lying just over ½ cable South of Linga.

Anchorages
Brindister Voe is long and hazards within the Voe consist of a rocky patch mid channel about three cables from the entrance, followed by a shoal patch extending from the West shore a further three cables in. The narrows, just over one mile from the entrance are bounded by a spit from the North and another shoal area on the South bank. Do not attempt to go beyond the pool just after the narrows.

Facilities
None.

Brindister Voe

MAINLAND SHETLAND – WEST COAST

West Burra Firth looking West over the harbour

West Burra Firth harbour

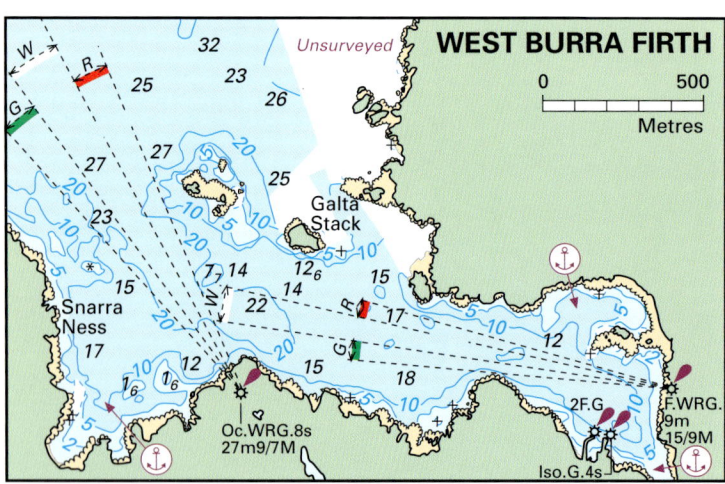

West Burra Firth

⊕ 60°18´·40N 001°34´·40W

CHARTS
3299, 3281

TIDES
-0210 Lerwick

LIGHTS
W Burra Firth Outer Oc.WRG.8s27m W9M, R7M, G7M; vis: 136°–G–142°–W–150°–R–156°. H24 60°17´·803N 001°33´·585W

W Burra Firth Inner F.WRG.9m W15M, R9M, G9M; vis: 095°–G–098°–W–102°–105°; H24 60°17´·806N 001°33´·141W

W Burra Firth T'port pier Iso.4s4m4M 60°17´·731N 001°32´·395W

Directions

West Burrafirth is entered between Lang Stack on Snarra Ness and Riv Skerries to the North East. A leading light situated on Snap Hevda Oc.WRG.8s shows the white sector on a bearing of 145°. This leads clear of all dangers, but note the rock one cable off the West shore. A further sectored leading light F.WRG.9s, bearing 100° leads to the inner firth.

Anchorages

There are several anchorages within this attractive area, but the most sheltered is within the harbour at Burraview. The ferry berth should be kept clear. Alternatively, anchor just North of the harbour in about 8–10m, or for shallower vessels anchorage may be found East of Ness of Brenda in about 3–4m, but note that the head of the Firth is very shallow for almost two cables.

The bay East of Holm of Tafts also offers anchorage in about 7–8m.
Note the shallow area to Port and the rocks to the starboard side of the entrance.
The bay at Snarra Ness offer temporary shelter from Southerly winds. Entry is achieved after following the first above mentioned leading light until the Southmost of the Riv Skerries is in line with the summit of The Heag. Anchor in 6–8m.

Facilities

Toilet, telephone, showers and fuel are all available. Ferry to Papa Stour.

Voe of Snarraness

⊕ 60°18´·50N 001°35´·27W

CHART
3281

TIDES
-0210 Lerwick

LIGHTS
None

Dangers
Very limited chart coverage, and there are several fish farms within the Voe. There is a shoal patch in the centre of the South arm of the Voe. Keep ½ cable clear of the shores.

Anchorages
The best anchorage is in the North East corner clear of the fish farm. Sheltered from all but strong Northerlies when some swell reaches the anchorage.

Facilities
Pier in North East corner.

Voe of Snarraness

MAINLAND SHETLAND – WEST COAST

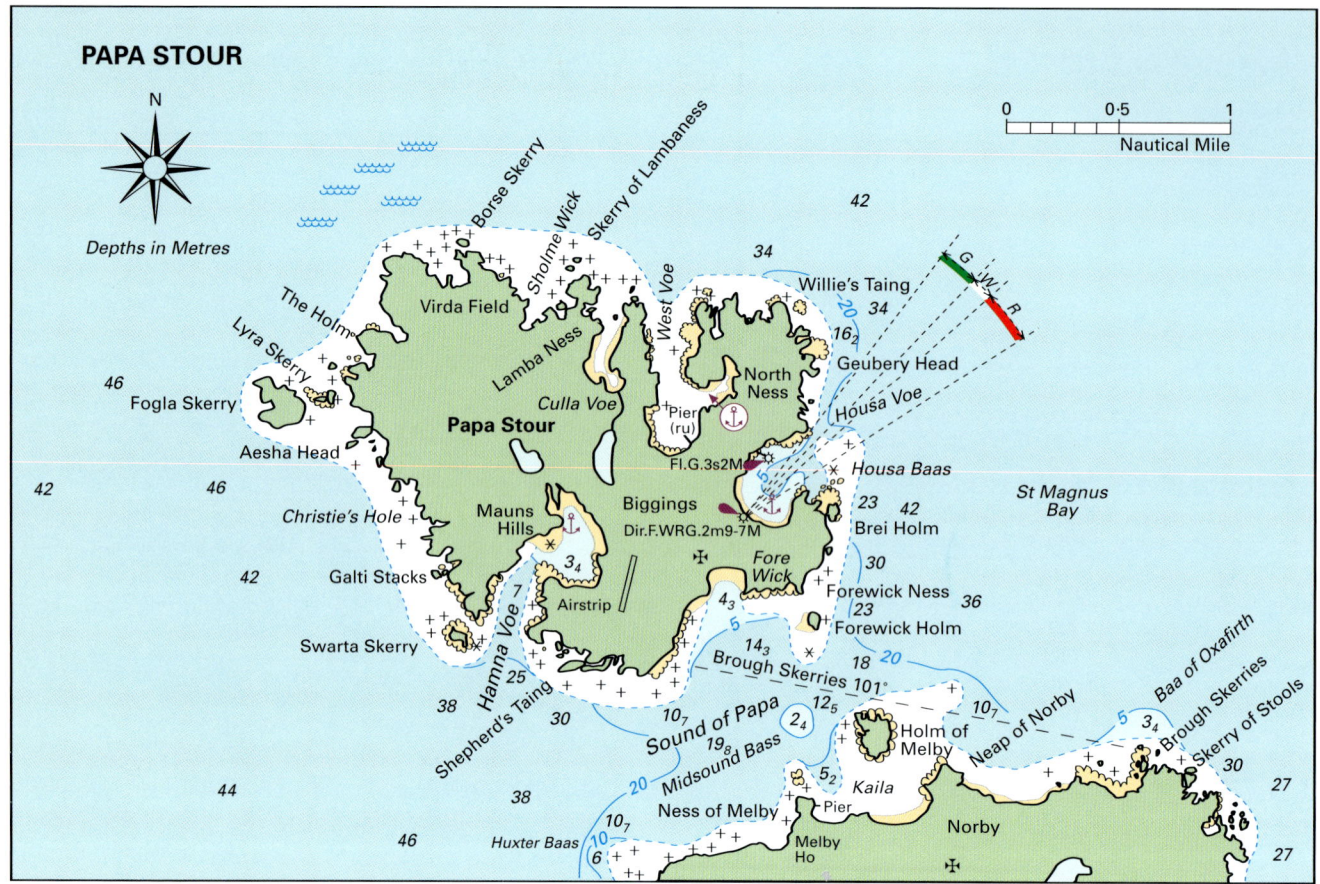

Sound of Papa

⊕ 60°19´·39N 001°38´·22W (East entrance)
⊕ 60°18´·36N 001°42´·80W (West entrance)

CHART
3281

TIDES
The tides in Papa Sound are strong and an important point is that the direction the flood tide changes in the western half of St Magnus Bay. This means that the flood tide goes through the Sound in a NE to SW direction. The flood starts at -0350 Lerwick and the ebb starts to flow NE +0350 Lerwick.

Note that the tides can reach nearly six knots and care must be taken to avoid being forced off course by a cross channel set when transiting the Sound.

LIGHTS
Papa Stour Housa Voe Dir Lt F.WRG.2m W9M, R7M, G7M; vis: 219°–G–226°–W–230°–R–239° 60°19´·589N 001°40´·496W

Dangers

Passage through the Sound is relatively strait forward if care is taken to avoid the various rocks that extend quite some distance into the channel. Passage is not recommended when wind is against the tide, and particularly if there is any strength in the wind.

Directions

From the East identify Holm of Melby and Forewick Holm. Steer for the N end of Holm of Melby on a course of not less than 240° until Brough Skerries over the N of Holm of Melby bears 101°. Do not go N of half way to Brough Skerries. Follow 281° until Forewick Holm bears 057°, then steer the reciprocal, 237° until clear of Huxter Baas with Hamna Voe bearing E of North.

From the West passage is the reverse of the above, but make sure that the mainland shore is given a berth of at least ⅓ M in order to avoid Huxter Baas. The Papa Stour shore is foul for nearly two cables. The above courses avoid Midsound Baas, and the dangerous rocks 1½ cables S of Forewick Holm and ⅓ M ENE of Holm of Melby.

PAPA STOUR

Hamna Voe,

⊕ 60°18'·71N 001°42'·90W

CHART
3281

TIDES
-0210 Lerwick

LIGHTS
None

Dangers
The west and north coasts of Papa Stour are dominated by the Ve Skerries, a rocky area some three miles to the northwest. The area between Ve Skerries and Papa Stour, although deep, is very turbulent with breaking seas on anything other than the calmest days at slack water. Keep at least ½ mile north or west of the Ve Skerries.

Anchorages
An attractive anchorage offering very good shelter. The entrance to the East of Swarta Skerry should not be attempted in strong Southerly winds due to breaking seas.

Note the two rocks off the East side of Swarta Skerry and on a North heading keep to mid channel until the Voe opens to the East. Identify the small Skerry off the Southern point and leaving this well to starboard steer for the pool. The bar at the Skerry has only 2m, but once into the pool, anchor either to the North or South end in 5–6m.

Facilities
At Housa Voe, a ½ mile walk.

Interest
Sea caves and volcanic formations have resulted in the area becoming a Special Area of Conservation.

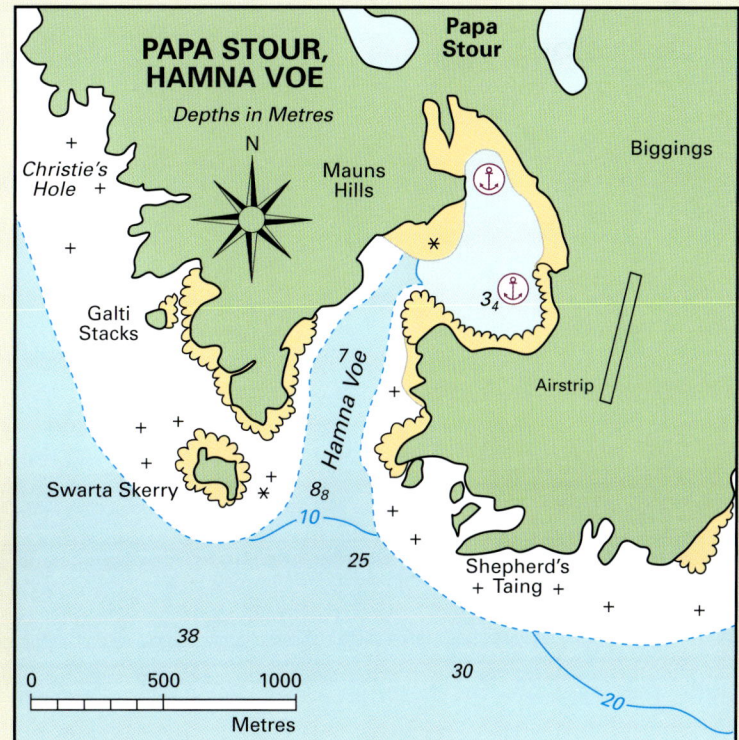

Housa Voe, Papa Stour

⊕ 60°20'·64N 001°38'·20W

CHART
3281, 3299

TIDES
-0210 Lerwick

LIGHTS
Housa Voe Dir Lt F.WRG.2mW9M, R7M, G7M; vis: 219°–G–226°–W–230°–R–239° 60°19'·600N 001°40'·498W **Ferry pier head** Fl.G.3s4m2M 60°19'·857N 001°40'·277W

Dangers
A course of 228° for the leading light clears all dangers. The sunken rock, Housa Baas, 1½ cables NNW of Lunga Stack is the main hazard, and is well within the red sector of the light.

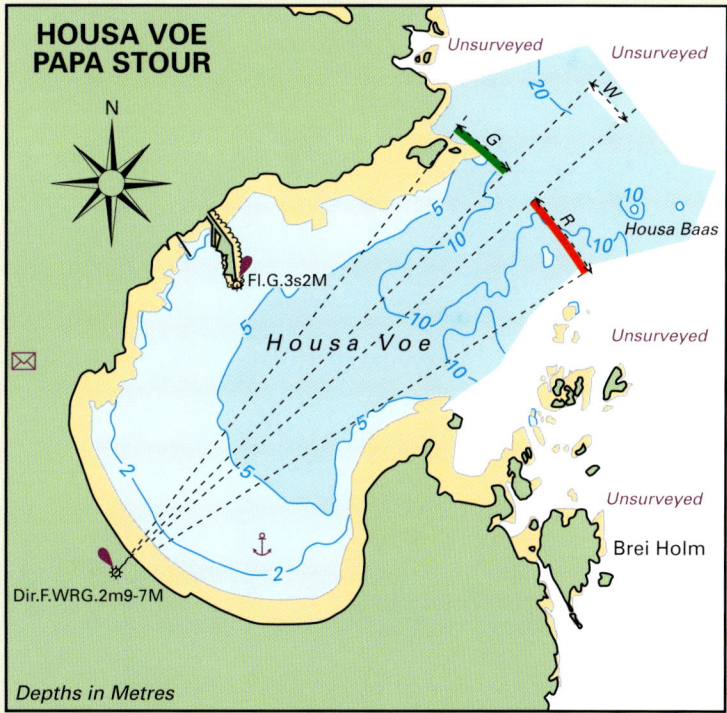

Anchorages
Alongside berthing is available at the small boat pontoon with 2·9m, alternatively anchor to best suit wind direction. Bottom sand with good holding. Exposed to the East and North.

Facilities
Water and toilets.

Interest
As above.

MAINLAND SHETLAND – WEST COAST

PAPA STOUR (CONTINUED)

West Voe

See plan page 64

⊕ 60°21'·01N 001°41'·23W

CHART
3281

TIDES
-0210 Lerwick

LIGHTS
None

Dangers
Keep to the west of centre when entering in order to avoid rocks off the east shore until the Voe opens to the east. Swell in northerly winds.

Anchorages
In the East arm of the Voe in 5m. Bottom sand.

Facilities
At Housa Voe.

Interest
As above.

Culla Voe

⊕ 60°20'·90N 001°41'·66W

CHART
3281

TIDES
-0210 Lerwick

LIGHTS
None

Dangers
Underwater rocks on both hands at the entrance, and one on the east side ¾ cable from the mouth of the Voe.

Anchorages
Keep to mid channel and anchor as near the head of the Voe as soundings permit.

Facilities
As above.

Interest
As above.

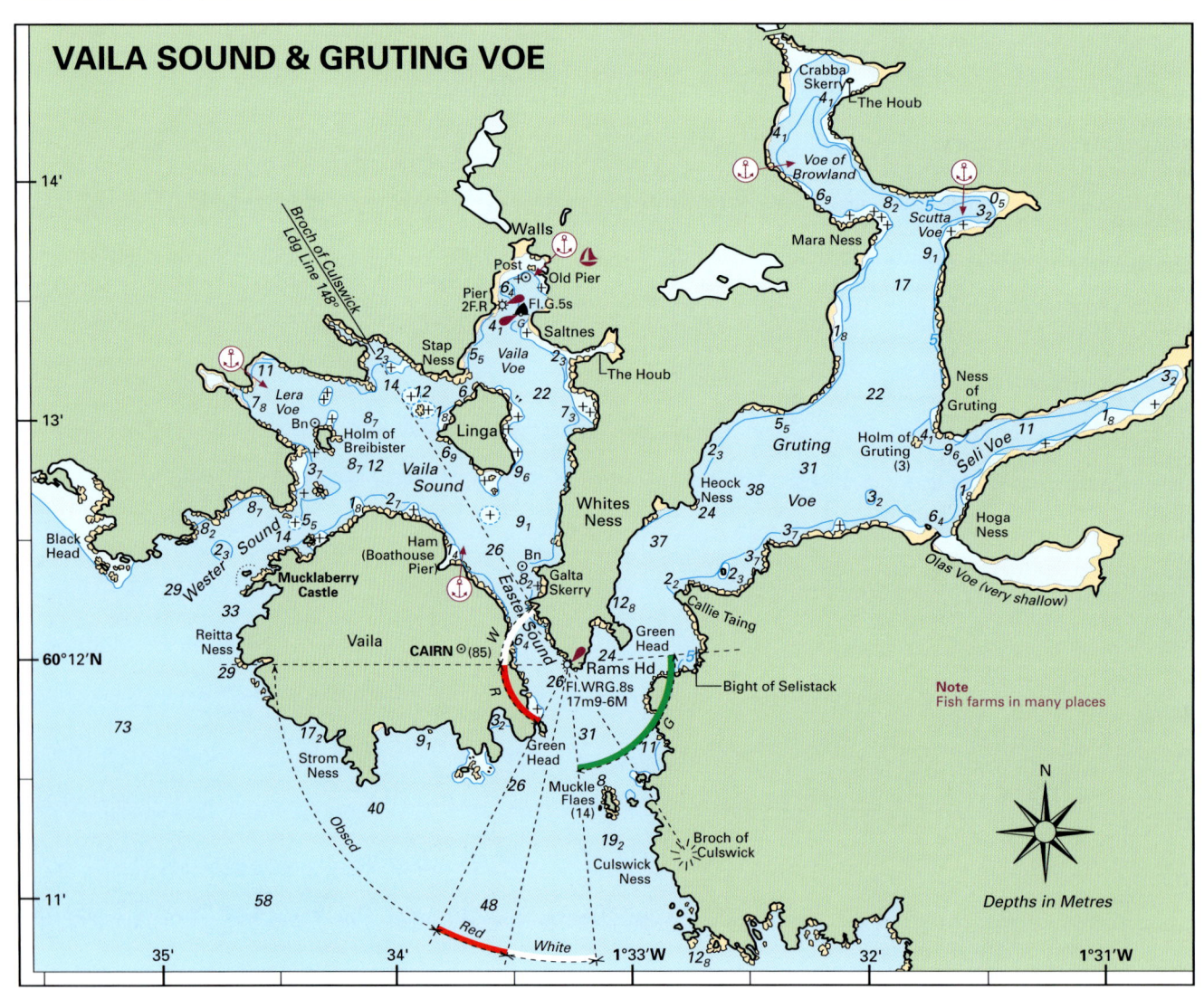

VAILA SOUND & GRUTING VOE

WALLS

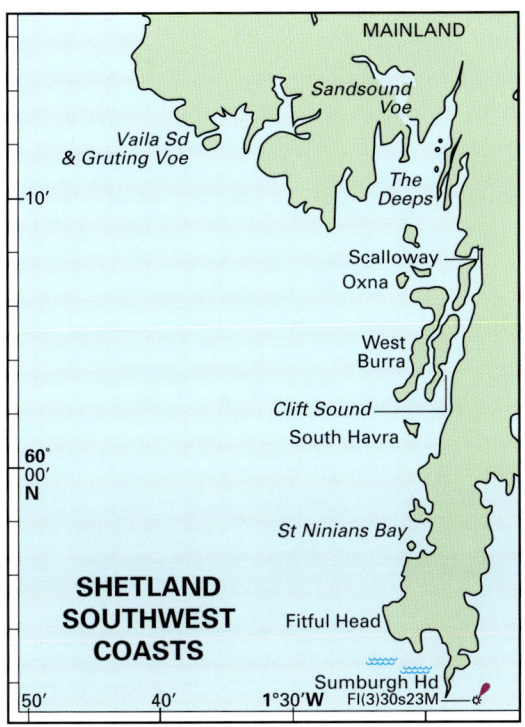

Vaila Sound

See plan page 66

⊕ 60°11´·00N 001°33´·89W

CHARTS
3295, 3281

TIDES
-0150 Lerwick

LIGHTS
Rams Head Fl.WRG.8s16m W9M, R6M, G6M; W house; vis 265°–G–355°–W–012°–R–090°–W–136° obsc by Vaila Is when brg more than 030° 60°11´·940N 001°33´·471W

Dangers

Wester Sound is narrow, and both shallow and littered with rocks. Passage through this Sound is only recommended with local knowledge and chart 3295.

Easter Sound is the main channel and although it narrows to almost one cable a course in the centre of the channel leads clear of dangers until the shoal patch at Galta Skerry is reached. This marked by a pillar beacon at its N end. ¼M NW lies the Baa of Linga, a dangerous rock. Leave on port hand if heading for Walls, or stay one cable off the Vaila shore if heading for Lera Voe.

Note the Skerries of Linga which extend fully one cable S of Linga.

Ham (Boathouse Pier)

See plan page 66

⊕ 60°12´·47N 001°34´·26W

CHARTS
3295, 3281

TIDES
-0150 Lerwick

LIGHTS
None

Dangers
Keep clear of submarine cables and beware of old moorings in the bay.

Anchorages
Anchor off pier in 3–4m. Tripping line recommended.

Facilities
None.

Interest
Pleasant walk to Vaila House along road.

Walls

See plan page 66

⊕ 60°12´·97N 001°33´·76W

CHARTS
3295, 3281

TIDES
-0150 Lerwick

LIGHTS
Rams Head Fl.WRG.8s16m W9M, R6M, G6M; W house; vis 265°–G–355°–W–012°–R–090°–W–136° obsc by Vaila Is when brg more than 030° 60°11´·940N 001°33´·471W
Vaila Voe pier 2F.R(vert)4m. SHM Fl.G.5s 60°13´·419N 001°33´·915W

Dangers

Keep a cable off the Linga shore and once Vaila Voe opens, head for the outer end of the pier. The marked channel will then be in sight.

Note the rock ½ cable N of the pier and a further rock marked by a R perch ¾ cable SW of the drying rocks in the centre of Walls bay. A SHM identifies the shoal that extends from Saltnesss.

Walls Pier

Walls marina for small craft only

Anchorages

There is a small marina with only 1·5m at the head of the bay and a pontoon berth on the N side of the pier with 4m. The area is sheltered and space permitting, anchor in 3–5m. Alternatively anchor off The Houb in 5–7m.

Facilities

Good hotel at Burrastow, five miles by road. Walls Shop ☎ 01595 809281. Bakery that supplies most of the Shetland Mainland. Toilets, showers, fuel, café and swimming pool.

Lera Voe

See plan page 66

⊕ 60°12´·99N 001°35´·17W

CHARTS
3295, 3281

TIDES
-0150 Lerwick

LIGHTS
Rams Head Fl.WRG.8s16m W9M, R6M, G6M; W house; vis 265°–G–355°–W–012°–R–090°–W–136° obsc by Vaila Is when brg more than 030°
60°11´·940N 001°33´·471W

Dangers

The channel N of Holm of Breibister is preferred but there are still several rocks to be avoided. These are located just over ½ cable N and just under 1½ cables N of Holm of Breibister leaving a channel les than a cable in width. A course with the rock off Stap Ness in line with the point at Skeo Taing leads through the channel.

Anchorages

Anchor as depths permit clear of the fish farms. The head of the Voe dries and is shoal beyond the narrows.

Gruting Voe

See plan page 66

⊕ 60°11´·40N 001°33´·51W

CHARTS
3295, 3281

TIDES
-0150 Lerwick

LIGHTS
Rams Head Fl.WRG.8s16m W9M, R6M, G6M; W house; vis 265°–G–355°–W–012°–R–090°–W–136° obsc by Vaila Is when brg more than 030°
60°11´·940N 001°33´·471W

Dangers

Keep at least ½ cable off Green Head and ¾ cable off the Bight of Selistack and the point at Callie Taing. A course from N of Callie Taing towards the N shore of Gruting Voe leads clear of dangers until the Voe opens to Voe of Browland to Port and Scutta Voe to Starboard. Shoals extend from the S points of both Voes. Keep at least a cable off the point at Mara Ness and 1½ cable of the S point at the entrance to Scutta Voe. There is much fish farming activity.

Anchorages

Scutta Voe provides an easy anchorage in 4–5m.
Voe of Browland is straight forward until the channel turns Northwards when it shoals from both shores. Stay mid channel and anchor as depth permits in about 5m.

Note the drying rocks at the entrance to The Houb.

Facilities

Shops at Bridge of Walls.

Seli Voe

See plan page 66

⊕ 60°12´·71N 001°30´·69W

CHARTS
3295, 3281

TIDES
-0150 Lerwick

Wester Sound looking SW.
Lera Voe is off the picture to the right

Entrance to Gruting Voe from north

Seli Voe is sheltered from north winds

SKELDA VOE

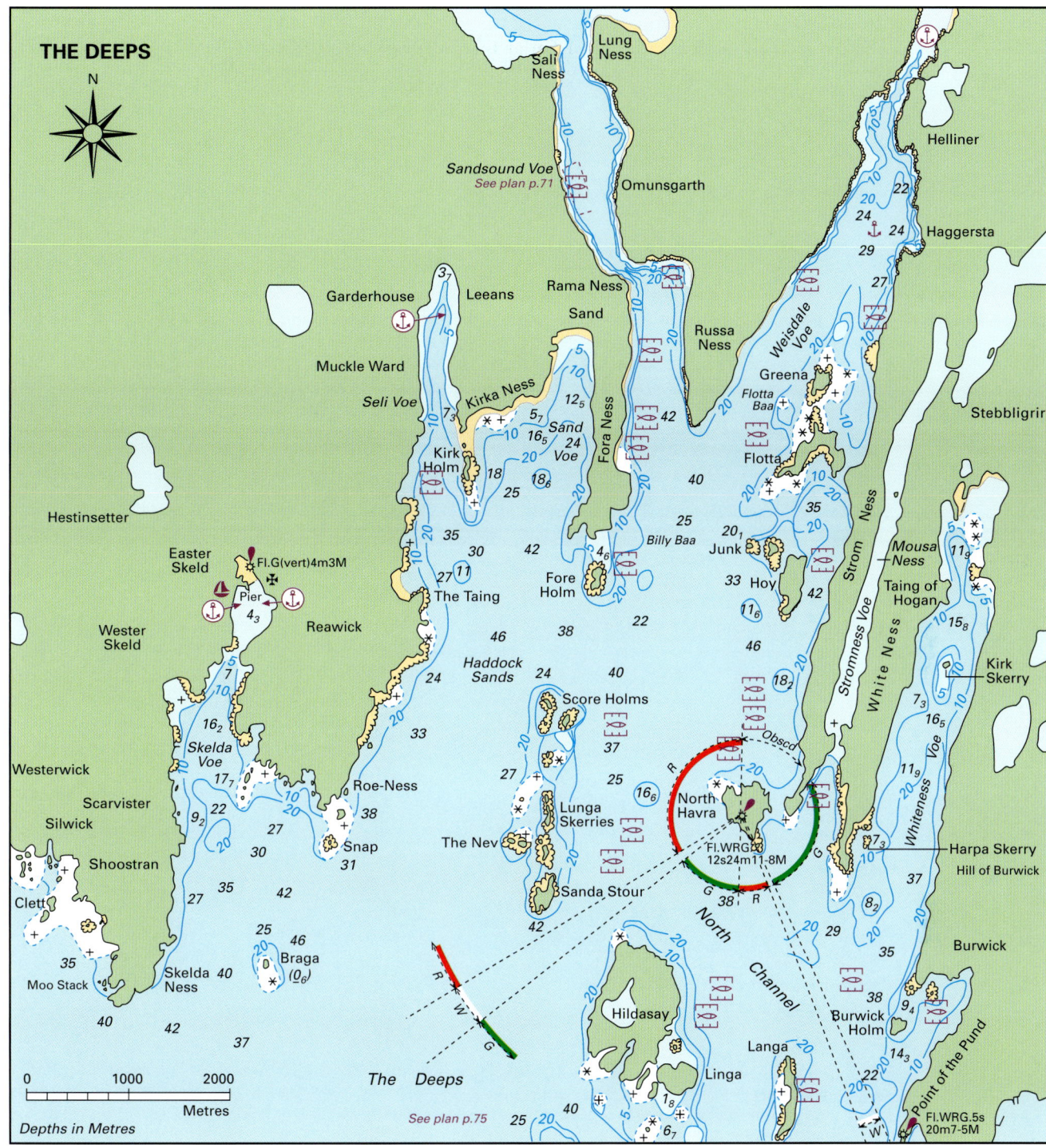

LIGHTS
None

Dangers
Do not pass between Holm of Gruting and Ness of Gruting if sailing from the N anchorages. A course ½ cable off the shores avoids any hazards although the head of the Voe shoals for nearly ½ M.

Anchorages
A rather uninteresting Voe but reasonable anchorage on mud in 5–7m off the slip on the N side.

Facilities
None.

The Deeps
The name given to the area covering the entrance to the delightful cruising ground west of Scalloway. There are no real difficulties caused by The Deeps provided all visible hazards are given a reasonable berth. Braga, Snap, the islets between Sanda Stour and the Score Holms and Fore Holm are all clear if course at least a cable off is held. More specific areas of note are described in the following sections covering the individual Voes.

MAINLAND SHETLAND – WEST COAST

Skeld Marina

Skelda Voe and Skeld Marina

Skelda Voe

See plan page 69

⊕ 60°08´·46N 001°26´·61W

CHART
3281

TIDES
-0150 lerwick

LIGHTS
North Havra Fl.WRG.12s24m W11M, R8M, G8M; W twr; vis: 001°–G–053·5°–W–060·5°–R–182°, 274°–G–334°–W–337·5° –R–001° 60°09´·836N 001°20´·272W
Skeld Pier 2F.G(vert)4m3M 60°11´·125N 001°26´·200W

Dangers

½ M east of Skelda Ness lies Braga, an isolated above water rock with a dangerous underwater rock one cable SSE. If approaching from the east beware Snap rock which lies ¼ mile south of Roe Ness, and take particular note of the rocky spit that extends fully ¼ mile offshore and lies 0·6 mile NW of Snap rock. 2M north of Skelda Ness lie the narrows. Keep to the centre of the channel then steer for the church to avoid the shoal patch on the west side.

Anchorages

Either at the marina which has visitors berths or anchor in the NE corner of the bay opposite in 4–5m. Both are sheltered from all but winter gales.

Facilities

Water, fuel, shower, toilets in marina.

Interest

Skeld Regatta is held during the third week of July and involves much Shetland hospitality.

Seli Voe

See plan page 69

⊕ 60°11´·05N 001°23´·42W

CHARTS
3294, 3281

TIDES
-0150 Lerwick

LIGHTS
North Havra Fl.WRG.12s24m W11M, R8M, G8M; W twr; vis: 001°–G–053·5°–W–060·5°–R–182°, 274°–G–334°–W–337·5°–R–001° 60°09´·836N 001°20´·272W
Seli Voe Pier 2F.G(vert) 60°12´·585N 001°23´·727W

Dangers

Entered North of Haddock Sands, the only real hazard are the rocks off Kirk Holm which are more of a problem if rounding to Sand Voe when Kirka Ness should be cleared to the south by ½ M. The shores of Seli Voe are clear of dangers if course is set ½ cable off until N of the pier where the Voe begins to shoal. Exposed to winds from the south, and obstructed by several fish farms.

Anchorages

Anchor as depths permit North of the pier and clear of the fish farms.

Sandsound Voe

See plan page 71

⊕ 60°11´·30N 001°20´·98W

CHARTS
3294, 3281

TIDES
-0150 Lerwick

LIGHTS
North Havra Fl.WRG.12s24m W11M, R8M, G8M; W twr; vis: 001°–G–053·5°–W–060·5°–R–182°, 274°–G–334°–W–337·5°–R–001° 60°09´·836N 001°20´·272W

Dangers

Keep at least two cables off the Fora Ness shore to avoid the shoal at Billy Baa over which seas break in strong winds. Apart from fish farming activity the entrance to Sandsound Voe is clear all the way to the first narrows between Rams Ness and Sandsound. The deep channel is only ½ cable wide and is slightly south of the centre of the visible gap. At the second narrows between Salt Ness and Lung Ness a dangerous spit extends for fully one cable NW of Salt Ness. The Firth opens beyond the second narrows.

Anchorages

Anchor in the bay North of Omunsgarth in 5–7m if not wishing to sail as far as the inner voes. Bottom is mainly mud, and there is a small pier where landing is possible.

Facilities

See Bixter Voe.

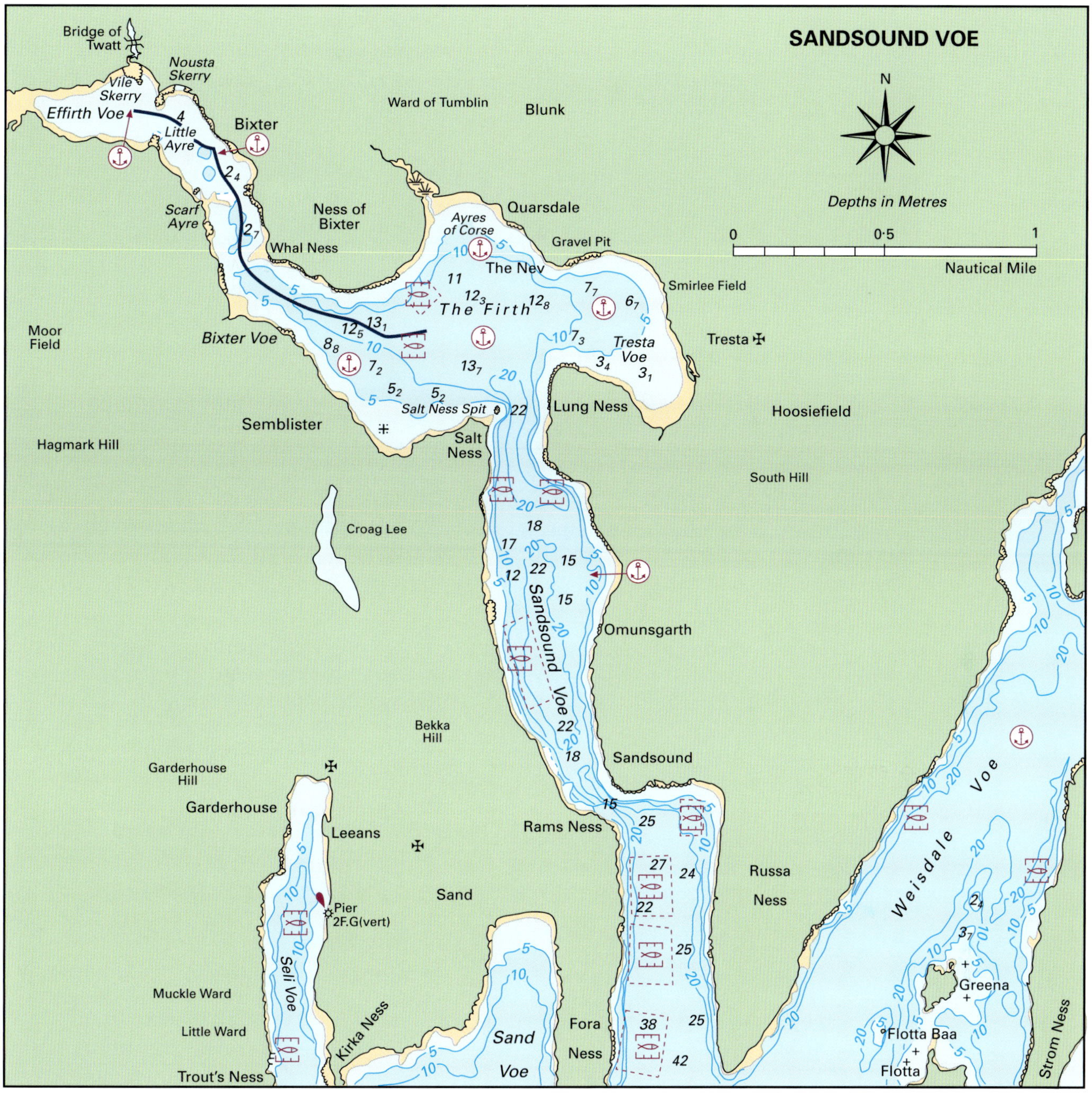

Tresta Voe

⊕ 60°14'·50N 001°22'·40W

CHARTS
3294, 3281

TIDES
-0150 Lerwick

LIGHTS
None

Dangers
The point at Lung Ness is shoal for a cable and the head of the Voe dries for some two cables.

Anchorages
As depths permit on sand and mud. In Westerly winds some shelter can be obtained at Ayres of Corse.

Facilities
Shops, water.

Tresta Voe and entrance from Sandsound Voe in the distance

Bixter Voe into Effirth Voe

Bixter Voe

See plan page 71

⊕ 60°14´·45N 001°23´·15W

CHARTS
3294, 3281

TIDES
-0150 Lerwick

LIGHTS
None

Dangers

There is a sandy shoal off the mouth of Laxa Burn at the entrance to Bixter Voe. This is immediately followed by a spit that runs out from the north shore at Whal Ness. This extends fully ⅔ of the way across the channel. Keep to the west shore. The second narrows at Scarf Ayre also extend almost ⅔ across the channel, but from the west side. Keep to the east shore but note the drying rocks on the east side at the north end of the narrowest part.

Anchorages

Anchor off Bixter as depths suit on sand and shingle. Alternatively, proceed past Little Ayre on the South side and Nousta Skerry on the north, giving both a clearance of at least ½ cable and enter Effirth Voe. Anchor no further West than Vile Skerry in 2–3m. Bottom mud with some rocks underneath, so a tripping line is recommended, although depths are such that the anchor can almost certainly be seen from on deck.

Facilities

Water, shop, petrol station.

Weisdale Voe

See plan page 69

⊕ 60°11´·37N 001°20´·71W

CHARTS
3294, 3281

TIDES
-0150 Lerwick

LIGHTS
None

Dangers

Keep a cable off the Hoggs of Hoy and two cables off Flotta.

Note the offlying rock at Flotta Baa and the extensive rocky shoal that extends both north and east of Greena. Do not attempt to pass through the Sound of Flotta. The west shore is clear of dangers from the point at Russa Ness and the east shore once clear of the shoal north of Greena.

Anchorages

Some shelter is available at Haggersta North of the point in 6–7m but the best anchorage is in the pool at the head of the Voe. The narrows present little difficulty if course is kept to mid channel. Anchor in 3–4m two cables North of the burn flowing from Loch of Hellister.

Facilities

Shops.

Weisdale Voe

WHITNESS VOE

Stromness Voe

⊕ 60°09´·31N 001°19´·79W

CHARTS
3294, 3281

TIDES
-0150 Lerwick

LIGHTS
North Havra Fl.WRG.12s24m W11M, R8M, G8M; W twr; vis: 001°–G–053·5°–W–060·5°–R–182°, 274°–G–334°–W–337·5°–R–001° 60°09´·836N 001°20´·272W

Point of the Pund Fl.WRG.5s20m W7M, R5M, G5M; W twr. vis: 350°–R–090°–G–111°–R–135°–W–140°–G–177° 267°–W–350° 60°07´·974N 001°18´·323W

Dangers

Note Havra Skerry to the south of North Havra, Foul Baas lyng 1½ cables south of Usta Ness and Silver Skerry lying to the west. At the entrance to the narrows a rock lies ⅓ cable offshore on the east side. Keep to the west side of the channel until the Voe begins to open then turn to the east side to avoid a second rock lying ½ cable north of where the shore turns to the west. Tides in the narrows run strongly at springs.

Anchorages

The bay immediately to starboard of the narrows is a popular anchorage and well sheltered. The alternative anchorages are as depths permit as far as Burra Holm beyond which there are many shoal patches. Mainly mud.

Whiteness Voe

⊕ 60°09´·02N 001°18´·73W

CHARTS
3294, 3281

TIDES
-0150 Lerwick

LIGHTS
North Havra Fl.WRG.12s24m W11M, R8M, G8M; W twr; vis: 001°–G–053·5°–W–060·5°–R–182°, 274°–G–334°–W–337·5°–R–001° 60°09´·836N 001°20´·272W

Point of the Pund Fl.WRG.5s20m W7M, R5M, G5M; W twr. vis: 350°–R–090°–G–111°–R–135°–W–140°–G–177° 267°–W–350° 60°07´·974N 001°18´·323W

Whiteness Voe

The head of Stromness Voe is well sheltered

Dangers

Beware Foul Baas 1½ cables off the point at Usta Ness and Harpa Skerry 2½ cables north just off the west shore. The Voe is clear on both sides for almost a mile beyond these easily avoided hazards, then pass the shoal around Kirk Skerry on either hand. The first narrows are easily negotiated if the shores are cleared by ½ cable. The navigable channel to the inner pool is less than ¼ cable wide. Keep to Port but beware the rock lying just off Mousa Ness.

Anchorages

The pool above Taing of Hogan provides reasonable shelter towards the North end in 5–7m South of Mousa Ness. The inner pool provides good shelter in the centre in 8–10m. Bottom is shingle over rocks so a tripping line is recommended.

Scalloway

See plans pages 75 and 76

⊕ North Channel 60°09'·40N 001°20'·87W
⊕ Middle Channel 60°08'·24N 001°22'·66W
⊕ South Channel 60°06'·03N 001°22'·99W

CHARTS
3294, 3283

TIDES
-0200 Lerwick

LIGHTS
North Channel:
North Havra Fl.WRG.12s24m W11M, R8M, G8M; W twr; vis: 001°–G–053·5°–W–060·5°–R–182°, 274°–G–334°–W–337·5°–R–001° 60°09'·836N 001°20'·272W
Point of the Pund Fl.WRG.5s20m W7M, R5M, G5M; W twr. vis:
350°–R–090°–G–111°–R–135°–W–140°–G–177° 267°–W–350° 60°07'·974N 001°18'·323W
Whaleback Skerry, North Cardinal Mark Q 60°07'·945N 001°18'·892W
Trondra Ness Fl(2)G.6s 60°07'·700N 001°17'·802W
Middle Channel:
Point of the Pund Fl.WRG.5s20m W7M, R5M, G5M; W twr. vis:
350°–R–090°–G–111°–R–135°–W–140°–G–177° 267°–W–350° 60°07'·974N 001°18'·323W
Trondra Ness Fl(2)G.6s at 60°07'·700N 001°17'·802W
South Channel:
Bullia Skerry Fl.5s5m5M steel pillar and platform 60°06'·658N 001°21'·562W
Fugla Ness Fl(2)WRG.10s20m W10M, R7M, G7M; W twr vis: 014°–G–032°–W–082°–R–134°–W–shore 60°06'·376N 001°20'·839W
Merry Holm SHM Fl(3)G.8s 60°07'·432N 001°18'·596W
Green Holm Fl(3)R.8s 60°07'·466N 001°18'·748W
Point of the Pund Fl.WRG.5s20m W7M, R5M, G5M; W twr. vis:
350°–R–090°–G–111°–R–135°–W–140°–G–177° 267°–W–350° 60°07'·974N 001°18'·323W
Trondra Ness Fl(2)G.6s 60°07'·700N 001°17'·802W
Scalloway Harbour:
Blacks Ness Pier SW corner Oc.WRG.10s10m W11M, G8M, R8M vis: 052°–G–063.5°–W–065.5°–R–077° at 60°08'·015N 001°16'·556W. PHM Fl.R.2s 60°07'·878N 001°17'·261W. PHM Fl(2)R.10s 60°07'·926N 001°17'·042W. SHM Fl.G.2s 60°07'·893N 001°17'·002W
Scalloway Marina Fl.R.5s 60°08'·059N 001°17'·061W
Scalloway Marina Fl(3)R.8s 60°08'·108N 001°17'·020W
Town slipway 2F.R(vert) 60°08'·175N 001°16'·840W
Commercial Quay Breakwater 2F.G(vert)3M 60°08'·101N 001°16'·594W
Northness Point SHM Fl(2)G.5s 60°07'·927N 001°16'·575W
Commercial Quay SE corner 2F.R(vert) 60°07'·996N 001°16'·470W
East channel SHM Fl(4)G 60°07'·991N 001°16'·265W
Commercial Quay E pier Oc.R.7s 60°08'·042N 001°16'·243W
East Voe Marina Fl.G.4s 60°08'·178N 001°16'·143W

Scalloway Boat Club vistors pontoon

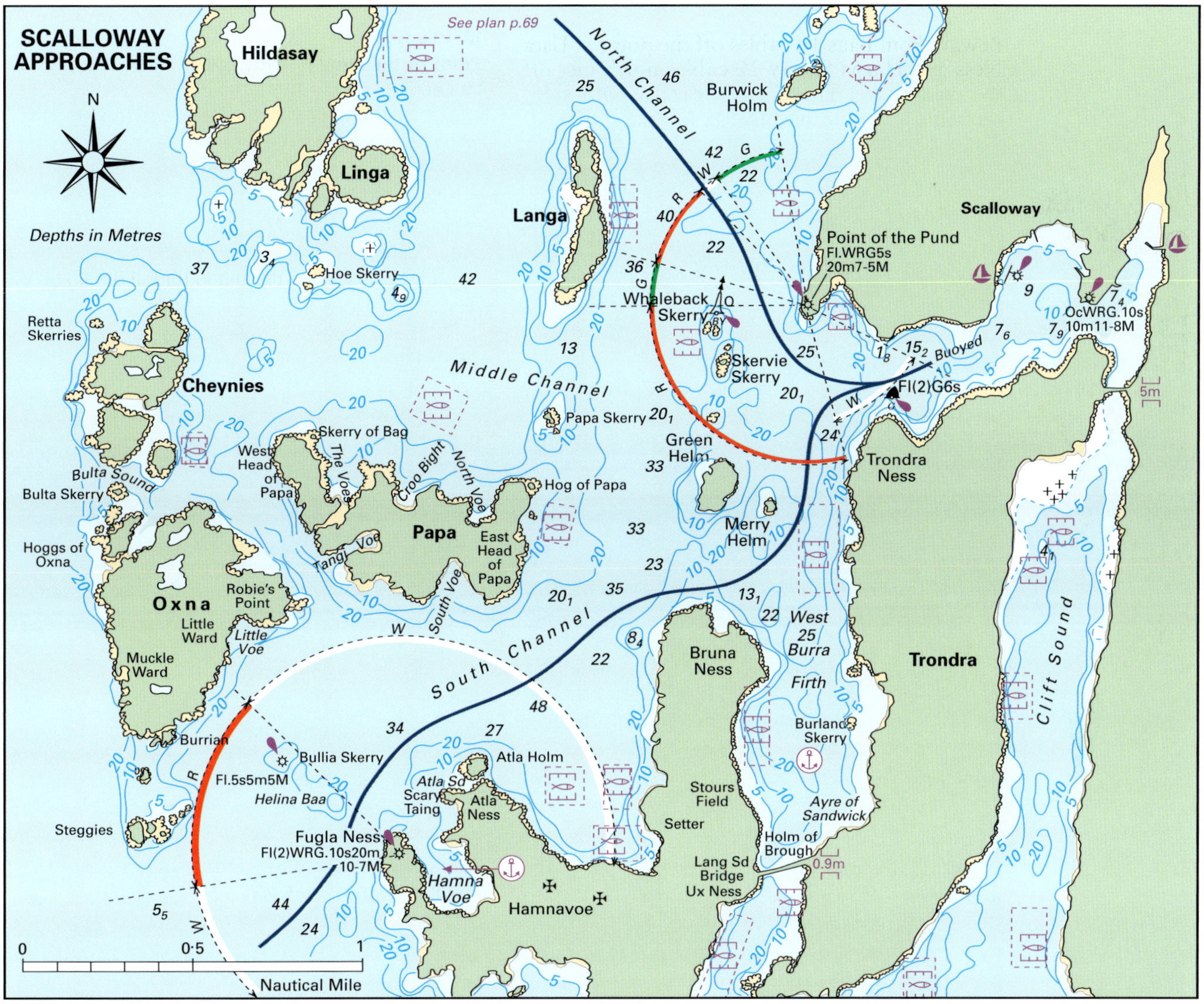

SCALLOWAY

Scalloway port and harbour

SHETLAND ISLANDS PILOT 75

MAINLAND SHETLAND – WEST COAST

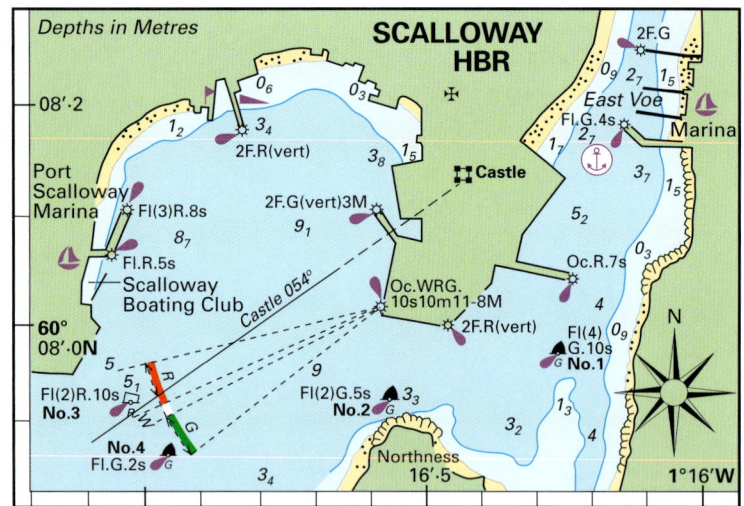

Scalloway Boating Club is located in the white building towards the right of the photo

West Burra Firth lies just to the west of Scalloway and Trondra Island

Dangers

The North channel is the easier and the lights are less confusing at night. The south channel needs care in strong winds, particularly from the southwest when the passage through the islands can be obscured by breaking seas right across the entrance. This makes identifying Bullia Skerry and Hellia Baa rather difficult, and both are dangerous. The mid channel is mainly used by boats with local knowledge, so best avoided for a first time visit to Scalloway.

Anchorages

Scalloway Boating Club maintains a pontoon just South of Scalloway Marina where visitors are welcome. Depths alongside range from 3–4m. Scalloway Marina is mainly for smaller boats and has few free berths. East Voe Marina is again a private marina but berths are sometimes available. Berthing alongside Blackness Pier is also available. Anchorage is also available in the harbour in 6–10m. Some local boats have moorings in Clift Sound North of the bridge, but the channel is shallow and a shoal extends 1½ cables NE of Northness Point.

Facilities

All facilities including marine engineers ☎ 01595 880215 and Scalloway Boating Club ☎ 01595 880409/880388.
Harbour VHF Ch 9, 12, 16. ☎ 01806 242551.

Interest

'Shetland Bus'. Museum on Main Street.

West Burra Firth

See plan page 75

⊕ 60°07'·19N 001°18'·41W

CHARTS
3294, 3283

TIDES
-0200 Lerwick

LIGHTS
Merry Holm SHM Fl(3)G.8s 60°07'·432N 001°18'·596W
Green Holm Fl(3)R.8s 60°07'·466N 001°18'·748W

Dangers

If approaching from the north note the shoal that extends over a cable off the east side of Merry Holm. There is a small islet off the east shore at the entrance to the Firth but apart from Burkland Skerry just under two cables further into the Firth the shores are clear if cleared by at least one cable. Fish farms operate in both the entrance and towards the head of the Firth. Exposed to winds from the north.

Anchorages

Anchor towards the head of the bay towards the West side in 6–8m. Mainly rocky bottom so trip line is recommended.

Facilities

Toilets, showers and fresh water. Road to Scalloway three miles away.

SAND WICK

Hamna Voe pier and anchorage

Hamna Voe

See plan page 75

⊕ 60°06´·61N 001°20´·96W

CHARTS
3294, 3283

TIDES
-0200 Lerwick

LIGHTS
Fugla Ness Fl(2)WRG.10s20m W10M, R7M, G7M; W twr vis: 014°–G–032°–W–082°–R–134°–W–shore 60°06´·376N 001°20´·839W

Dangers
The tides across the entrance are strong so beware being pushed onto either Fugla Ness or Scarva Taing. Keep to the west side in order to avoid the shoal patch off Scarya Stack one cable from the entrance. The head of the bay is shoal for ½ cable.

Anchorages
Almost completely landlocked, Hamna Voe offers good shelter from all but strong North West winds when some swell enters the bay. Many moorings, both on the surface and sunk, so trip line recommended, but a local mooring may be available. A small marina is planned 2007, to be located by the existing pier.

Sand Wick

⊕ 60°05´·06N 001°21´·33W

CHARTS
3294, 3283

TIDES
-0200 Lerwick

LIGHTS
None

Dangers
If approaching from the north beware the dangerous reef ¾ mile south of Fugla Ness, and also note Inner Skerry and West Skerry. Do not go more than half way into the Wick.

Anchorages
At best a temporary anchorage completely exposed to the West, but a possible lunch stop.

Facilities
None.

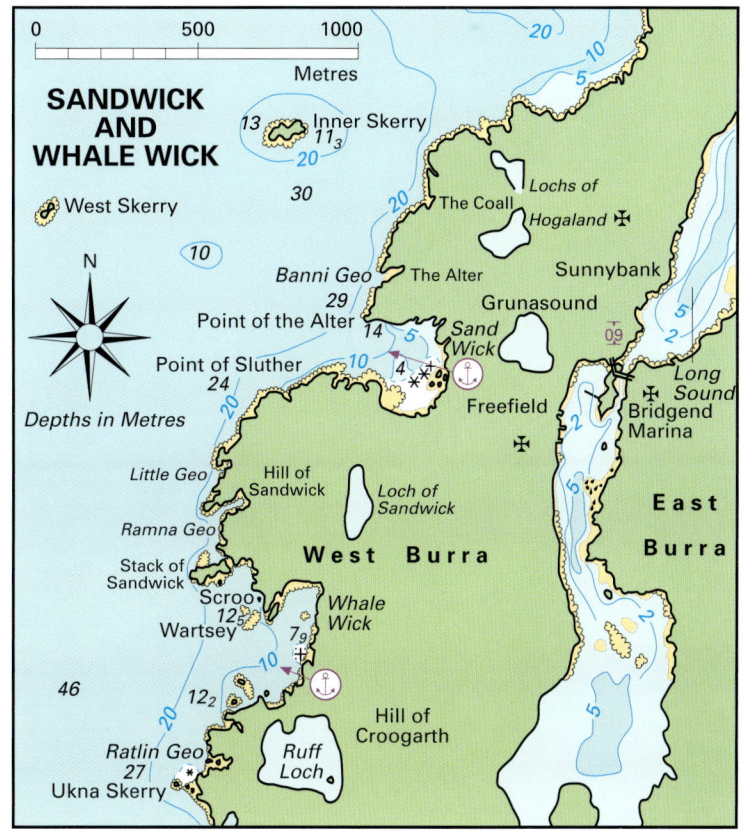

OXNA

See plan page 79

⊕ 60°07′·50N 001°21′·87W

CHART
3294

TIDES
–0150 Lerwick

LIGHTS
None

Dangers

Best approached from the east, either through the channel between Oxna and Papa, or to the south of Hildasay. If using the Oxna to Papa channel leave Robie's Point at least a cable off in order to avoid the rock lying to the east of the point. If approaching south of Hildasay keep four cables south of the Hogg of Linga in order to clear Hoe Skerry and its offlying rocks.

Anchorages

South of Spoose Holm at the entrance to Hogg Sound. From the East leave the fish farm to starboard and anchor due South of Spoose Holm just short of the entrance to the Sound.

Hogg Sound is shoal and passage should not be attempted. Bulta Sound to the North is narrow but passable with great care. Tripping line recommended.

Facilities

None.

Interest

Uninhabited islet with numerous tiny lochs.

CHEYNIES

See plan page 79

⊕ 60°07′·70N 001°22′·06W

CHART
3294

TIDES
-0150 Lerwick

LIGHTS
None

Dangers

See comments on approach to Oxna south of Hildasay. Exposed to winds with any east and anchorage is close north of fish farm equipment. Ensure sufficient swinging room when anchoring.

Anchorages

Anchor 1 cable North of the fish farm in the bay to the East of Cheynies. Keep the West coast of Hildasay just closed of Cheynies. Anchor in 5–6m.

Facilities

None.

PAPA

North Voe

See plan page 79

⊕ 60°07′·51N 001°20′·32W

CHART
3294

TIDES
–0150 Lerwick

LIGHTS
None

Dangers

Temporary anchorage only, completely exposed to the north.

Anchorages

Anchor in centre of bay in 5–6m. Tripping line recommended.

Facilities

None.

South Voe

See plan page 79

⊕ 60°07′·01N 001°20′·41W

CHART
3294

TIDES
–0150 Lerwick

LIGHTS
None

Dangers

Apart from the tides which run strongly through South Channel there are no real hazards in the approaches to South Voe. *See also the passage notes for South Channel leading to Scalloway.*

Anchorages

In centre of bay in 5–6m. Tripping line recommended.

Facilities

None.

MAINLAND SHETLAND – WEST COAST

Whale Wick

See plan page 77

⊕ 60°04´·43N 001°21´·64W

CHARTS
 3294, 3283

TIDES
 -0200 Lerwick

LIGHTS
 None

Dangers
Rocks off both points at the entrance and several rocks in the bay make this a rather undesirable anchorage. Completely exposed to the west.

Anchorages
Temporary anchorage only slightly south of the centre of the bay in 8m.

Facilities
None.

West Voe

⊕ 60°02´·33N 001°21´·12W

CHARTS
 3294, 3283

TIDES
 -0200 Lerwick

LIGHTS
 None

Dangers
If rounding Kettla Ness from the north keep at least 1½ cables off to avoid Red Skerries and their offlying rocks.

Anchorages
West Voe is entered between Groot Ness and Point of Stakka and the first bay on the west side gives some shelter from northwest winds. Beyond this, navigation in the Voe is very hazardous with many underwater rocks and shoals.

Facilities
None.

Bridgend Marina

See plan page 81

⊕ 60°04´·80N 001°19´·96W

CHARTS
 3294, 3283

TIDES
 -0220 Lerwick

LIGHTS
 None

Dangers
Many hazards in the approach make this marina suitable only for local, shallow draft boats.

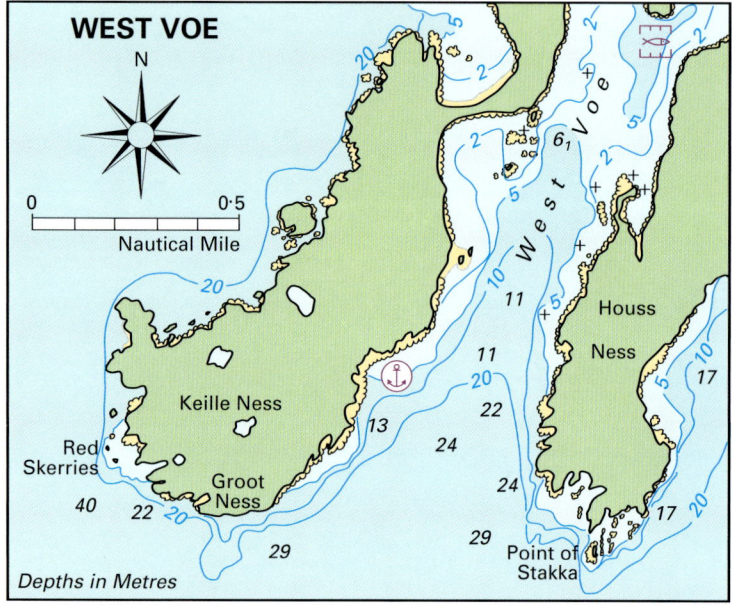

Bridgend Marina and some of the shoals in the approach

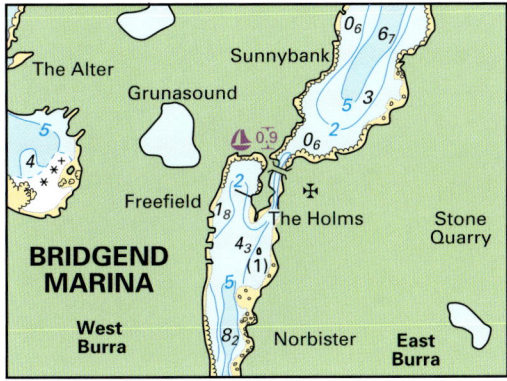

Anchorages

Possibly a berth may be available for a trailer/sailer which could be used to explore the upper part of South Voe.

Facilities

Outdoor Centre, toilets, showers and laundry.

Clift Sound

⊕ 60°02´·11N 001°19´·52W

CHARTS
3294, 3283

TIDES
−0130 Lerwick

LIGHTS
None

Dangers

Keep well off the Stacks of Houssness at the west side of the entrance to Clift Sound, but otherwise the shores are clean beyond one cable until north of Stream Sound nearly 4M into the Sound. There the west shore shoals six cables due north of West Voe of Quarff and the head of Sound is shoal for the last ½ mile. The northwest corner is littered with rocks which can be avoided by keeping due south of the west end of Clift Sound bridge. The passage under the bridge is only suitable for small craft. Charted depth is only 1·8m and air draft 5m.

Anchorages

The first anchorage is at Voe of North House, and although shallow, particularly in the North part of the bay, gives good shelter. Beware Scarf Skerry in the middle of the entrance and anchor clear of the fish farm equipment as depth permits. On the West side, the entrance to Stream Sound offers reasonable shelter from West winds. Anchor East of the islet in the Sound in about 5–7m. Passage through Stream Sound should not be attempted without local knowledge. West Voe of Quarff opposite Stream Sound offers better shelter in East winds. Anchor due South of Crooie Taing in 5m clear of the underwater cables.

Facilities

No local facilities, but Scalloway is on the other side of Clift Sound bridge.

Interest

See Scalloway.

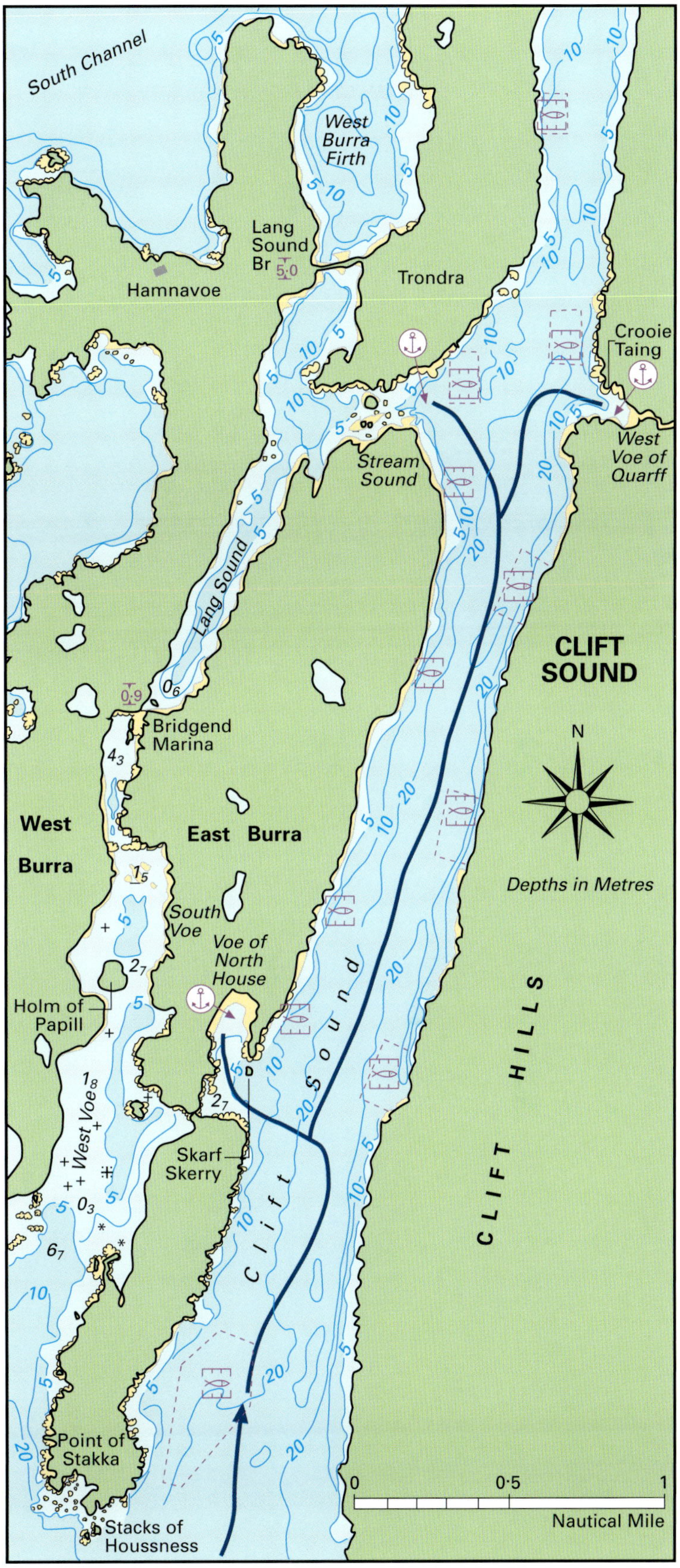

MAINLAND SHETLAND – WEST COAST

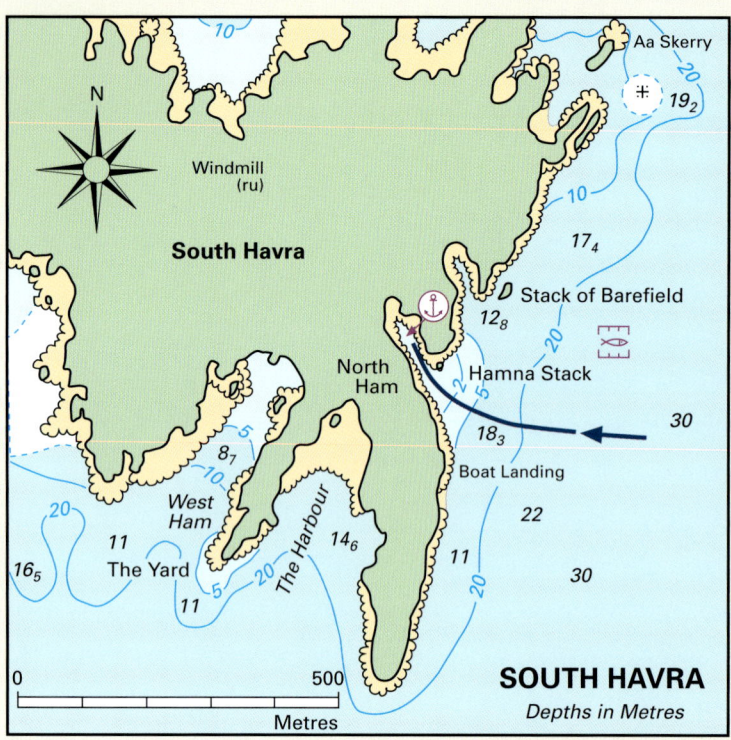

SOUTH HAVRA

⊕ 60°01′·35N 001°20′·68W

CHARTS
3283, 3294

TIDES
-0145 Lerwick

LIGHTS
None

Dangers
If approaching from the north, note the isolated rock ½ cable southeast of Aa Skerry. Avoid the north inlet on the east side of the island as it is completely foul with rocks. The inlets on the south coast named West Ham and The Harbour are both foul with rocks.

Anchorages
A lovely anchorage if extremely narrow. The South inlet on the East side of South Havra provides anchorage in 2m. Lay a stern anchor at the entrance before entering the inlet and then lead bow warps to the rings ashore. Use the stern anchor to reverse out.

Facilities
None.

Interest
Ruined windmill on the island's summit.

Maywick

⊕ 60°00′·80N 001°20′·10W

CHARTS
3294, 3283

TIDES
-0120 Lerwick

LIGHTS
None

Dangers
An isolated rock 1½ cables south of Holm of Maywick must be avoided, but otherwise a course at least one cable off leads clear of dangers. The head of the bay shoals and the east side is littered with rocks, one of which is a full cable offshore.

Anchorages
Useful shelter in South winds but exposed to the North. Anchor in 3–5m on sand over rocks. Trip line recommended.

Facilities
None.

Bigton Wick

See plan page 83

⊕ 59°59′·18N 001°21′·07W

CHART
3283

TIDES
-0115 Lerwick

LIGHTS
None

Dangers
Keep at least a cable off when rounding Loose Head and just a cable off the west side of the bay to avoid the rocks on the mainland side. Seas break on the shallow area (5m) at the entrance in strong winds.

Anchorages
Towards the West side at the head of the bay gives most shelter. Bottom sand. Exposed to the North in which case St Ninian's bay on the other side of the sand bar which leads to St Ninian's Isle is a good alternative.

Facilities
Shop.

Loose Head at the entrance to Bigton Wick

Bigton Wick

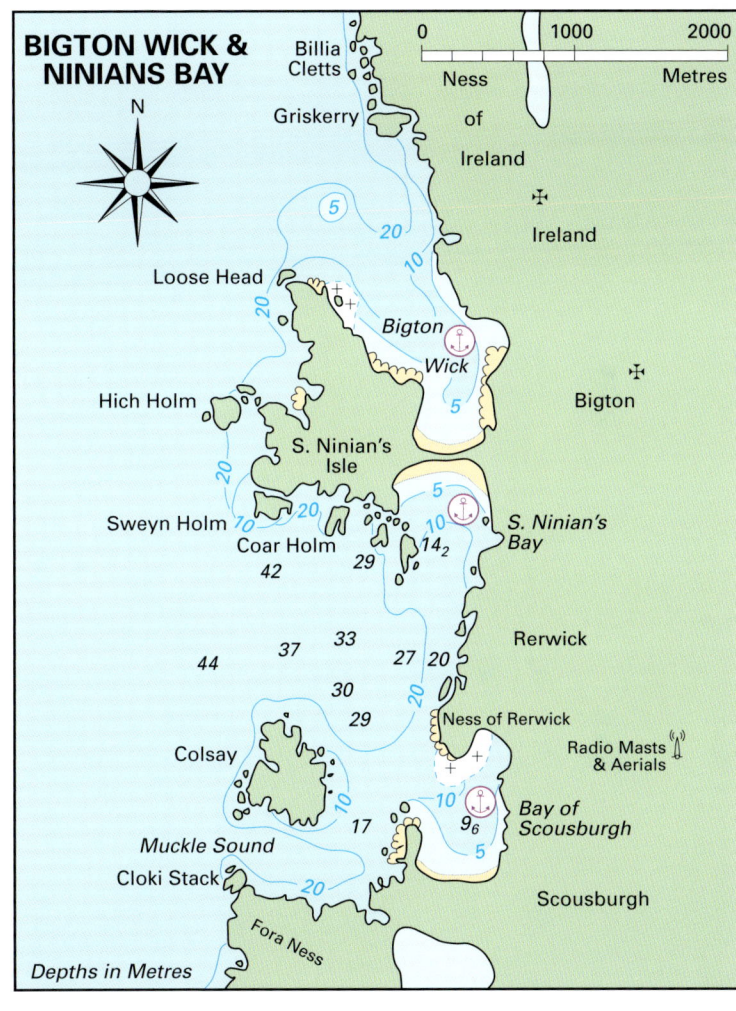

St Ninians Bay

⊕ 59°57′·64N 001°21′·23W

CHART
3283

TIDES
-0115 Lerwick

LIGHTS
None

Dangers
A course at least a cable off St Ninian's Isle and the outlying islets leads clear of dangers.

Anchorages
Good anchorage on sand towards the west side in 4–5m. Better shelter from Westerly winds than Bigton Wick.

Facilities
Shops at Bigton.

St Ninians Bay with the head of Bigton's Wick in the foreground

Spiggie Beach at the sound end of Scousborough

Bay of Scousborough

See plan page 83

⊕ 59°57′·64N 001°21′·23W

CHART
3283

TIDES
-0115 Lerwick

LIGHTS
None

Dangers

Colsay should be cleared by at least a cable, and keep to SW half of entrance to avoid a rock off Ness of Rerwick.

Anchorages

In centre of bay in 7–8m. Botom sand. Can also be reached by Muckle Sound, the channel South of Colsay with no dangers more than a cable offshore.

Facilities

Spiggie Hotel ☏ 01950 460409, a ½ mile walk.

Fitful Head

See plan page 85

⊕ 59°53′·97N 001°26′·32W

CHART
3283

TIDES
Tides run strongly past this area and can create extremely rough conditions particularly when wind is against the tide. Fitful Head is the name give to the stretch of coast between The Nev and Siggar Ness. The N-going flow starts at +0200 Lerwick and the S-going flow at -0500 Lerwick. Rates can reach over three knots.

LIGHTS
None

Dangers

Except in very settled and calm conditions the safest course past Fitful Head is to keep at least two miles off. This leads clear of the worst of the tide and the heavy seas that result from the uneven bottom closer inshore.

Colsay Island beyond the Bay of Scousborough

Bay of Quendale

⊕ 59°52´·30N 001°21´·08W

CHARTS
3295, 3283

TIDES
+0100 Lerwick

LIGHTS
None

Dangers
The approach between Garths Ness and Lady's Holm is clear of any unseen hazards but keep a cable north of the latter. There is a dangerous rock, Oxfoot Rock, lying four cables northeast of Lady's Holm and this is at the southern end of a shoal which extends from the shore and some three cables to the north. Completely exposed to the south.

Anchorages
The best anchorage is in the North West corner in 5–7m on sand. Useful anchorage in suitable wind directions to wait for a fair tide when rounding Sumburgh Head, or heading North past Fitful Head.

Facilities
See Sumburgh.

Horse Island

See plan page 12

⊕ 59°51´·39N 001°19´·48W (West side of channel)

CHART
3283

TIDES
The tides run generally NW and SE through the channel inside Horse Island. The flood starts at +0200 Lerwick and the ebb at -0500 Lerwick.

LIGHTS
Sumburgh Head Fl(3)30s91m23M 59°51´·214N 001°16´·499W

Dangers
The passage inside Horse Island is useful if rounding Sumburgh Head and avoids the need to go many miles offshore in order to avoid the Sumburgh Rost. Keep ⅓ of the way across the channel from Hog of Ness to Horse Island. This course avoids the rocks that extend beyond half way NE from Horse Island.

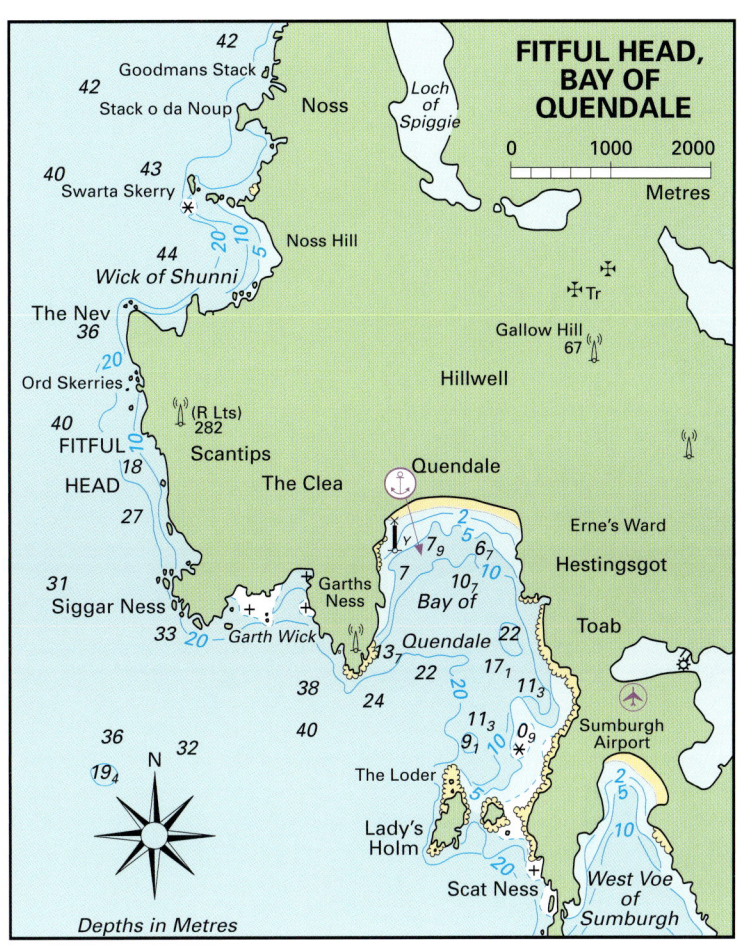

Sumburgh Head

See plan page 12

⊕ 59°51´·04N 001°16´·50W

CHART
3283

TIDES
The west-going stream starts at +0200 Lerwick and the east-going stream at -0500 Lerwick.

LIGHTS
Sumburgh Head Fl(3)30s91m23M 59°51´·214N 001°16´·499W

Horse Island. The passage inside the island is clear of the Sumburgh Rost

MAINLAND SHETLAND – WEST COAST

West Bay of Sumburgh with Bay of Quendale and Fitful Head

Dangers
The infamous Sumburgh Rost is to be avoided in all but the very calmest of weather, and even then the seas will be best avoided, partcicularly if there is any wind against the tide. Either stay at least five miles off on all sides or use the inshore route close in under the cliffs. Keep no more than 1½ cables off, and time passage to coincide with slack water. This leads to the passage inside Horse Island.

Facilities
At *Sumburgh*, hotel ☏ 01950 460201. Shops at Dunrossness ☏ 01950 460676. *See also Grutness Voe and Virkie.*

FOULA

Ham Voe

⊕ 60°08′·50N 002°00′·00W

CHARTS
3283, 3281, 1239

TIDES
-0135 Lerwick

LIGHTS
South Ness Fl(3)15s36m18M W twr; vis: obscured 123°–221° 60°06′·740N 002°03′·859W
Ham Voe pier 2F.G(vert)6m3M 60°08′·048N 002°02′·893W

Dangers
If approaching from the east and heading for Ham Voe, keep well north of Foula Shoal, 4½ miles east of the island. Seas break dangerously here in strong winds. This course will also avoid Hoevdi Grund and Hoevdi Rock, an area of shoals and dangerous rocks extending almost three miles east of South Ness.

Anchorages
The only haven on Foula is at Ham Voe and even this does not provide any shelter from winds other than West. There are rocks on both sides of Ham Voe and to the East, seaward, side of the pier. Aim for the South west corner of the pier on a course of 295° until the inner, West, face of the pier is visible.

Note that there is only 1·8m towards the inner end of the pier. Even the fairly substantial mail boat is lifted out of the water on arrival, but a yacht can lie alongside the pier for a short stay in settled weather. If the wind changes it is essential to clear out.

Facilities
Water alongside. No supplies, but local items of interest can be purchased at the Smiddy.

Interest
Spectacular scenery and wildlife.

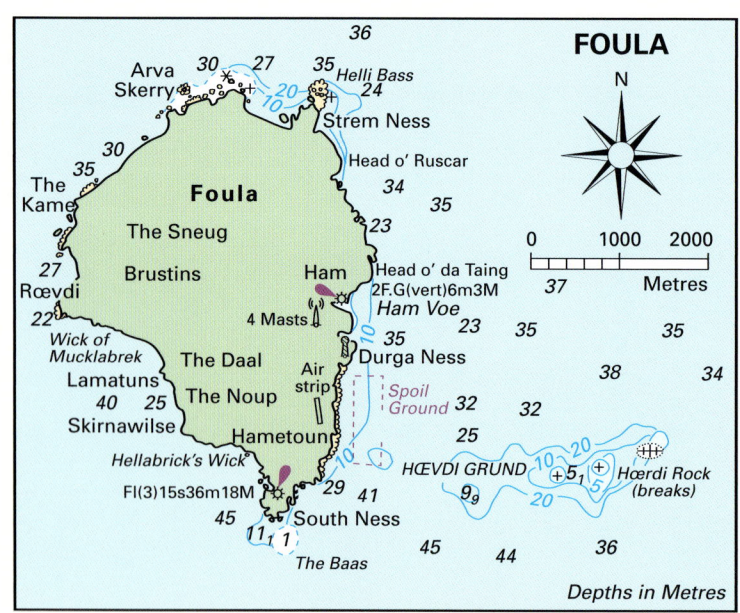

YELL

Ulsta

See also plan page 41

⊕ 60°29´·45N 001°10´·39W

CHARTS
3292, 3282

See Plan on page 41.

TIDES
-0025 Lerwick

LIGHTS
Ulsta Ferry Term, Bkwtr Head Oc.RG.4s7m R5M, G5M; vis shore–G–354°; 044°–R–shore. Same structure; Oc.WRG.4s5m W8M, R5M, G5M; vis: shore–G–008°–W–036°–R–shore 60°29´·736N 001°09´·471W.
Bay of Ulsta Fl(2)G.4s 60°29´·523N 001°09´·424W

Dangers
Beware the area ½M southwest of the Bay of Ulsta where seas break and overfalls occur particularly with wind against tide. Otherwise the entrance to the bay is clear of unmarked hazards.

Anchorages
There is a small pontoon behind the ferry terminal with two berths, mainly used by local fishing boats.

Note that depths alongside are limited. Only really of use as a stop when meeting crew from the ferry.

Facilities
Ferry terminal for the main Yell-Mainland ferry. Some shops and fuel.

Southladie Voe

See also plan page 41

⊕ 60°33´·35N 001°11´·70W

CHARTS
3298, 3282

TIDES
-0025 Lerwick

LIGHTS
Ness of Sound Fl(3)WRG.12s18m W9M, R6M, G6M; vis shore–G–345°–W–350°–R–160°–W–165°–G–shore 60°31´·337N 001°11´·272W

Dangers
Exposed to winds from the south, but otherwise sheltered.

Note that seas break on Southladie Bank. Give Head of Brough a berth of at least two cables.

Anchorages
The head of the Voe beyond half way in is shallow although there is pool with 1½m beyond Urabug, the spit that extends from the East side. Bottom mud.

Facilities
Post Office.

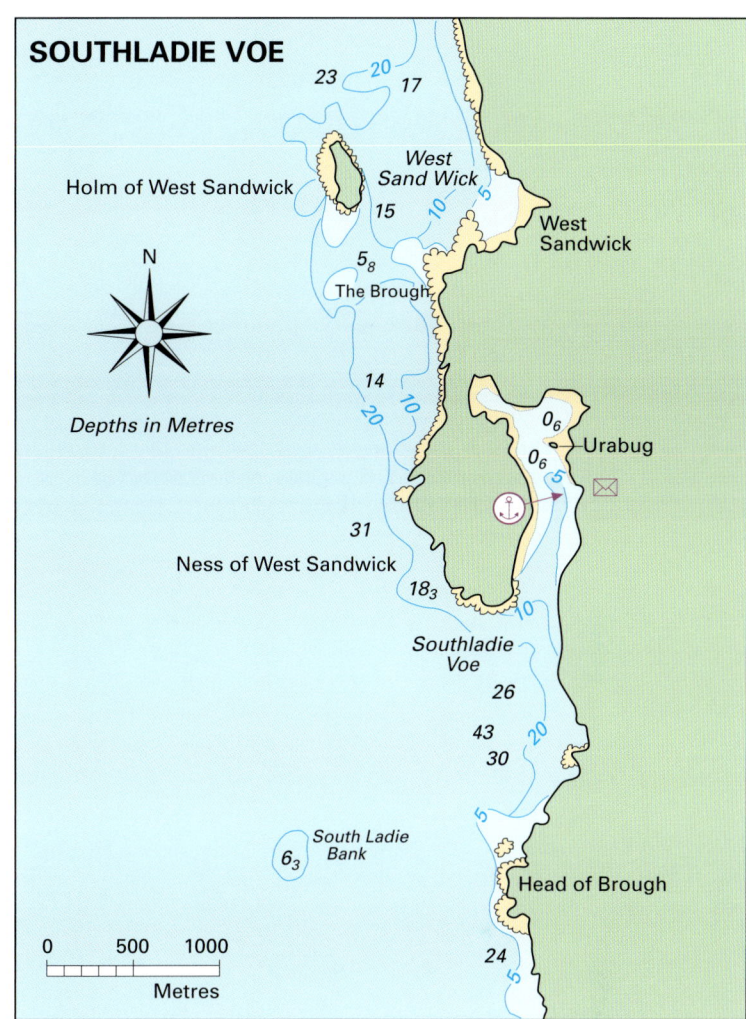

Southladie Voe from the north. Shallow but sheltered

Ness of Sound, Yell

Whale Firth

See also plan page 41

⊕ 60°39´·97N 001°08´·98W

CHARTS
3298, 3282

TIDES
-0025 Lerwick

LIGHTS
Point of Fethaland Fl(3)WR.15s65m W24M, R20M vis 080°–R–103°–W–160°–206°–W–340° 60°38´·045N 001°18´·691W
Gruney Is. Fl.WR.5s53m W8M, R6M; W twr, vis 064°–R–180°–W–012°. Racon(T)14M 60°39´·147N 001°18´·168W
Bagi Stack Fl(4)20s45m10M 60°43´·530N 001°07´·530W

Dangers

Entered between Stuis of Graveland and Gorset Hill there is a dangerous underwater rock 1¼ cables north of the outermost of the Stacks of Stuis. Keep to the east side of the entrance until the Firth turns east then note the rock ½ cable off the south side. Thereafter keep to mid channel. Several fish farms.

Anchorages

The best anchorage is at the head of the Firth some 3½ miles from the entrance in 5m. An alternative anchorage in winds other than North can be obtained in the bay on the West side where the Firth turns to the East, but note the rock off the point at the east side of the bay.

Facilities

None, but Mid Yell is two miles away.

Wick of Whallerie (Gloup Voe)

See also plan page 89

⊕ 60°44´·31N 001°05´·33W

CHARTS
3298, 3282

TIDES
-0130 Lerwick

LIGHTS
Bagi Stack Fl(4)20s45m10M 60°43´·530N 001°07´·530W

Dangers

Exposed to the north, and the tide race off Gloup Holm and The Clapper which must be cleared to the north make access a much longer voyage than might be assumed at first sight.

Anchorages

Only for those who are prepared to explore uncharted and potentially dangerous waters.

Facilities

None.

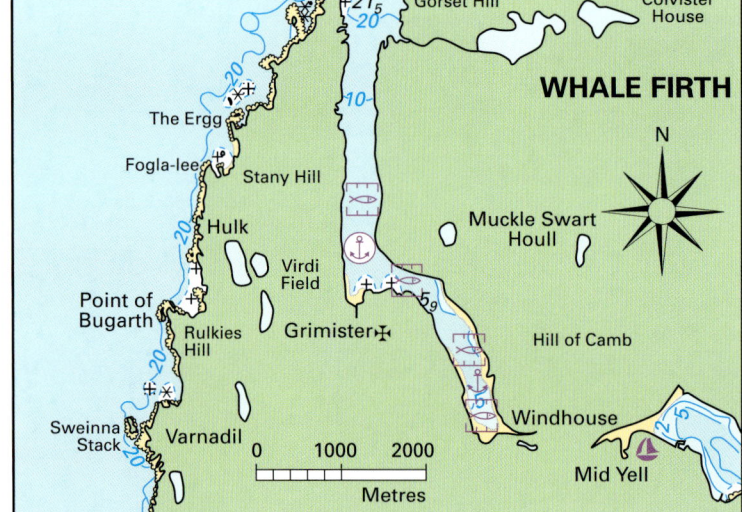

Whale Firth, Yell

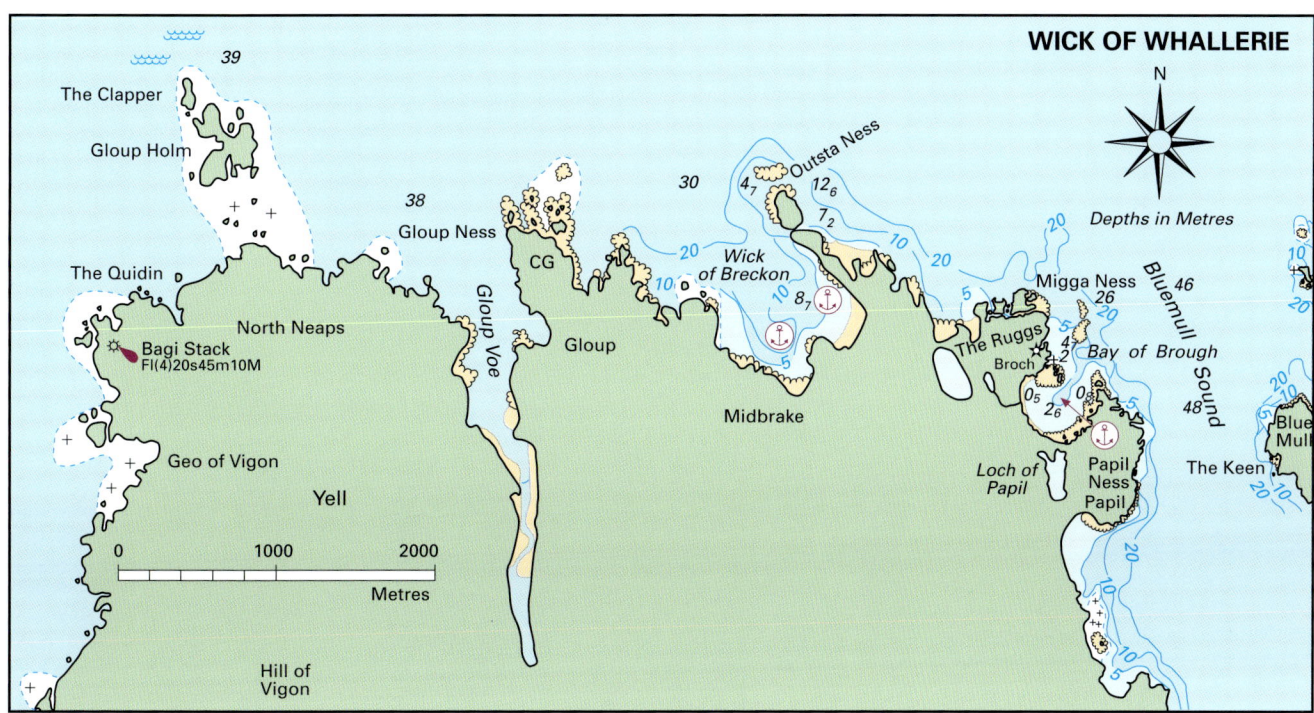

Wick of Breckon

⊕ 60°44′·15N 001°03′·58W

CHARTS
3292, 3282

TIDES
-0130 lerwick

LIGHTS
Bagi Stack Fl(4)20s45m10M 60°43′·530N 001°07′·530W

Dangers
Exposed to the north and west, and the head of the bay dries further than suggested on chart 3292. Give the drying rocks 1½ cable NW of Outsta Ness a wide berth.

Anchorages
Only usable as a temporary anchorage due to its exposed position. Anchor in either of the two small bays in 5m. Weed and sand over rock. Tripping line recommended.

Facilities
None.

Bay of Brough

See also plan page 90

⊕ 60°43′·60N 000°59′·95W

CHARTS
3292, 3282

TIDES
-0130 Lerwick

LIGHTS
None

Dangers
An anchorage only for those who like rock hopping.

Note the shoal area 1½ cables off The Ruggs and the drying rocks off both points of the bay. The rocks at the southeast point extend further than those from the opposite point.

Anchorages
Once the bay has been positively identified along with the rocks on each point, a course of 220° leads into the pool. Anchor in 6m on weed over rock and shingle. Trip line recommended.

Facilities
None.

Wick of Breckon, Yell

YELL

Blumull sound from Yell

Bluemull Sound

See also plan page 90

⊕ **North entrance** 60°44′·02N 000°59′·70W

⊕ **South entrance** 60°39′·71N 000°56′·86W

CHARTS
3292, 3282

TIDES
South-going flow starts at -0420 Lerwick
North-going flow starts at +0140 Lerwick

LIGHTS
Cullivoe Bkwtr Hd Fl(2)WRG.10s3m4M vis:
080°–G–294°–W–355°–R–080° 60°41′·856N
000°59′·693W
Gutcher Bkwtr Oc.WRG.8s4m2M and
2F.R(vert)7m2M 60°40′·404N 000°59′·750W
Wick of Belmont Pier 2F.G(vert)6m2M 60°40′·979N
000°58′·070W

Dangers
Apart from the tidal flow which can reach six knots at springs there are no hazards in the Sound if a distance of at least two cables from the shores is maintained. The area south of the entrance to Cullivoe is prone to severe turbulence particularly in wind against tide situations. When entering the Sound from the north keep The Keen off Blue Mull bearing less than 180° in order to avoid rocks at Round Holm and The Vere.

Papil Bay

See also plan page 90

⊕ 60°42′·81N 000°59′·71W

CHARTS
3292, 3282

TIDES
-0140 Lerwick

LIGHTS
None

Dangers
Only the north part of the bay is usable due to underwater rocks known as the Skerries of Kellister which occupy almost ⅔ of the bay. Fish farms occupy much of the rest of the bay.

Anchorages
As depths permit clear of the fish farm. Bottom is mainly sand.

Facilities
None.

Cullivoe

See also plan page 90

⊕ 60°41′·65N 000°59′·18W

CHARTS
3292, 3282

TIDES
-0140 Lerwick

LIGHTS
Cullivoe Bkwtr Hd Fl(2)WRG.10s3m4M vis:
080°–G–294°–W–355°–R–080° 60°41′·856N
000°59′·693W SHM Fl.G.5s 60°41′·878N
000°59′·558W
Pier NE corner 2F.R(vert)4m3M

Dangers
Tides run strongly across the entrance and severe turbulence may be encountered south of the Ness of Cullivoe.

Anchorages
Anchor North of the conspicuous ice plant situated on the pier in 3–5m but note that this is a busy fishing port. Leave ample room for boats to access the pier. Alternatively, a berth may be available on the pier. Check availability with Roger Moore on ☏ 01806 244200. There is a small and shallow (1·2m) marina at the head of Cullivoe bay where a shallow draft boat may find a vacant berth.

Facilities
Telephone, shop, bus, care hire, taxi, and most yacht services.

Interest
First weekend in July is 'Party at the Pier' where the hospitality is not for the faint hearted.

Gutcher

See also plan page 92

⊕ 60°40′·49N 000°59′·54W

CHARTS
3292,3282

TIDES
-0100 Lerwick

LIGHTS
Gutcher Bkwtr Oc.WRG.8s4m2M and
2F.R(vert)7m2M 60°40′·404N 000°59′·750W

Dangers
A busy ferry terminal. The bay is mostly shallow and exposed to the east.

Cullivoe with small boat harbour, the main pier at extreme left

YELL

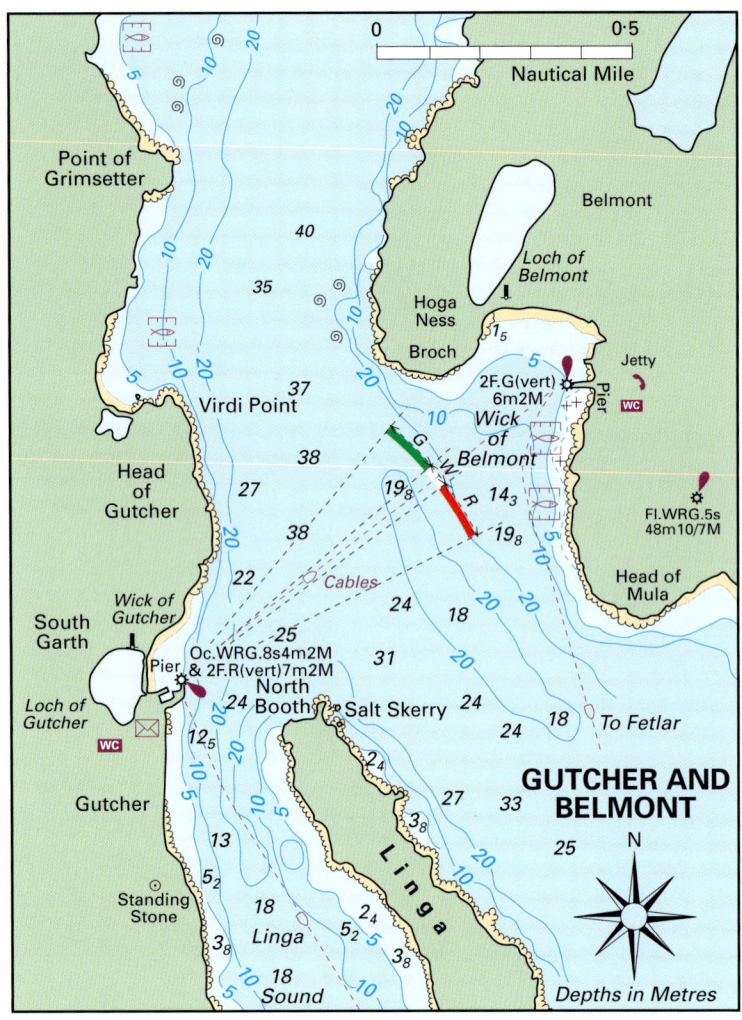

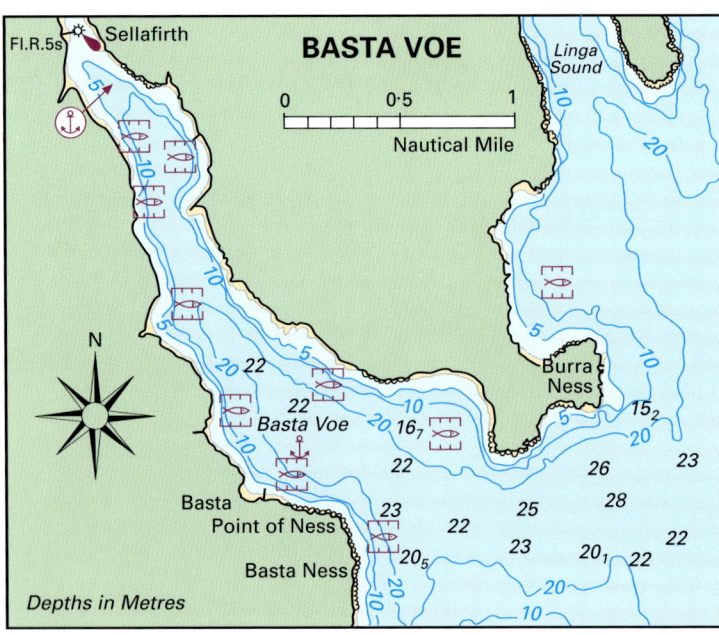

Basta Voe. The small pier is opposite Sellafirth

Anchorages
There is space to anchor in 3–4m to the North of the ferry pier.

Facilities
Ferry to Unst. Café with small shop.

Linga Sound

⊕ 60°40´·39N 000°59´·52W (North entrance)

CHARTS
3292, 3282

TIDES
-0100 Lerwick

LIGHTS
Gutcher Bkwtr Oc.WRG.8s4m2M and 2F.R(vert)7m2M 60°40´·404N 000°59´·750W

Dangers
Tides run strongly through the Sound, but the shores are clear of dangers if course is maintained a cable offshore.

Basta Voe

⊕ 60°37´·76N 000°58´·02W

CHARTS
3292, 3282

TIDES
-0040 Lerwick

LIGHTS
Sellafirth Pier Fl.R.5s 60°39´·721N 001°03´·838W

Dangers
A spit runs almost a cable west from the point at North Ayre of Cunnister, and the Voe is home to much fish farming activity.

Anchorages
At the head of the Voe in 4–5m.

Note that the area beyond the small pier shoals, but otherwise quite sheltered.

Facilities
Hotel.

Hascosay Sound

⊕ North entrance 60°37´·45N 001°00´·43W

CHARTS
3292, 3282

TIDES
-0040 Lerwick

LIGHTS
None

Dangers
Kay Baa lying ⅔ way through the channel from the north is the only real hazard, and is easily avoided by keeping to the eastern half of the Sound. Keep a look out for the fish farms, particularly on the east side.

HASCOSAY

Housa Wick

⊕ 60°35′·34N 000°58′·63W

CHART
3292

TIDES
−0040 Lerwick

LIGHTS
None

Dangers
The main hazard encountered when approaching Housa Wick is Baa of Hascosay, a dangerous rock three cables SSE of Ba Taing, the most southerly point on Hascosay. Keep well to the south, and do not attempt to pass inshore of the Baa.

Anchorages
A temporary anchorage in the centre of the bay in 8–10m. Exposed to South and East winds, and a rocky bottom. Tripping line recommended.

Facilities
None.

YELL

Mid Yell Pier

Wick of Vatsetter

See also plan page 93

⊕ 60°35′·63N 001°01′·41W

CHARTS
3292, 3282

TIDES
-0040 Lerwick

LIGHTS
None

Dangers
A small bay with a stony bottom, that is shoal almost half way from the head of the bay. Keep to mid-channel. Exposed to north winds.

Anchorages
Anchor in the centre of the bay in 5m. Tripping line recommended.

Facilities
None.

Interest
View through Hascosay Sound.

Mid Yell Voe

See also plan page 93

⊕ 60°36′·04N 001°01′·79W

CHARTS
3292, 3282

TIDES
-0040 Lerwick

LIGHTS
None

Dangers
Entered between Kay Holm and Ness of Lussetter the channel is clear of dangers if course is maintained a cable off. The south shore has many offlying rocks, but all are within one cable of the shore. The head of the Voe dries for some distance in the northwest corner. The pier is surrounded by shallow water, but can be approached from the north in line with the pier.

Anchorages
A sheltered area offering good anchorages either off the pier, or between the pier and the marina in 6–9m. Bottom is mud and sand. The pier is in constant use by the local fish farms, but a berth may be available. Call Roger Moore ☎ 01806 244200 for information. The marina has limited space for visiting yachts, and is shallow. Keep close to the breakwater when entering. Call Angus Petrie ☎ 01957 702317 for availability of a berth and information on depths.

Facilities
Leisure centre, bar ☎ 01957 702333, shop ☎ 01957 702026 and post office.

Interest
Wildlife.

South Sound

See also plan page 93

⊕ 60°35′·73N 001°01′·04W

CHARTS
3292, 3282

TIDES
-0040 Lerwick

LIGHTS
Whitehill lighthouse Fl.WR.3s24m W9M, R6M; vis: shore–W–163°–R–211°–W–349°–R–shore 60°34′·792N 001°00′·217W

Dangers
The only serious hazard is the shoal ground off the point of Ba Taing that leads out to Baa of Hascosay some four cables to the southeast. Otherwise a course a cable off the shores leads clear of dangers.

Interest
Birdlife around Hascosay and Fetlar.

Otters Wick

See also plan page 95

⊕ 60°32′·53N 001°00′·55W

CHARTS
3292, 3282

TIDES
-0035 Lerwick

LIGHTS
None

Dangers
Beware the isolated Wick Skerry which lies ¼M northeast of Ness of Gossabrough. Black Skerry, the small islet on the north side of the bay should be left to starboard when entering. The

Mid Yell Voe. The marina can just be seen in the middle of the photo channel between the islet and Yell is littered with rocks and not recommended. There is a drying patch and rock just under one cable off the west shore, and another rock a cable off the north shore.

Anchorages
Due to the rocks mentioned above, anchor in not less than 6m North West of Black Skerry. Sand over rock. Tripping line recommended.

Facilities
Otterswick ½ mile.

Wick of Gossabrough
⊕ 60°32´·40N 001°00´·99W

CHARTS
3292, 3282

TIDES
-0035 Lerwick

LIGHTS
None

Dangers
Beware the isolated Wick Skerry which lies ¼M northeast of Ness of Gossabrough. There is a shoal patch and sunken rock extending over ½ cable off the south shore located 1½ cables east of the small pier in the southeast corner of the bay. The west shore line has many rocks up to ½ cable offshore. Exposed to east winds.

Anchorages
Anchor in the North west corner in 5–6m.

Facilities
Gossabrough.

Burra Voe
See also plan page 96

⊕ 60°28´·53N 001°03´·01W

CHARTS
3292, 3282

TIDES
-0030 Lerwick

LIGHTS
Burravoe Breakwater 2F.R(vert) 60°29´·851N 001°02´·548W

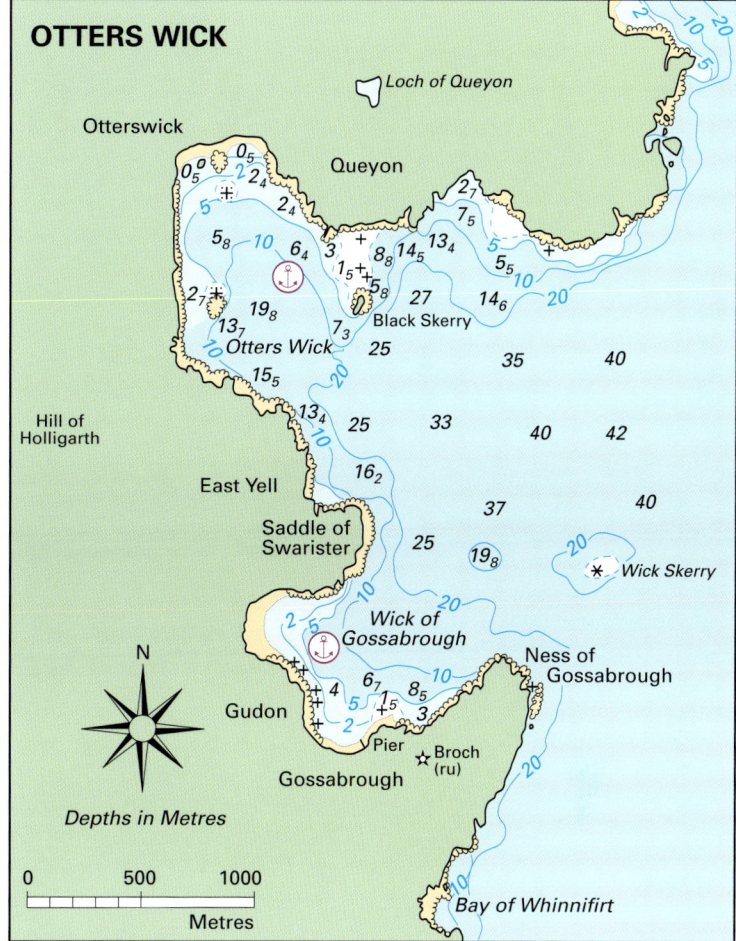

Dangers
There are numerous hazards in the approaches, the furthest offshore being Cloa Rock (1·8m) ½ mile southwest of Muckle Skerry of Neapaback. If approaching from the south keep the Western tip of Heoga Ness bearing between 344° and 360° until abeam Greem Holm. This course also avoids the shoal at Burga Skerry, ¼M to the southwest of Green Holm. There is another shoal patch 1½ cables northeast of Green Holm. This bounds the west side of the entrance to the Voe. The east side is bounded by Heoga Ness with a shoal and underwater rock ¾ cable off the point. The church at Burravoe in line with the warehouse at the root of the pier (brg 006°) leads into the Voe. There is a bar at the entrance with 2·4m, thereafter green and red posts lead

Wick of Gossabrough

YELL

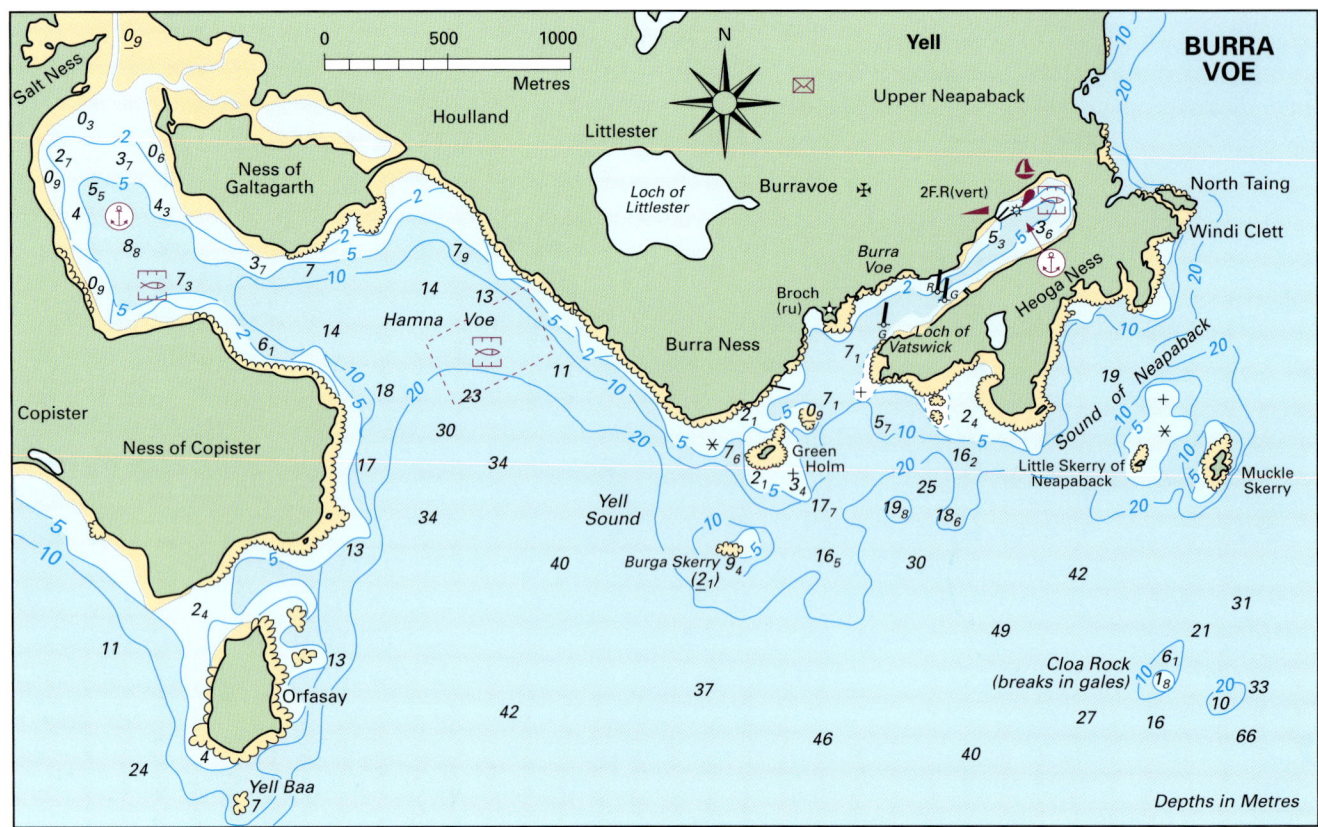

Burra Voe

into the anchorage and marina. If approaching from the east either round Cloa Rock well to the south or pass 1½ cables south of Muckle Skerry of Neapaback. The Sound of Neapaback is usable in settled weather by keeping one cable off the Heoga Ness shore, but beware being set onto the rocks off Little Skerry of Neapaback.

Anchorages

The inner part of the Voe provides sheltered anchorage on good holding in 5m. There is a pier with 2m alongside and also a marina.

Facilities

Leisure centre, swimming pool, bar, and shop as well as water and fuel etc. Pier contact Dan Thomson ☎ 01957 722201 and marina contact Robert Odie ☎ 01957 722315.

Interest

The Old Haa Museum and Heritage Centre.

Hamna Voe

⊕ 60°28´·61N 001°04´·78W

CHARTS
3292, 3282

TIDES
–0030 Lerwick

LIGHTS
The Rumble Fl.10s8m4M 60°28´·165N 001°07´·265W

Dangers

Keep four cables South of Burra Ness in order to clear the rocks at Burga Skerry and two cables off both The Rumble and Orfasay Island to clear the rocks to the south and east of these hazards. There is some fish farming activity within the Voe. Exposed to the southeast.

Anchorages

Anchor West of Ness of Galtagarth as depths permit. Good holding on sand with some weed.

UNST

Belmont

See Plan on page 92

⊕ 60°40´·84N 000°58´·51W

CHARTS
3292, 3282

TIDES
-0120 Lerwick

LIGHTS
Head of Mula Fl.WRG.5s48m W10M, G7M, R7M; metal framework twr; vis: 292°–G–357°–W–002°–R–157°–W–161·5° 60°40´·749N 000°57´·569W
Wick of Belmont ferry Terminal 2F.G(vert)6m2M 60°40´·979N 000°58´·076W
Gutcher Bkwtr Oc.WRG.8s4m2M and 2F.R(vert)7m2M 60°40´·404N 000°59´·750W

Dangers
Fish farms and rocks immediately south of the pier are the only hazards.

Anchorages
Temporary anchorage in the North of the bay clear of the ferry in 4–5m. Exposed to South winds and only really useful if transferring crew.

Facilities
Toilets, telephone, water. Ferry to Gutcher on Yell.

Lunda Wick

See Plan on page 90

⊕ 60°43´·57N 000°59´·06W

CHARTS
3292, 3282

TIDES
-0130 Lerwick

LIGHTS
None

Dangers
Exposed to north and west. Keep a cable to the west of The Vere and enter Lunda Wick between Blue Mull and The Vere. The northeast part of the bay is foul with both drying and submerged rocks.

Note that the tide flows at up to six knots in Bluemull Sound and care must be taken to avoid being set off course when entering the Wick.

Anchorages
Anchor in the South part of the bay on mud and sand in 6–8m.

Muckle Flugga

⊕ 60°51´·31N 000°55´·16W (1 mile West of Muckle Flugga Light)

CHART
3282

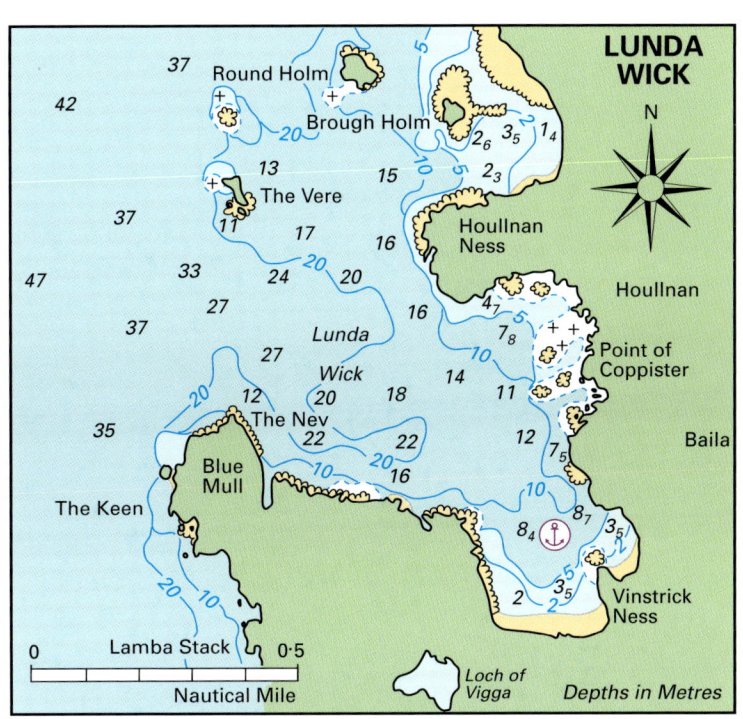

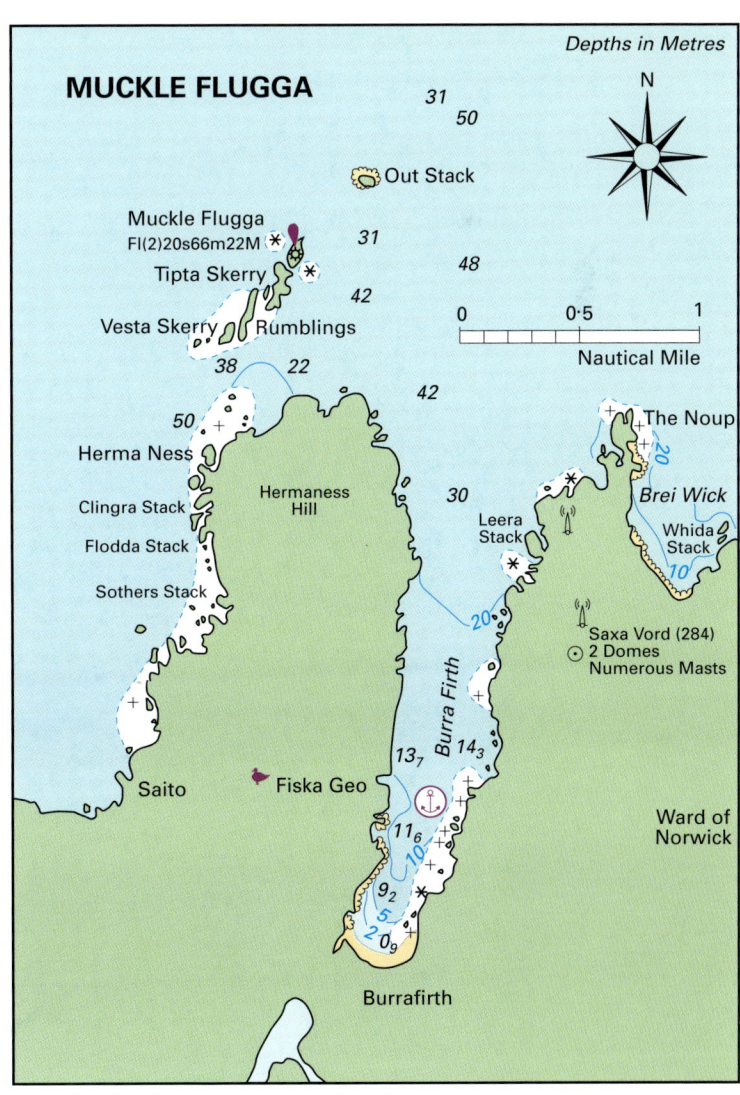

SHETLAND ISLANDS PILOT 97

UNST

Lunda Wick, Unst

Burra Firth, Unst. Muckle Flugga is just beyond the headland

TIDES
The flood tide (East-going) starts -0350 Lerwick
The ebb tide (West-going) starts at +0140 Lerwick

LIGHTS
Muckle Flugga Fl(2)20s66m22M 60°51′·302N 000°53′·113W
Holm of Skaw Fl.5s8m8M 60°49′·847N 000°

Dangers
The main hazard in rounding Muckle Flugga is the strength and flow of the currents. Not only does the flow reach 6–7 knots, but the changes in direction produce powerful eddies. Great care should be taken to avoid being pushed onto the many rocks that lie offshore on the north coast of Unst. The passage between Out Stack and Muckle Flugga is a useful shortcut, but it is essential to have adequate visibility to ensure that a course in the centre of the channel is maintained.

Interest
The cliffs and birdlife that are such a feature of the most Northerly inhabited British Isle are well worth the effort of making the passage.

Burra Firth
See plan page 97

⊕ 60°51′·00N 000°51′·30W

CHARTS
3282, 1239 (small scale passage chart)

TIDES
-0110 Lerwick

LIGHTS
Muckle Flugga Fl(2)20s66m22M 60°51′·302N 000°53′·113W
Holm of Skaw Fl.5s8m8M 60°49′·847N 000°46′·317W

Dangers
The shores are generally steep to and there are several rocks off the east shore. These can be avoided by keeping at least one cable off. Exposed to north winds which cause a substantial swell to set into the bay. Beware the cross tides at the entrance.

Anchorages
Chart 3282 shows an anchorage in 13–15m, but holding is good towards the sandy beach at the head of the bay in about 5m. Bottom sand.

Facilities
The Hermaness Visitor Centre is located on the West shore.

Interest
Wildlife.

Holm of Skaw

⊕ 60°50´·05N 000°40´·00W

CHART
3282

TIDES
The flood tide (South-going) starts -0340 Lerwick
The ebb tide (North-going) starts +0130 Lerwick

LIGHTS
Holm of Skaw Fl.5s8m8M 60°49´·847N 000°46´·284W

Dangers

Skaw Roost is the dominant feature if rounding the northeast corner of Unst. The above waypoint is approximately three miles offshore and can be considered the nearest safe approach to the coast due to the force and turbulence within the Roost. Heavy breaking seas occur, particularly on the ebb tide, and the whole area is best avoided. There are also reports of heavy breaking seas covering the bank that extends 2·5M NNW of Holm of Skaw.

Nor Wick

⊕ 60°48´·30N 000°45´·40W

CHART
3282

TIDES
-0105 Lerwick

LIGHTS
Holm of Skaw Fl.5s8m8M 60°49´·847N 000°46´·284W

Dangers

Completely exposed to the east and only suitable as a temporary anchorage. If entering from the north, do not turn towards the bay until Lamba Ness is bearing at least 300° and then set course for the centre of the bay.

Anchorages

Anchor just North of the middle of the bay in 8–10m. Bottom manily sand.

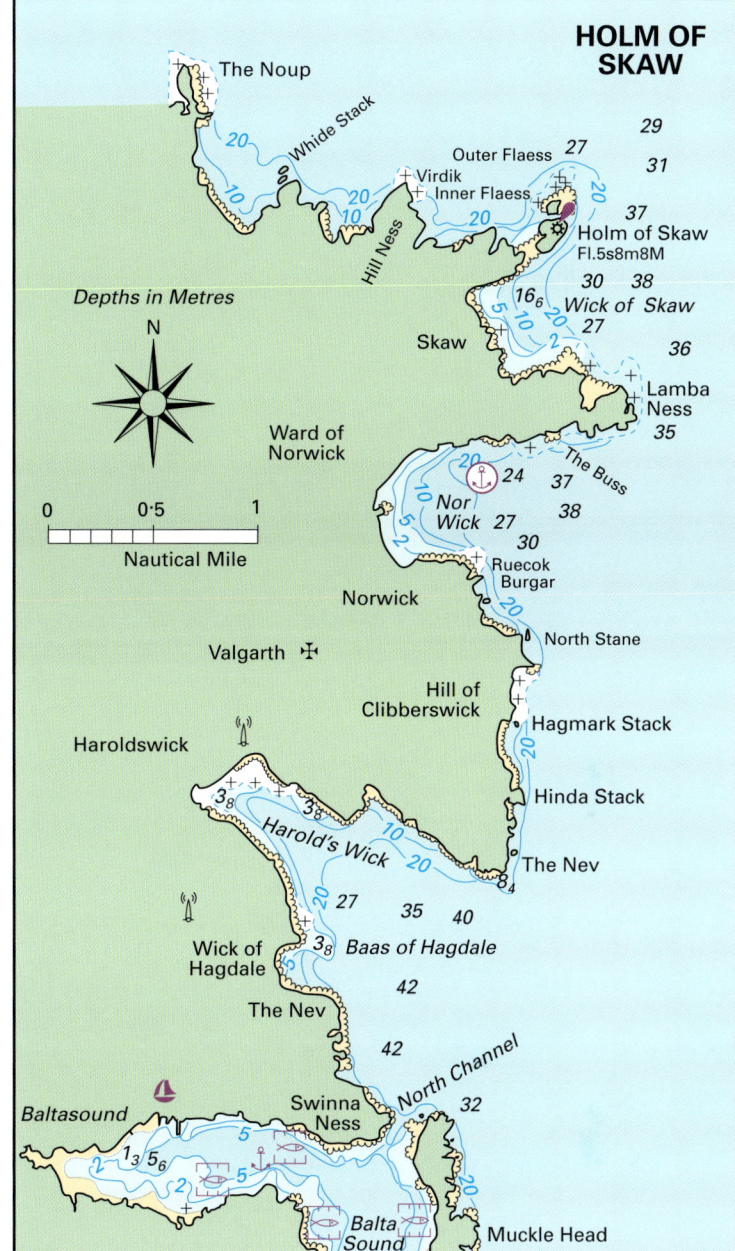

Nor Wick, Unst

UNST

Harold's Wick, Unst. Beware rocks in middle of bay at head

Harold's Wick

See plan page 99

⊕ 60°46´·17N 000°46´·61W

CHART
3282

TIDES
-0105 Lerwick

LIGHTS
None

Dangers

The north shore has several rocks which are easily avoided by keeping slightly south of mid-channel. Exposed to the south and east.

Anchorages

At the head of the bay in the Southern half in 4–5m. Bottom is rock and stones. Tripping line recommended.

Interest

Unst Boat Haven is well worth a visit with its displays of Shetland boats and artefacts.

Unst Boat Haven, Harold's Wick

Balta Sound

⊕ **North channel** 60°45´·96N 000°47´·74W
⊕ **South channel** 60°44´·03N 000°47´·70W

CHARTS
3282, 3299

TIDES
-0100 Lerwick

LIGHTS
Balta Sound Fl.WR.10s17m W10M, R7M vis 249°–W–008°–R–058°–W–154° 60°44´·425N 000°47´·681W
Balta Pier Oc.WRG.10s5m2M vis 272°–G–282°–W–287°–R–297° 60°45´·532N 000°50´·269W
Baltasound Pier Head 2Fl.G(vert)7m2M 60°45´·522N 000°50´·324W
Balta Marina Breakwater Fl.R.6s2m2M 60°45´·564N 000°50´·379W. PHM Fl.R.5s 60°45´·289N 000°48´·781W. SHM Fl.G.5s 60°45´·403N 000°48´·977W. PHM Fl(3)R.10s 60°45´·445N 000°49´·685W

Dangers

North Channel lies between Swinna Ness on Unst and Balta Island and although narrow is easily passed in daylight, there being no useful lights. Keep ½ cable off the Unst shore to avoid the shoal area SW of the Black Skerries of Balta which lie just over ½ cable off the NW corner of Balta Is. The beacon South of Swinna Ness bearing 220° leads clear of the shoals. Leave the beacon to starboard.

South Channel is wider and more widely used. Apart from breaking seas in strong SE winds the entrance presents no hazards if course is maintained at least 1½ cables off the shores.

Note the channel marks when turning west towards Balta Harbour. Many fish farms and the bottom at the head of the Sound is reported to be foul with kelp.

Do not attempt to pass between Huney and Unst.

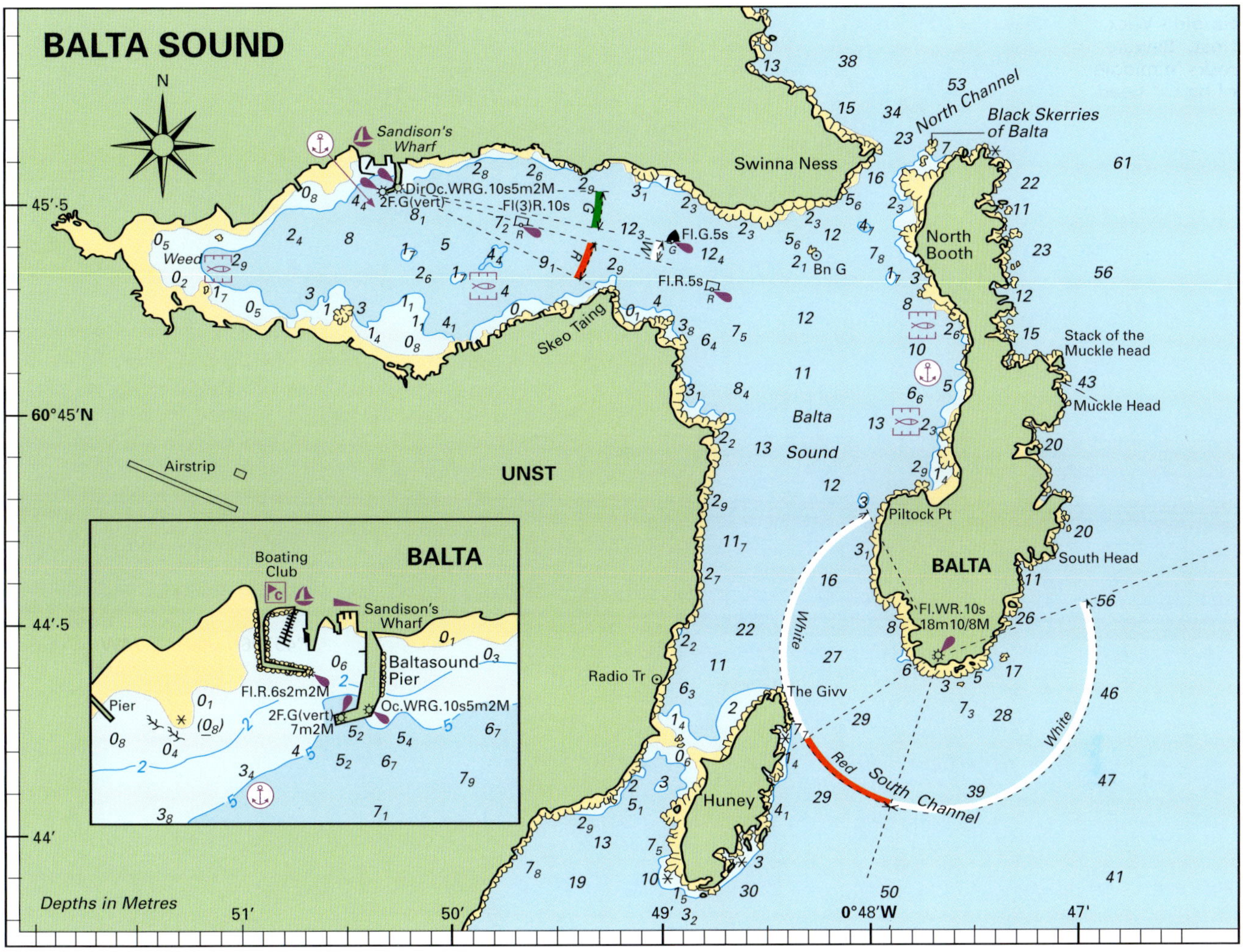

BALTA SOUND

Anchorages

The small boat marina has restricted depths, but a pontoon is available alongside the main pier where depths are suitable for all but the very largest yachts. Alternatively anchor in 5–6m SW of the breakwater.

Facilities

The main harbour on the East side of Unst, Baltasound has most facilities, power, water, showers and fuel are available either on the pontoon or close by. Contact ☎ 01957 711444. General store, and Post Office are within walking distance. Unst Inshore Services offer repair facilities. ☎ 01957 711881. Hotel ☎ 01957 711334.

Interest

Music evenings are regularly held in the village hall, and there is an annual regatta.

Balta Sound harbour and marina

Balta Sound

SHETLAND ISLANDS PILOT

Balta (Island)

⊕ 60°45´·08N 000°48´·05W

CHART
3299

TIDES
-0055 Lerwick

LIGHTS
Balta Sound Fl.WR.10s17m W10M, R7M vis 249°–W–008°–R–058°–W–154° 60°44´·425N 000°47´·681W
Balta Pier Oc.WRG.10s5m2M vis 272°–G–282°–W–287°–R–297° 60°45´·532N 000°50´·269W
Baltasound Pier Head 2Fl.G(vert)7m2M 60°45´·522N 000°50´·324W
Balta Marina Breakwater Fl.R.6s2m2M 60°45´·564N 000°50´·379W. PHM Fl.R.5s 60°45´·289N 000°48´·781W. SHM Fl.G.5s 60°45´·403N 000°48´·977W. PHM Fl(3)R.10s 60°45´·445N 000°49´·685W

Dangers
See notes for entry to Balta Sound. There is extensive fish farming activity in the bay. There is a shallow area one cable SW of North Booth, the ruin at the north end of the bay.

Anchorages
The bay on the West side of Balta Island provides good shelter when the wind is from the East. Anchor towards the centre of the bay as depths permit and clear of the fish farms. Bottom is mainly sand. Good holding but some kelp.

Facilities
At Baltasound.

Skuda Sound

⊕ 60°40´·32N 000°48´·92W (Passage North of Haaf Gruney)
60°39´·19N 000°51´·18W (Passage between Haaf Gruney and Wedder Holm)

CHARTS
3292, 3282

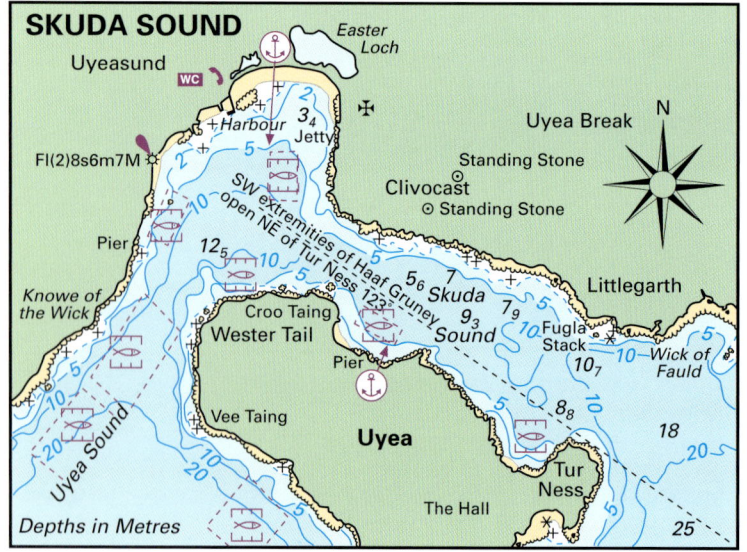

TIDES
-0105 Lerwick

LIGHTS
Uyea Sound Fl(2)8s6m7M 60°41´·139N 000°55´·467W

Dangers
If approaching from the north keep The Vere bearing less than 360° until Skuda Sound is open of Ness of Ramnageo, otherwise a course at least a cable off leads clear until into Skuda Sound.

Note that seas break heavily in the area south of Ness of Ramnageo during gales, particularly from south or southeast.

Note the shoal area off Croo Taing on Uyea. There are several magnetic anomalies in the area.

Uyeasound

⊕ 60°41´·00N 000°54´·80W

CHARTS
3292, 3282

TIDES
-0105 Lerwick

LIGHTS
Uyea Sound Fl(2)8s6m7M 60°41´·139N 000°55´·467W

Dangers
There are sunken rocks one cable E and 1½ cables SW of the small pier at Uyeasound. There are several fish farms in the area, mostly unlit.

Anchorages
In the bay to the W of the jetty on the E shore in 4–5m. Bottom sand and mud. Exposed to winds with any Southerly component.

Uyea

PIER ANCHORAGE
⊕ 60°40´·76N 000°54´·11W

CHARTS
3292, 3282

TIDES
-0105 Lerwick

LIGHTS
Uyea Sound Fl(2)8s6m7M 60°41´·139N 000°55´·467W

Dangers
Restricted swinging room behind the fish farm.

Anchorages
Off the pier between the shore and the fish farm.

Facilities
None.

Uyeasound, Unst looking NW

Uyeasound harbour

Hawks Ness

⊕ 60°39′·51N 000°53′·75W

CHARTS
3292, 3282

TIDES
-0105 Lerwick

LIGHTS
None

Dangers

Temporary anchorage completely exposed to the south.

Note the isolated rocks S of Scarf Stack and NW of Wedder Holm.

Anchorages

Between Winna Ness and Hawks Ness inshore of the fish farm in 3–5m. Tripping line recommended.

Facilities

None.

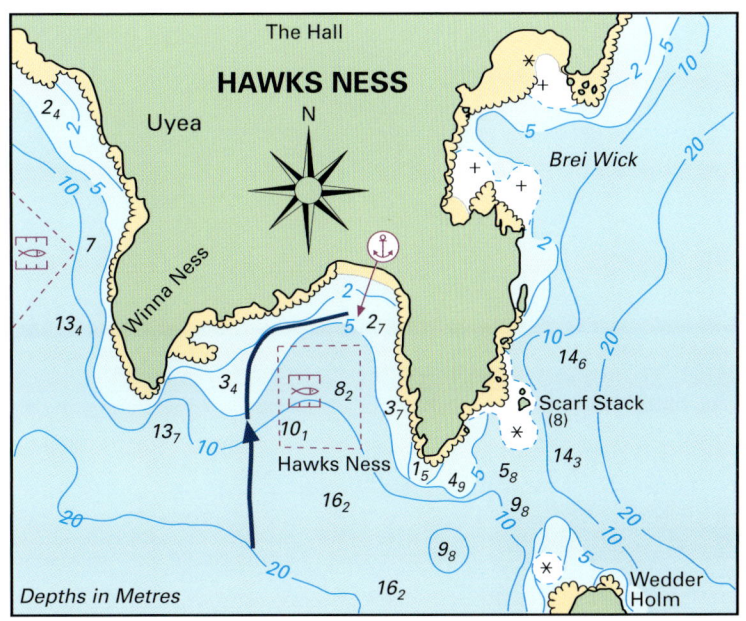

FETLAR

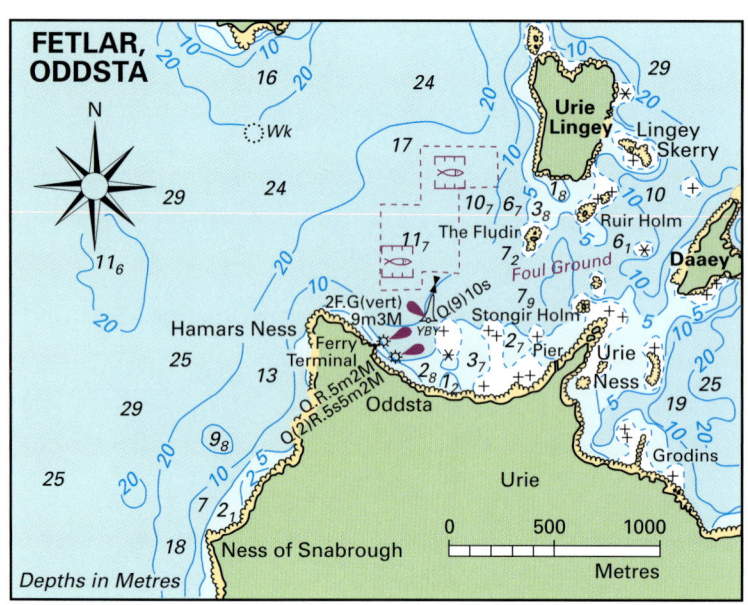

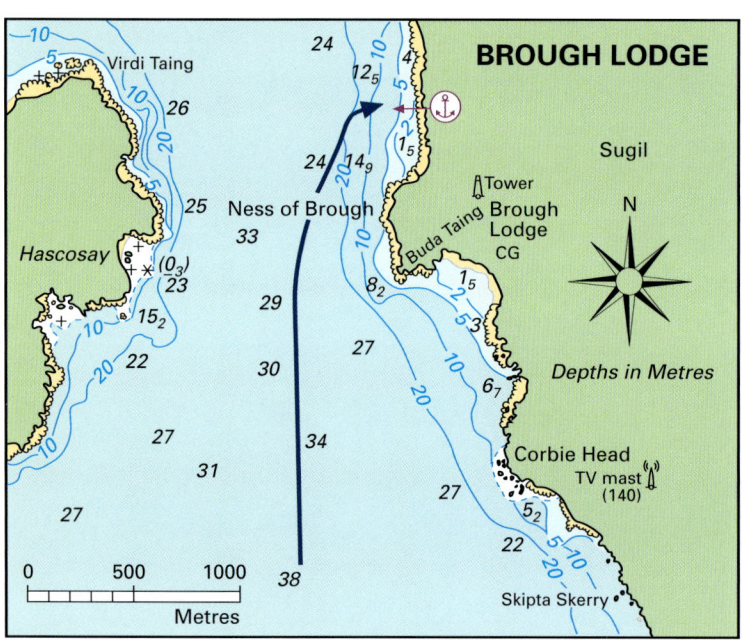

Oddsta

⊕ 60°38´·09N 000°55´·94W

CHART
3292

TIDES
-0100 Lerwick

LIGHTS
Ferrry terminal 2F.G(vert)9m3M 60°37´·770N 000°55´·804W **WCM** VQ(9)10s at 60°37´·828N 000°55´·528W

Dangers
The bay east of the WCM is foul. And the pier is reserved for the ferry.

Anchorages
None.

Facilities
Ferry to Yell.

Brough Lodge

⊕ 60°36´·40N 000°56´·73W

CHARTS
3292, 3282

TIDES
-0045 Lerwick

LIGHTS
None

Dangers
Temporary anchorage at the north of Colgrave Sound. Submarine cables to the south of Buda Taing.

Anchorages
Off the pier North of Ness of Brough in 5m.

Facilities
None.

Wick of Tresta

⊕ 60°34´·22N 000°50´·12W

CHARTS
3292, 3282

TIDES
-0045 Lerwick

LIGHTS
None

Dangers

If rounding Lamb Hoga from the North keep ¼ mile offshore, particularly at Helliers Ness and Rams Ness. There is an isolated rock ¼ mile east of Head of Lambhoga. Exposed to winds from east and south. If approaching from the east keep at least a cable off The Snap, the point at the SE corner of Fetlar.

Anchorages

The head of the bay is shoal for two cables, but otherwise anchor as depths permit. Bottom is sand with some rocks. An alternative temporary anchorage is South of the pier at Houbie in 7–10m.

Facilities

Water and shop at Houbie.

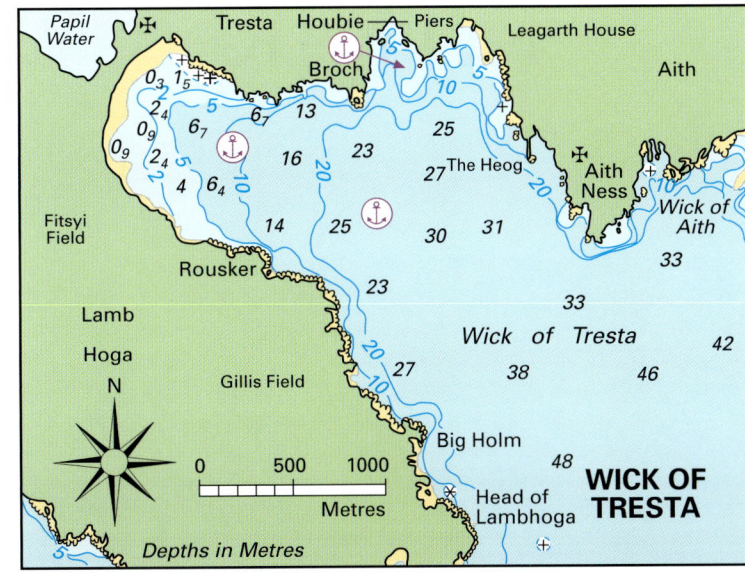

Wick of Gruting

⊕ 60°36´·90N 000°48´·31W

CHART
3282

TIDES
-0050 Lerwick

LIGHTS
None

Dangers

Keep at least a cable off Outer Brough, the islet lying to the N of Strandborough Ness, and the same distance off the shores until approaching the anchorage.

Anchorages

Anchor in 5m off the East shore half way to the head of the bay to the East of Ness of Gruting Tripping line recomended. Alternatively, anchor to the West of Ness of Gruting in 10–12m.

Facilities

None.

Interest

Wildlife.

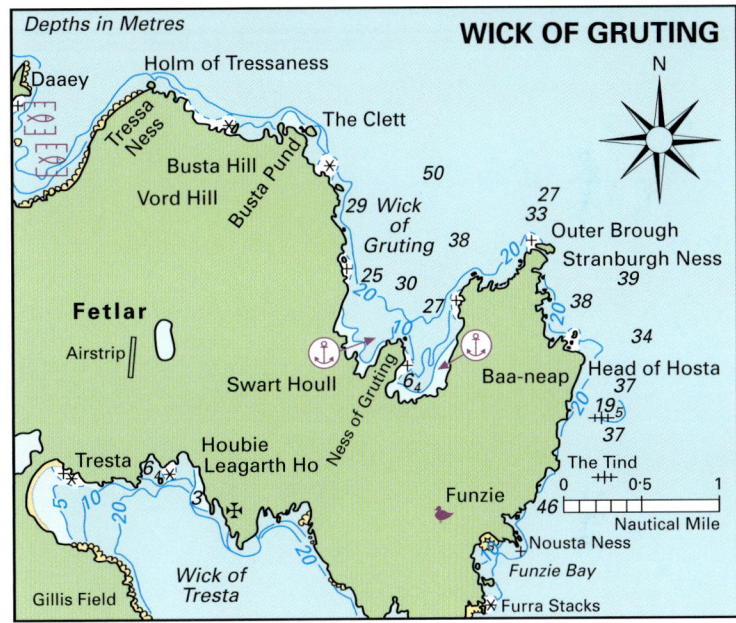

OUT SKERRIES

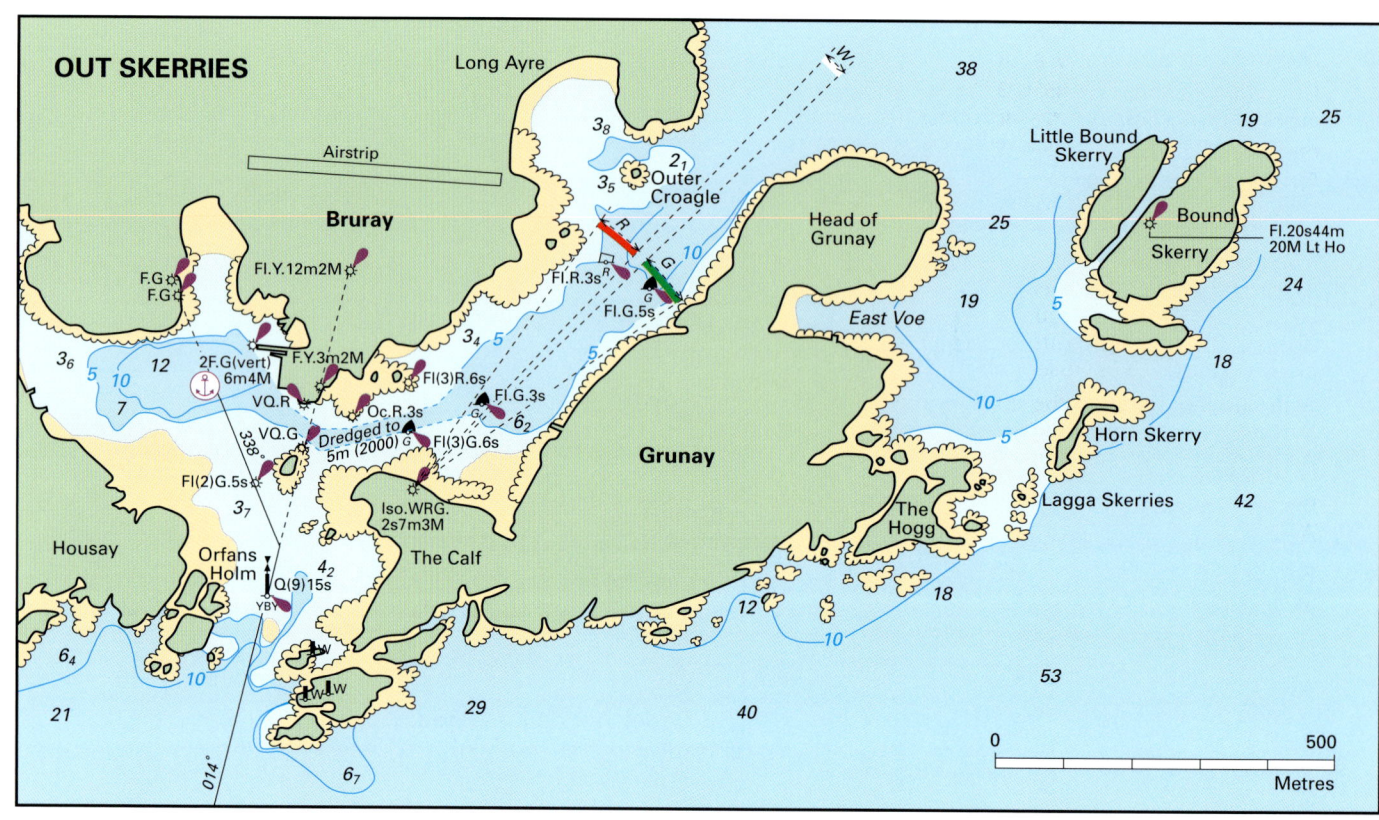

Northeast mouth

⊕ 60°25′·90N 000°43′·62W

CHARTS
3284, 3282

TIDES
-0030 Lerwick

LIGHTS
Bound Skerry Lighthouse Fl.20s44m20M 60°25′·467N 000°43′·680W
Grunay Ldg Light Iso.WRG.2s7m3M vis 215°–R–223°–W–226°–G–234° 60°25′·250N 000°44′·865W. SHM Fl.G.5s 60°25′·412N 000°44′·481W. PHM Fl.R.3s 60°25′·431N 000°44′·549W. SHM Fl.G.3s 60°25′·318N 000°44′·749W. SHM Fl(3)G.6s 60°25′·298N 000°44′·870W
Pillar Lt Fl(3)R.6s 60°25′·336N 000°44′·870W
Pillat Lt Oc.R.3s 60°25′·306N 000°44′·958W. VQ.G 60°25′·284N 000°45′·038W. VQ.R 60°25′·318N 000°45′·038W
Breakwater head 2F.G(vert)6m4M 60°25′·364N 000°45′·115W

Dangers
The channel is quite straight forward but note that the direction of buoyage is NE. Strong onshore winds cause large seas and some swell can reach the harbour pool of Bod Voe.

Anchorages
Either berth alongside the pier where charges are very reasonable, or anchor in the bay West of the pier in 7–8m. Use of a tripping line is recommended as the bay has many moorings including disused ones.

Facilities
There are two shops, toilets, showers, fuel and fresh water. There is a small boat marina, used mainly by local boats. This is located just North of the bridge to Housay in String Voe and has restricted depths.

Interest
Sealife in the approaches to the islands, and during July a fishing competition, followed in August by the local yacht race.

South Mouth

⊕ 60°24´·78N 000°45´·30W

CHARTS
3284, 3282

TIDES
-0030 Lerwick

LIGHTS
Leading lights bearing 014°, front F.Y.3m2M 60°25´·333N 000°45´·010W. Rear F.Y.12m2M 60°25´·424N 000°44´·966W. Both towers W Or.WCM Q(9)15s 60°25´·166N 000°45´·093W. Leading lights bearing 338°, front F.G 60°25´·404N 000°45´·237W, rear F.G 60°25´·415N 000°45´·249W. Both towers R Gy.
Pillar Light Fl(2)G.5s 60°25´·254N 000°45´·113W

Dangers
Severe swell can make entry by South Mouth hazardous in strong winds and it is essential to identify the leading lights before entering. The plan on chart 3284 is essential.

Note the shoal area to the south of the WCM in the entrance, and then identify the second set of leading lights that lead into the harbour area.

Anchorages
As above.

Facilities
As above.

Interest
As above.

North Mouth (String Voe)

⊕ 60°26´·18N 000°44´·98W

CHARTS
3284, 3282

TIDES
-0030 Lerwick

LIGHTS
None

Dangers
There is no adequate chart coverage of the Voe.

Anchorages
Very restricted swinging room but the anchorage in the pool North of the bridge West of the small boat marina offers good shelter although some swell can enter in strong North winds.

Facilities
As above.

Interest
As above.

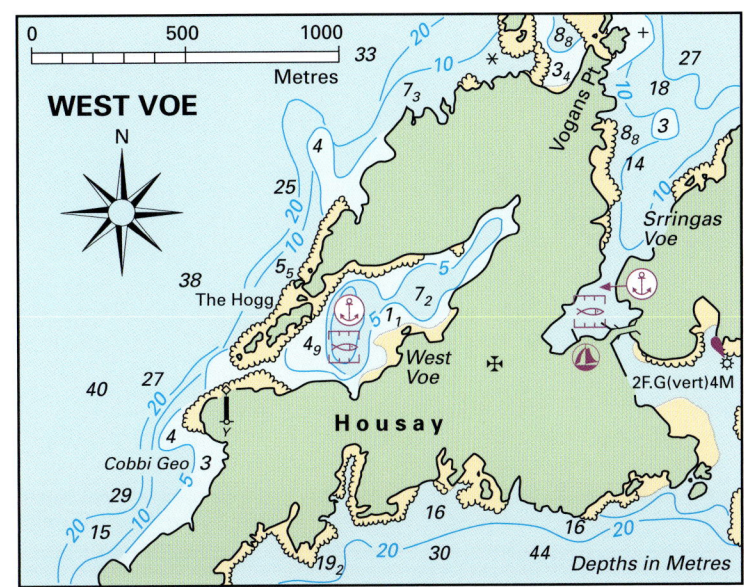

Housay (West Voe)

⊕ 60°25´·42N 000°47´·53W

CHARTS
3284, 3282

TIDES
-0030 Lerwick

LIGHTS
None

Dangers
The pool is almost landlocked and the entrance to the south of The Hogg has less than 1m with rocks on both sides of the very narrow entrance. Definitely one for the serious rock hoppers.

Anchorages
In the centre of the pool in 6–8m clear of the fish farm.

Facilities
None.

INDEX

Aith Voe (Bressay), 20, 21
Aith Voe (NW Mainland), 59-60
Aith Voe (SE Mainland), 16-17
Albert Dock (Lerwick), 24
anchors, 1
approaches to Shetland, 2, 3, 6

Balta (Is.), 102
Balta Sound, 100-101
Baltasound (Unst), 101
Bard Head (Bressay), 20
Basta Voe (Yell), 92
Bay of Brough (Yell), 89
Bay of Fladdabister, 17
Bay of Ollaberry, 45, 46
Bay of Quendale, 85, 86
Bay of Scousborough, 84
bearings, 6
Belmont (Unst), 92, 97
Bigga (Is.), 40, 41, 42, 43
Bight of Haggrister (Sullom Voe), 46
Bigton Wick, 82, 83
Bird Observatory, 3, 11
Bixter Voe, 72
Blackness Pier (Scalloway), 76
Bluemull Sound (Yell), 90, 91
Boathouse Pier (Vaila), 67
Boatsroom Voe, 33, 35
Boddam, 13
Brae, 46, 57
Brae Wick (NW Mainland), 52
Breckon, Wick of (Yell), 89
Brei Wick (SE Mainland), 18, 19
Bressay (Is.), 20, 21
Bridge of Walls, 68
Bridgend Marina, 80-81
Brindister Voe, 61
brochs, 5
Brother Isle (Yell Sound), 40, 41, 43
Brough, Bay of (Yell), 89
Brough Lodge (Fetlar), 104
Browland, Voe of (Gruting Voe), 68
Bruray (Out Skerries), 106
Burra Firth (Unst), 98
    see also East Burrafirth; West Burra Firth
Burra Voe (NE Mainland), 48-9
Burra Voe (Yell), 95-6
Burrastow, 68
Burraview, 62
Busta Voe, 57

Caledonian Canal, 3
Cape Wrath, 3
car hire, 4
Cat Firth, 27, 29
chandlery, 5, 7
Channer Wick, 14
charts, 1, 6, 7
Cheynies, 78, 79
Clift Sound, 81
Clousta, Voes of (N & S), 61
Coastguard, 7

Colla Firth (N of Quey Firth), 47-8
Colla Firth (W of Swining Voe), 38
Colsay Is., 84
Cribba Sound (Vementry), 60
Crog Holm, 55
Culla Voe (Papa Stour), 66
Cullivoe (Yell), 90, 91

Dale Voe (Sullom Voe), 44
Dales Voe (NE Mainland), 34, 38
Dales Voe (SE Mainland), 26
Deeps, The, 69
Delting Boating Club, 46
depths, 6
distances, 6
Dock of Lingness, 31
Drongs, The, 53
Dunrossness, 86
Dury Voe, 31-2

East Burra (Is.), 77, 80-81
East Burrafirth (Aith Voe, NW Mainland), 59
East Ham (Mousa), 15
East Ness of Brenda, 62
East Voe of Quarff, 17
East Voe of Skellister, 31
Easter Sound (Vaila), 67
Effirth Voe, 72
Egilsay (Is.), 54
Ell Wick (Sullom Voe), 46
Elvis Voe (Bressay), 20
equipment, 1, 7
events, 4

facilities, 7
Fair Isle, 3, 6, 8-11
Fethaland, Point of, 49
Fetlar (Is.), 104-5
Firths Voe, 34, 39
fish farms, 6
Fitful Head, 84, 85, 86
Fladdabister, Bay of, 17
Foraness Voe, 27
Fort William, 3
Foula (Is.), 86
fuel, 1, 7

Garths Voe (Sullom Voe), 44
Gletness, 29-30
Gloup Voe (Yell), 88
Gluss Isle, 44
Gluss Voe, 46
Gon Firth, 58
Gossabrough, Wick of (Yell), 95
Gremista, 7, 25
Grunay (Out Skerries), 106
Gruney (Point of Fethaland), 49
Grunna Voe, 31, 32
Gruting, Wick of (Fetlar), 105
Gruting Voe, 66, 68
Grutness Voe, 12, 13
Gulberwick, 18

Gunnister Voe, 54
Gutcher (Yell), 91-2

Haggrister, Bight of (Sullom Voe), 46
Ham (Vaila), 67
Ham, South (Muckle Roe), 55, 56
Ham Voe (Foula), 86
Hamar Voe (Ura Firth), 54
Hamna Voe (NE Mainland), 33, 35
Hamna Voe (NW Mainland), 52
Hamna Voe (Papa Stour), 65
Hamna Voe (West Burra), 77
Hamna Voe (Yell), 96
Harold's Wick (Unst), 100
Hascosay (Is.), 93
Hascosay Sound, 92
Hawks Ness (Unst), 103
health centre, 7
Hermaness (Unst), 98
Hillswick, 53
history, 4-5, 7
Hogg Sound (Oxna), 78, 79
Holm of Skaw (Unst), 99
Holm of Tafts, 62
Horse Island, 85
Hos Wick, 14
Houb of Lunnister (Sullom Voe), 46
Houbansetter, Sound of, 58
Housa Voe (Papa Stour), 65
Housa Wick (Hascosay), 93
Housay (Out Skerries), 107

Isle of Fethaland, 49

Jarlshof, 5, 13

Kirkwall (Orkney), 3
knitwear, 5

Laxfirth, 27, 28
Laxo, 32
Lera Voe, 68
Lerwick, 3, 5, 6, 7, 22-5
Lerwick Boating Club, 3, 4, 7, 24
Lerwick Port Authority, 7, 24
Lerwick Tourist Office, 1, 7, 25
Leven Wick, 13-14
Linga Sound (Mainland), 37-8
Linga Sound (Yell), 92
Lingness, Dock of, 31
Little Holm (Cat Firth), 29
Little Holm (Yell Sound), 40
Lunda Wick (Unst), 97
Lunna Voe, 33-5
Lunning Sound, 31, 32, 36-7
Lunnister, Houb of (Sullom Voe), 46

Mangaster Voe, 54
Maywick, 82
Mid Yell Voe (Yell), 94
mobile phones, 6
Mousa (Is.), 5, 15
Mousa Sound, 15

INDEX

Muckle Ayre, 26
Muckle Flugga (Is.), 97-8
Muckle Holm (Yell Sound), 40
Muckle Roe, 55, 56
museums, 4-5
music scene, 4, 5

navigation, 6
Ness Boating Club, 13
Nesti Voe (Noss), 21
Nor Wick (Unst), 99
North East Mouth (Out Skerries), 106
North Haven (Fair Isle), 3, 9, 10, 11
North Mouth (Out Skerries), 107
North Roe, 49
North Voe (Papa), 78, 79
North Voe of Clousta, 61
North Voe of Gletness, 30
Noss (Is.), 21
Noup of Noss, 21

Oddsta (Fetlar), 104
Old Scatness, 5, 13
Ollaberry, Bay of, 45, 46
Olna Firth, 57
Orka Voe, 42, 43
Orkney Islands, 3, 6
Otters Wick (Yell), 94-5
Out Skerries, 106-7
Oxna, 78, 79

Papa, 78, 79
Papa, Sound of, 64
Papa Little, 56, 58
Papa Stour (Is.), 62, 65-6
Papil Bay (Yell), 91
Point of Fethaland, 49
Pool of Virkie, 13
provisions, 1, 7

Quarff, East Voe of (SE Mainland), 17
Quarff, West Voe of (Clift Sound), 81
Quendale, Bay of, 85, 86
Quey Firth, 47

repairs, 7
Roe Sound, 54-5
Ronas Hill, 51
Ronas Voe, 50-51
Rost, The (Sumburgh), 3, 85, 86
routes, 3, 6

St Ninian's Bay, 83
Samphrey (Is.), 40, 41, 42, 43
Sand Voe (NW Mainland), 50
Sand Voe (SW Mainland), 70
Sand Wick (NW Mainland), 53
Sand Wick (SE Mainland), 14, 15
Sand Wick (West Burra), 77-80
Sandsound Voe, 70, 71
Sandsayre, Wick of, 16

Scalloway, 4, 5, 74-6
Scalloway Boating Club, 74, 76
Scatsta, Voe of (Sullom Voe), 46
Scousborough, Bay of, 84
Scutta Voe (Gruting Voe), 68
Seli Voe (Gruting Voe), 68
Seli Voe (SW Mainland), 70
Shetland Bus, 4-5, 35
shopping, 1, 5, 7
Skaw, Holm of (Unst), 99
Skeld Marina, 70
Skelda Voe, 70
Skellister, Voes of (E & W), 30-31
Skuda Sound (Unst), 102
Snarra Ness, 62
Snarraness, Voe of, 63
Sound, Voe of, 18
Sound of Houbansetter, 58
Sound of Papa, 64
South Gletness, 29-30
South Ham (Muckle Roe), 55, 56
South Harbour (Fair Isle), 11
South Haven (Fair Isle), 11
South Havra (Is.), 82
South Head (W of Ronas Voe), 51
South Mouth (Out Skerries), 106
South Nesting Bay, 27, 30-31
South Sound (Yell), 94
South Voe (Papa), 78, 79
South Voe of Clousta, 61
Southladie Voe (Yell), 87
Spiggie Beach, 84
Spoose Holm (Oxna), 78
stores, 1, 7
Stream Sound, 81
String Voe (Out Skerries), 107
Stromness Voe, 73
Sullom Voe, 40, 43-6
Sumburgh Head, 3, 4, 12, 85
Sumburgh Rost, 3, 85, 86
Suthra Voe (Vementry), 60
Swarbacks Minn, 56
Swining Voe, 35-7
Symbister (Whalsay), 36, 37

Tafts, Holm of, 62
tides, 1, 3
Tofts Voe, 34, 39
Tourist Office, 1, 7
transport links, 3, 6
Tresta Voe (Mainland), 71
Tresta, Wick of (Fetlar), 105
Trondra (Is.), 76

Ulsta (Yell), 87
Unst Boat Haven, 5, 100
Unst (Is.), 92, 97-103
Up-Helly-Aa, 4
Ura Firth, 52, 53
Uyea (Is.), 102
Uyea Sound (Swarbacks Minn), 60
Uyeasound (Unst), 102, 103

Vaila Sound, 66, 67
Vassa Voe, 29
Vatsetter, Wick of (Yell), 94
Vementry (Is.), 60
Victoria Harbour (Lerwick), 7, 23, 24, 25
Vidlin Voe, 32, 33
Virkie Marina, 13
Voe (Clift Sound), 81
Voe (Olna Firth), 57, 58
Voe Bay, 13
Voe of the Brig (Colla Firth), 48
Voe of Browland (Gruting Voe), 68
Voe of the Mels (Noss), 21
Voe of Scatsta (Sullom Voe), 46
Voe of Snarraness, 63
Voe of Sound, 18
Voes of Clousta (N & S), 61
Voxter Voe (Sullom Voe), 46

Wadbister Voe, 27, 28-9
Walls, 67-8
waste disposal, 7
weather, 1, 3
Weisdale Voe, 72
West Bay of Sumburgh, 86
West Burra (Is.), 77-81
West Burra Firth (NW Mainland), 62
West Burra Firth (SW Mainland), 76
West Ham (Mousa), 15
West Linga (Is.), 36, 37
West Lunna Voe, 33-5
West Voe (Out Skerries), 107
West Voe (Papa Stour), 66
West Voe (SW Mainland), 80
West Voe of Quarff, 81
West Voe of Skellister, 30
Wester Sound (Vaila), 67, 68
Whale Firth (Yell), 88
Whale Wick, 77, 80
Whallerie, Wick of (Yell), 88
Whalsay (Is.), 31, 32, 36-7, 39
Whalsay Boating & Sports Club, 36, 36-7
Whiteness Voe, 73-4
Wick of Belmont (Unst), 92, 97
Wick of Breckon (Yell), 89
Wick of Gossabrough (Yell), 95
Wick of Gruting (Fetlar), 105
Wick of Sandsyre (SE Mainland), 16
Wick of Tresta (Fetlar), 105
Wick of Vatsetter (Yell), 94
Wick of Whallerie (Yell), 88
wildlife, 3, 4
winds, 1, 3
World War II, 4-5, 35

yacht races, 4
Yarfils Wick (Sullom Voe), 44
Yell (Is.), 87-96
Yell Sound, 40-42